PACAL'S PORTAL TO
PARADISE AT PALENQUE

YELSRAEK

Autobiographical Note:

Graeme R. Kearsley is an architect who has maintained a life-long interest in archaeology. He was born in New South Wales in Australia and began his architectural training at the University of New South Wales in Sydney. After five years he travelled to the U.K. and after some years recommenced his architectural studies at Thames Polytechnic (Greenwich University) in London where he graduated in 1977 with first class honours.

Front Cover Illustration: Pacal's funerary slab coloured to correspond with coding known from other buildings of the ceremonial site at Palenque. The background and skin colouring for rulers is usually red but here the skin toning is lightened to clarify the physical form of Pacal. See illustrations *3.49* and *4.02*.

ISBN 0-9541158-1-3

E-mail: mayangenesis@btinternet.com

Web Page: **www.mayan-genesis.com**

First published in the United Kingdom by the Yelsraek Publishing in the year 2002.

Yelsraek Publishing
P.O. Box 19697
London
SE19 2BZ

Printed and bound by    www.dd.com.pl

PACAL'S PORTAL TO PARADISE AT PALENQUE

THE INCONOGRAPHY OF INDIA AT PALENQUE AND COPAN

GRAEME R. KEARSLEY

YELSRAEK

PHOTOGRAPHIC SOURCES AND COPYRIGHT

Where possible throughout this work the original and earliest photographs available have been used since they are often the only source of many cultural aspects and iconographic elements which reflect the original context in which the ceramics, supporting panels, monoliths and walls supporting the elements of iconography of interest had been found. Some reflect crafts or social contexts which are no longer found.

The owners of the copyright of those photographs that have been incorporated and are still within that copyright have been notified where necessary depending on the varying regulations applicable at the time of publication. Because many of the photographs utilised have appeared in publications longer than seventy years ago or more attempts to trace the origins, or contact those who might still have right of copyright have not always succeeded. Continuing attempts to contact such owners are still being undertaken and will be negotiated when that right has been established.

Old photographs have a charm of their own but their broad inclusion in this work, as for all photographic, sketch and graphic aspects, is to illustrate elements of iconography which are similar in India, Indonesia and Mesoamerica and associated cultural regions. The problem with early photographs is they often lack clarity of detail, but, for the most part, only those which depict related elements of iconography illustrated reasonably clearly has been included. Comparisons for the most part are achieved by juxtaposition where possible but since many illustrations depict more than one pertinent element of iconography the major element takes precedence in the photographic arrangement.

CONTENTS

INTRODUCTION

Among the high cultures of the Americas the discovery of Palenque in the early nineteenth century with its remarkable architecture and reliefs initiated some of the wildest speculations in attempting to explain possible cultural influences and origins in the history of archaeology. Located in the dense tropical forests of South East Mexico in the state of Chiapas this ceremonial site is located in one of the most romantic of settings sited above the Usumacinta River flood plain in a natural amphitheatre with the surrounding hills as a backdrop. In some of the earliest reports it is known that Hernandez Cortez, the Spanish conqueror of Mexico, passed close by Palenque in his search for gold and initiating the subjugation of the Mayan tribes in the Yucatan and Chiapas. After the excesses of the early Spaniards in their zeal to convert the Mayans in Southern Mexico and their levelling of the existing cultural institutions and buildings the later friars and administrators pursued a policy of brainwashing to eliminate what they considered to be the devilish attractions of the Mayan's ancient past. This was to result in the great loss of continuity with the original high culture which the contemporary Maya of today are the inheritors and rather impoverished remnants.

In 1773 the canon of the Cuidad Real in Chiapas, Friar Ramon de Ordonez y Aguilar, was informed by an Indian that there was a great city which had been abandoned so long ago that it had become overgrown by the surrounding jungle. He was told of beautiful carvings and fine stonework and was so enamoured with the story that he decided that he should himself go in search of the ruins to determine whether there was any truth in the report. Undoubtedly he was also motivated by the fame, and perhaps treasure, which may ensue from such a discovery and he set out in a palanquin for the village of Santo Domingo del Palenque sixty miles away. Arriving at the site to discover that the rumours were certainly true he sent off a report to his superior in Guatemala City. Ordonez then wrote a volume entitled "A History of the Creation of Heaven and Earth" in which he preserved what he knew about the ruins and from whence he considered their founders had come[1].

Unfortunately the book must be accepted on face value, if at all, in part or whole since there is no verification of the reports upon which Ordonez based his opinions. He recorded in this work that the city of Palenque had been founded by a culture hero named Votan who had arrived from overseas on the east coast of Mexico. Among his stated sources is the claim that the local Mayan belief in a hero of this name is based on the fact that he had seen a copy of part of a book, said to have been written by Votan himself, in which his origins and association with Palenque were derived. The copy had apparently been the work of the Bishop of Chiapas - Nunez de la Vega, who himself had burned the original in 1691, but who had allowed Ordonez access to the copy some time later. The copy of the book by Votan, written in Quiche-Mayan, is said to have indicated that this culture hero had arrived from a land named Valum Chivim. This arrival in the Yucatan was believed to have been from the east across the Atlantic, although this is not specifically stated, having in transit visited the "Dwelling of the Thirteen" which some have identified with the Canary Islands. The hero was also recorded as residing for a time on a large island, perhaps Cuba or Hispaniola or one of the lesser islands, before arriving in South East Mexico.

It was said to be recorded that Votan returned to this land of his origin called Valum Chivim four times which Ordonez identified with the Phoenician city of Tripoli on the East Mediterranean shores. After one of these return voyages Votan is said to have recorded that he had visited a great city near his own land where a great temple was being constructed with the intent of reaching heaven in the sky but that it was doomed by a confusion of languages. The early Spanish chroniclers were not slow in identifying this place with the Biblical Tower of Babel. It was attested by both Ordonez and Nunez in considering the book of Votan, in consultation with the local Mayan Indians of the region, that these foreign culture-bearers from Chivim were in fact the Biblical Hivites, the descendants of Heth, the great grandson of Noah. These Hivites were said to have been expelled by the Philistines, and by the Israelites and later conquered Sidon and founded Tyre, and from here Votan was said to have sailed to the Americas.

It was apparently recorded that Votan and his followers were dressed in long robes and that they were accepted by the Indians as the leaders of the communities they set up with them and these strangers were given their daughters to create new clans or dynasties. But Ordonez was not to be the sole author recording Votan's existence since Bishop Nunez de la Vega also wrote his own version of the events described in the original book he had himself destroyed. This he entitled "Constituciones Diocesianos de Chiapas" and he claimed in this publication that Votan had recorded all the places he had visited in his journey to the Americas. One of the places named was Huehueta where it was said that this hero had deposited a treasure in a dark underground location and then appointed a woman as the "priestess" or "keeper" with other guards to ensure her safety. The bishop recorded that he had searched the whole province where the treasure was believed to be secreted and that he had indeed located it, or so he believed, and that he had found only "lidded" clay jars, green stones and manuscripts. These cult objects the bishop destroyed and the manuscripts he had burned.

In a Quiche-Mayan manuscript written in 1554 it is said that the three Quiche nations of Indians considered themselves to be descended from the "Ten tribes of the Kingdom of Israel". These tribes of Israel were those which had been made captive by the Assyrians and, to escape perpetual servitude, they decided to emigrate. It is said that they came "from where the sun rises" and they recognised the local customs to be those identical with those of ancient Israel. In signing the document they also asserted that this was the tradition which their forefathers had handed down to them and whose ancestors had come from "Givan-Tulan" adjacent to Babylonia. The document was obviously a homily to justify some believed line of descent in an attempt to associate themselves with the new religion imposed upon them by the Spanish and such homilies are certainly not new in the social history of the world's people. However, there are certain references which do not fit the Biblical pattern and will be considered in a later publication.

Estacheria, after the report received from Ordonez, commissioned the mayor of Santo Domingo del Palenque, Jose Antonia Calderon, to survey the ruins with an Italian architect in Guatemala named Antonio Bernasconi. Their report was forwarded to Charles III of Spain who, interested in Greek and Roman ruins, was excited by the possibility of finding other, perhaps related ruins in the Americas and ordered the Mexican ruins to be explored. Estacheria appointed a captain stationed in Guatemala City named Don Antonia del Rio to "rescue" the ruins at Palenque and to date and determine why they were abandoned. In arriving at the site del Rio found the forest covering had so enveloped the ruins that he had to hire two hundred Indians to assist in the clearance of the palaces, temples and pyramids soon to be revealed. Del Rio was accompanied by an artist named Ricardo Armendariz who made sketches of the sculptures reliefs and buildings as they emerged and resulted in twenty five plates and his own report records his opinion that the ancient Romans may have visited the Americas. He also quoted Father Jacinto Garriod who believed that the ancient Greeks, English and others also visited the Americas.

Del Rio's report did not initiate any other explorations since Charles III had been succeeded by his son Charles IV who was little interested, but a copy of his report in Guatemala City did interest a visiting Italian, Dr. Paul Felix Cabera who edited this copy and inserted his own impressions ascribing the ruins at Palenque to West Asian influences. He also inserted his version of Siguenza and Boturini who suggested that Carthaginians had arrived on the East Coast of Mexico and colonized the region, before the First Punic War, interbreeding with the local women to form the first great civilisations of Mesoamerica.

After Baron von Humboldt's researches in the Americas he returned to Europe to greatly advertise the existences of the newly found civilisations which were worthy of note. Charles IV of Spain who had earlier so conspicuously lacked interest in any explorations felt obliged to order a broad exploration of Mexican antiquities. He delegated the explorations to a retired army officer, Captain Guillermo Dupaix, and he in turn selected a young Mexican, Jose Luciano Castenada, who was something of a collector of pre-Columbian remains and who had been consulted by Humboldt himself. As a team Dupaix and Castenada travelled through the wild country of Mexico suffering from sickness, bandit attacks and hostilities from local peoples but still managed to explore many of the now famous sites such as Cholula, Xochicalco, Oaxaca and lastly ending their researches in Palenque. Among the description of the achievements of these ancient builders Dupaix noted the glyphs surviving at Palenque which did not appear to relate to any of the known Classical scripts of the Old World. He therefore concluded that they were dealing with an unknown race who were not necessarily considered to be the ancestors of the local Mayan peoples and suggested that these forefathers of the Mexican cultures may have been an unknown people from Atlantis.

From Cabrera's review of Del Rio's work he interestingly notes that one of Castenada's drawings represented either Votan or a Hivite and that he was called a "culebra" or serpent which suggests that he was also identified with Kukulcan the famous winged serpent deity of the Maya. Castenada later became the professor of drawing and architecture at the University of Mexico. These early explorers were frequently embroiled, although not directly, in the political upheavals in pre- and post-independence Mexico and their work, against the most daunting odds, did not receive deserved recognition. Following Dupaix and Castenada the Frenchman named Jean-Frederic Maximilien Waldeck was inspired by engravings he had seen by Ricardo Armendariz and determined to see the sites illustrated for himself. He took up residence in Mexico City as the Count of Waldeck. He set about collecting rare books and objects and also wrote an unpublished history of the Nahua. He eventually managed to arrange a subsidy for himself to travel to Palenque to explore and record the ruins and set out and arrived there in 1832. In the time his sketching ability proved prodigious since he completed ninety drawings and this production of records was only interrupted by revolution which engulfed Tabasco. Waldeck decamped to the Yucatan where he continued producing more drawings but he heard that the Mexican government suspected him of being a British spy and, hearing they were about to seize his work, his remarkable response was to copy them and allow these copies to be confiscated. He then smuggled the originals to England later following to publish them in a folio of twenty-one plates along with text. Waldeck's conclusion as to the origins of the constructors of Palenque was that it was culture-bearers from Chaldea and the Hindus of India who were responsible for its construction and iconography. Problematically Wadeck's reputation was tarnished by his other earlier illustrations of Egyptian pyramids indulgently decorated with Romanesque statues. His later Mexican illustrations tend to suffer from stylisation rather than as exact copies of the subjects intended.

Although Waldeck was considered suspect and his work was somewhat over-romaticised he was soon eclipsed by a new breed of explorers whose records were to initiate the first of the purposeful "new age" of anthropology and archaeology based on more scientific and carefully observed researches. One of Waldeck's volumes had been shown to the thirty-two years old John Lloyd Stephens in New York. He was so impressed that he determined to mount his own enterprise to finally check out for himself whether the drawings of Waldeck were a record of ruins which existed in Central America or whether they were in fact, as reputed, a hoax. Stephens invited his English friend Frederick Catherwood, a fine artist and draughtsman, to venture with him to these mysterious sites. Although also dubious of Waldeck's claims Catherwood decided to join him in this risky undertaking. Because of political instability in Central America Stephens and Catherwood set out for Belize, then a part of the short-lived Central American Republic, in late 1839, with the intention of finding a place noted on the contemporary map, but not confirmed, which was soon to become famous as the Mayan site of Copan. The location of Copan had become known from a report by an Irishman who had adopted the name of Colonel Juan Galindo. He had declared that this site was created by a civilisation greater than any other known in the Americas and to verify this claim, therefore, became a priority for Stephens and Catherwood over Palenque or other sites.

On struggling through the dense jungle in one of the wettest regions in the Western Hemisphere they arrived at the site near the village of Copan tò discover stelae, plazas, pyramids and temples with abundant sculptures still largely in their original places the like of which neither had seen before. To be able to work with fewer problems than having to deal with difficult proprietors Stephens managed to purchase the site for fifty dollars and he and Catherwood then spent weeks in exploring, clearing and sketching the site. However, the attraction of their original intention three hundred miles to the north, Palenque, was too great and pressing and they set off on mule-back across the mountain range which forms part of the great volcanic spine which extends from the high massif of the Mexican plateau and separates Guatemala from South Mexico forming the modern border. In arriving at Palenque Stephens and Catherwood realised that none of the earlier reports, and those of Waldeck in particular, had not been exaggerations. In fact Stephens in his writings appeared to be more impressed by Palenque rather than by Gallindo's reference to Copan as being the most outstanding of the ancient ruins in the Americas.

In their survey of the ruins at Palenque Stephens discovered Waldeck's name scratched in the surface of the so-called "Palacio" accompanied by the date of 1832. Perceptively he also considered there to be a close connection between Copan from whence they had so recently travelled to the culture which had created Palenque. For the weeks Stephens and Catherwood spent at Palenque, the former measuring and the latter sketching, they were incessantly assailed by tropical forest diseases such as malaria and the malevolent insects associated with such hot and damp climes. Although suffering seriously from malaria they emerged from the jungle to successfully reach New York where Stephens' book illustrated with Catherwood's sketches was to prove such a great hit. This publication entitled "Incidents of Travel in Central America, Chiapas, and Yucatan" was to finally focus attention on the ruins then so little known and on the homeland of the Maya which has still to yield many of its ancient towns and cities.

Both Stephens and Catherwood returned to the Yucatan and Campeche once they had fully recovered to investigate other reports of ruins which were located in less infested areas of the tropical forest to the north of Palenque. Stephens was able to obtain a Spanish transcription of the Mayan pre-Conquest beliefs and he also learnt the Mayan means of computing time from a book written by a Spaniard named Don Pio Perez. He further noted that there were similarities between this system and that of the Aztec and came to the conclusion that these were the result of an indigenous system to Central America. Because of these comparisons he declared that the Mediterranean peoples could not have been responsible for the great pyramids, temples and palaces covering such a large area in this region.

The writings of Stephens popularised the ancient ruins of Central America among the educated peoples of America and Europe and among those who were enthralled by the new discoveries was a Flemming from Dunkirk named Charles Etienne Brasseur de Bourbourg. Realising that the question of who had actually built the ruins of Southern Mexico and Guatemala was still a vexing problem he decided to take on board, as his personal mission, the determination of the origins of these ancient builders. At the age of thirty-one he set off for America on route to Mexico in 1845 having just been ordained into the priesthood. In Mexico City he was able to find the necessary assistance to obtain access to, and read all of the available manuscripts such as Ixtlilxochitl's history of the Aztecs. He also learnt Nahuatl, the language of the Aztecs, before embarking for the forests of Southern Mexico. Brasseur travelled on mule in the footsteps of Dupaix and he found and translated two remarkable and important manuscripts, the "Annals of the Chakchiquel" and the "Popol Vuh". When he returned to Paris he published the Popol Vuh in French and as a result he was given access not only to the Aubin collection of Mexican manuscripts and codices but also to those in the Spanish collection in Paris. For the first time the work of translation of the hitherto unknown works into more readily understood languages was begun. Of special importance was the fact that among the Spanish collections he discovered in the Academy of History archive Bishop Diego de Landa's now famous work "Relacion de las Cosas de Yucatan" which provided vital keys in translating the Mayan script. The Mayan script has been the focus of many futile, but some fruitful hours in the attempt to translate the glyphs which still cast their spell over many scholars and lay-people but Brasseur de Bourbourg was not as successful as he first anticipated he might be. A great deal of progress has now been made in the translation of many of the Mayan glyphs but when Brasseur de Bourbourg first made his attempts he perceived in some manuscripts the revelation of the sinking of Atlantis. This he determined from the joint halves of the Tro-Cortesianus Codex from which he dated its believed submergence to 9937 BC. The basis for reading of the glyphs has shifted radically from his time one hundred and fifty years ago and although his translations are mostly of historical interest he did in fact release these important manuscripts to allow those more able to eventually understand their relevance to Mayan history.

A young Americanised Frenchman from New Orleans, Claude Joseph Desire Charnay, was enamoured with Mexico, and in 1850 he returned to France to attempt to persuade Napoleon III's minister of fine Arts, Eugene Viollet-le-Duc, to commission him to photograph the ruins which had now become of such interest. In this he succeeded which is of special interest since the art of photography was in its infancy as the less than spectacular resulting illustrations proved. Charnay was something of an opportunist and was not considered up to the standard of an academician and after his first foray into the world of ancient Mexican ruins he spent another twenty years in attempting to find a backer for further explorations. Charnay did, however, realise that a more in-depth knowledge of the ancient cultures was required and could only be obtained by excavations and not solely by the pretty illustrations which had up until that time had been all that was available on which to judge these early peoples.

In 1880, after succeeding to convince the less than scrupulous Pierre Lorilard to back him, Charnay arrived in Veracruz on his way to Mexico City. When there he developed the theory that there had been a great empire ruled by the Toltecs which extended not only over most of central Mexico, taking in not only the better known sites of Teotihuacan, but also Xochicalco, Cholula and even extending to the Yucatan site of Chichen Itza. He became convinced from fragments of manuscripts and myths and stories he had heard that the legendary ancient capital of the Toltecs was in fact a reality. He set off to discover its location believing that it was to be found near the town of Tula, North-West of Teotihuacan. Charnay's excavations were fruitful and he noted that some of the monuments and sculptures uncovered were reminiscent of those he had seen twenty years earlier at Chichen Itza confirming his belief that there were in fact cultural connections which had existed over these vast distances. Of special interest were the "wheeled toys" which were so very similar to those found from the Indus civilisation in India through to the present day.

Charnay's second visit to Palenque, two decades after his first, resulted in his determination to record the reliefs there by papermache whereby six layers of wet pulp were overlaid, and pressed upon the wall carvings and allowed to dry. These he sent off to Paris following frescoes he had peeled off earlier at Teotihuacan. The work was urgent and necessary since he noted from his last visit that the ruins had become noticeably more broken or decayed and many of the frescoes and sculptures had been looted. After Palenque Charnay travelled under military escort, because of the unstable political climate of the day, to Chichen Itza where he noted that the friezes and carvings reminded him of Hindu India, but also of Java, Malaya and Cambodia. He was one of the first to note the blood rites among the Mayans depicted in their reliefs which were considered by him to be closely similar to those of Siva and Kali in India. Such clearly depicted symbolic blood rites or rituals at Bonampak and Yaxchilan were to be carefully ignored by later generations of researchers except as works of art who considered the Mayans to be among the most enlightened and peaceful of the world's ancient peoples - how wrong they were!!! He also considered that there might have been Greek and Chinese elements in the Mayan culture. But Charnay was not satisfied with his already mounting achievements and wished to seek out the legendary city of Yaxchilan considered by Stephens as being only a "phantom" in the imaginations of dreamers but reputedly the greatest of the Mayan cities. He made his way to its believed location on the Mexican-Guatemalan border formed by the Usamacinta River only, to his amazement, to find an Englishman already there busing himself with recording this exceptional site.

The Englishman was no other than Alfred Percival Maudslay, one of the greatest of the early names in Mayan research. He considered himself an amateur but made seven voyages to Central America where he spend some time at the sites besides Yaxchilan, at Palenque, Copan, Quirigua, Tikal and Chichen Itza. He also made, besides his many sketches, plaster castes of the reliefs and statues and these eventually reached the Victoria and Albert Museum in London. His books and illustrations, both photographic and drawn, are still utilised by researchers and historians to this day.

Pacific Contacts with Palenque:

In terms of iconography it is of special note that there were contacts not only between Copan and Palenque but both exhibiting elements of iconography found in their ancestral form at the site of Izapa near modern-day Tapachula. It is now recognised that the deity known as the "Long-lipped god" is first depicted at Izapa on the Pacific Coast of extreme South-East Mexico and who is depicted as part human and part fish. This god is the prototype designated as God G1 of Palenque and is the early form of the god of rain and lightning, Chac[2], and is one of several elements indicating early contacts between Palenque and the Pacific Coast.

The basic planning structure of ceremonial sites, the so-called "triadic" pattern, formed by a primary pyramid with two others flanking and facing with their ceremonial stairs extending from the central plaza is found in a later form at Palenque. This fundamental planning form is believed to be based on a symbolic structure but also occurs earlier at other Mayan centres such as Tikal, Uaxactun, Lamanai and Cerros[3]. The city of Palenque is one of the smallest of the Mayan sites but is renown because of its architectural or structural "innovations". Water was supplied to the complex by a corbel-vaulted aqueduct and the overall planning is focused by its unique four-storey tower. The site is particularly known for its remarkable carved stucco murals and wall reliefs and the colour coding of red skin toning for humans and blue for deities is of special interest[4]. In three of the temple-pyramids, that of the Foliated Cross, the Sun, and the Cross the reliefs are of special interest since they exhibit elements which must have convinced the earlier explorers to believe so intently that there had to be connections with far-distant India. But it is in under the Temple of the Inscriptions at Palenque, the name given to the temple built atop the main stepped pyramid, that the chamber housing Pacal's funerary coffin and sepulchral slab was found that is of particular interest for this study.

The art forms of the Maya in the later phases in the second half of the first millenium A.D. seem to have progressively adopted more unique styles in figurative art and architecture. Although there was a tradition among the Maya in relief carvings and murals this was extended particularly at Palenque toward a more naturalistic reflection of the human form. They even excelled at the most difficult representation of all - that of sculptured three-dimensional realistic portraiture[5]. Of some concern is that there appears to be little to indicate a development of these arts both in this difficult aspect of sculpture and architectural styles and planning suggesting that these were in fact introduced from outside although such a proposition would be fiercely opposed by many Mayanists. It is of interest that Copan developed also at this time, in the Late Classic, other three dimensional sculptural forms and their subject matter appears closely similar to aspects of iconography in the Ganges Delta in India. Palenque however has elements which have survived the many centuries of ruinous decay and looting indicating very specific cultural intrusions that must have been derived from India and these are reflected in the iconography of Pacal's slab. It is also of interest that some of the artefacts of the Maya, such as certain designs and votive figures, seem to have close similarities with those in the same time frame in Ecuador in South America and this aspect also will be of interest in a future work.

The mythic figures depicted on ceramics and recorded in the Mayan myths are of great interest to modern-day researchers. It has been discovered through excavations that the pre- and post-Conquest literary records, originally doubted as to their veracity, have been vindicated through the study of the more recent finds depicting these mythical beings and scenes illustrated so faithfully centuries before, as well as immediately before and after the Conquest.

One of the great problems in considering the surviving iconography is the lack of associated myths with the imagery or elements of it and the long forgotten sites where examples of it were found. Some aspects of myths and traditions relating to iconography have survived in remote Mayan tribes but all too much of it has to be gleaned from the few surviving documents from the pre-Conquest era and those surviving written after the conquest. Those surviving remnants of the high civilisation of the Maya are few considering the great number of records which the early Spanish friars admitted to torching in their chronicles or other writings. In India, however, the story is different since, although there was an enormous destruction of monuments and lack of maintenance in those that survived in India over the millennia the iconography remained recognizably the same over those millennia as did the cultures and writings engendering their existence. It is also of the greatest good fortune that from the earliest contacts some of the British officers and officials were interested in the existing cultures they encountered throughout the Indian Sub-continent and many undertook to recording the many variations in literature, myths, religions and peoples which made up the life of India as they saw it. Their records are still of great value and therefore the related iconography can be assessed to a greater degree as formalized aspects carved in stone intended to be projected by the priests for the patrons and the devotees in the masses as the attributes didactically descriptive of the gods and deities represented. Because of the survival and accessibility of myths and religious aspects associated with the iconography of India and the more limited references associated with the Mayan the following text tends to appear to reflect a bias toward India. This is not intended to indicate that India alone was the progenitor of Mayan culture since there appears to be some evidence that China was also in contact with Central America in the same time frame. There is some evidence also that there was a counter-flow of cultural influences from Central America to Indonesia and India in which the Maya appear prominent.

In the overall study of cross-Pacific contacts this small volume must be considered as an extension of the previous book by the same author entitled "Mayan Genesis - South Asian Myths, Migrations and Iconography in Mesoamerica". The many cross-references in this present volume to items in "Mayan Genesis" are too many to allow for a brief augmentation of the data to be included and only the reference itself to the book as "Mayan Genesis" generally or with an indication to a page of photo-page is noted.

CHAPTER 1
PALENQUE and COPAN
NAMES and SYMBOLS

Archaeologists in recent decades have noticed the close similarities between the local development of the Maya culture at Palenque with that at Copan and there is evidence indicating that they probably formed an alliance or were related in some way from the middle of the first millennium A.D., in the Late Classic period. Aspects of a possible alliance are found at Copan located on the western boundary of the modern state of Honduras, and nearby Quirigua in Guatemala adjacent the same border. It appears that at least one bride was sought for the ruler of Palenque in Copan and this may suggest that there were tribal connections through origin or that it was Copan's ruling dynasty who had an elevated status with whom it was desirable to be associated.

The iconography surviving from both these Mayan cities, and indeed also at Quirigua, indicates that culturally both drew from a common origin. It is this iconography which is of particular interest to the theme of this book and although not exclusive to these sites is more clearly demonstrated here than among the rest of the Mayan settlements, at least in terms of surviving architectural and artefactual remains.

Imagery at these Mayan ceremonial sites frequently bears more than a superficial resemblance to that of India but was considered by several early European explorers to be only "accidentally" similar to that of Asia. The iconography displayed appears always to be applied with definite meaning and purpose of intent and apparently never entirely as decoration in the modern Western sense. The elements of this iconography seems to reflect that in India more than anywhere else emphasising a common origin with Asian cultures and it will be shown that this resemblance is more than superficial. This connection would indicate that there were conduits by which this flow of culturally significant themes and symbols could enter Mesoamerica. The question should be asked as to why such foreign elements should be considered of such importance that the ruling Mayan dynasties had it applied with less than complete assimilation into what might be considered the generality of Mayan culture.

The adoption of elements of iconography so completely from India suggests that there were three conduits through which such influences may be introduced into Mesoamerica and in certain cities, or ceremonial sites, in particular. One is via primary introduction through migration by sea across the Pacific Ocean Counter Current which flows directly from Asia, and Indonesia in particular to the western Central American coast. This current washes directly on to the Mayan territory of El Salvador for Copan, and perhaps more significantly on to the adjacent Guatemalan coast allowing access to the Highland Mayan site of Kaminaljuyu. From this important trading site access would thence be east or north-eastwards to the Usumascinta River to Palenque and the other lowland Mayan sites. A little further west from Guatemala the same current delivers mariners and traders to the South Mexican site of Izapa.

Trade influences are very important in many cultures of the world and their influence permeates through regular or occasional contact over generations. It would be expected that the traders' influence would not necessarily appear in the ruling dynasties unless they traded in prestige goods which would be specifically aimed at their acquisition and this was noted later in the Aztec empire. These later traders were called Pochtecas but their appearance and deity name - Ek-Chauh[1] - may have been derived from India (see "Mayan Genesis"). Traders could, and did elsewhere, form alliances and intermarried with local people and on the Pacific coast of Central America they may have achieved sufficient power and alliances to extend their own rule and government systems beyond their local areas of domicile. In this way they would introduce their influence upon the more established dynasties or through alliances into other regions of the Mayan heartland.

A second means of entry into Mesoamerica for Asian iconography is by missionaries such as those sent out by the great Mauryan emperor Asoka in the 3rd century B.C. India whose influence was of such importance within and beyond his empire, and clearly visible to this day in the island of Sri Lanka. If successful, as in the Sri Lankan model, the external influence would be reflected in the buildings constructed, both civil and religious, and the iconography adorning such structures and applied to ceramics and other artefacts.

The third means of introduction of Asian iconography is for the Mayans or other Central American traders to have travelled themselves to Indonesia, China and India either as mariners, craftsmen or pilgrims and returned to their homeland with new ideas through association with the ancient religions of India. They are likely to have learnt new means and principles of building construction to regenerate their own institutions and perhaps some of the pilgrims proselytised on behalf of foreign religions having undergone conversion in these foreign lands.

In studying these possibilities it would appear that there are elements of all three options which are evident among the Mayan. It is most likely that the traders from Asia reached the Americas at least by the first millennium B.C. Because of the vast distances involved some of these probably formed permanent or temporary liaisons with the women of local tribes and become integrated with them, or formed new clans elsewhere. There is much to suggest that this occurred on the west coast of Central America and Southern Mexico, and was probably an essential element of the social structure of Kaminaljuyu in the Mayan Highlands. This site is located near the Pacific Coast and the surrounding and coastal sites such as El Baul and Bilbao on the coastal strip itself and Izapa further to the north. The so-called "pot-bellied" monoliths, bas-reliefs, mushroom stones and other elements of carving and iconography have been shown to closely correspond to those known in Indonesia - Sumatra in particular[2]. These appear in the beginning of the first half of the first millennium A.D. or earlier corresponding with their appearance on the Pacific Coast of Guatemala and shown in "Mayan Genesis"[3]. These carvings also suggest the importation into Central America of a strong religious element which appears to have been largely Buddhist.

The likelihood of targeted destinations by the Buddhists is a real possibility since, as already mentioned and widely known, the adherents of this religion were recorded as having set out, or were sent to proselytise abroad. It is also recorded that some rulers of foreign kingdoms actually applied to either the emperor Asoka or in later times to the North Indian monasteries for missionaries to be sent to convert their subjects. Pilgrimage in India was known by at least as early as the beginning of the first millennium A.D. and was receiving pilgrims from China by the middle of that millennium. It is the record of these Chinese pilgrims, Fa Hsien and Hsuan-Tsang in particular, which has been of use in defining the state of the Sub-continent in those centuries but also of interest because of their record of the long and dangerous sea-voyages back to China via Indonesia lasting sometimes for many years.

Wherever Buddhism had successfully taken root it resulted in a great desire for those with sufficient means or will to undertake a pilgrimage to Bodh Gaya and Nalanda. The former of these sites is the location of the sacred banyan tree under which the Buddha was said to have attained enlightenment and the latter the great university which for centuries had been the educational centre of India. These sites are located within a day's walk of each other, a little distant north of the Ganges River in what is now Bihar. Also of importance were the Ajanta Caves north of modern Auragabad in western India near one of the tributaries of the sacred Godavari River which flows right across Central India to the Bay of Bengal.

The Buddhist caves of India were sites of important pilgrimage in their times since many of the contemporary and historic saints of that religion were associated with, and lived in hermitages adjacent or within these cave complexes. The Ajanta Caves are of special interest since they were, and a few still are extensively covered in the finest murals existing in India today dating from about the 5-6th., centuries A.D. These caves give an unprecedented insight in the daily religious life of India at that time. The fact that so many of the paintings have survived into the beginning of the third millennium A.D is remarkable and of particular importance to this study is the fact that they display the evidence for the origin of the so-called sky-band of

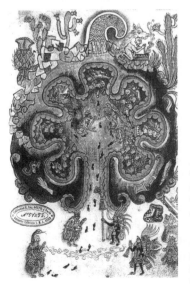

1.02 Panorama of the Ajanta gorge on the Waghore River. The caves are spread from the entrance at the bottom right all around the visible curve of the gorge on the other side of the river. Ajanta, West Central India, 3rd., century BC- 6th., century, AD.

1.01 Codex depiction of sacred "Seven Caves" known as Chicomotzoc in Mexico. Historia Tolteca-Chichimeca, Pre- or Post-Conquest Mexico.

1.03 Plan of the Ajanta Caves showing the caves disposed around the curve of the gorge of the Waghore River. 3rd., century, BC - 6th., century, AD.

Mesoamerica being evident here in Ajanta.

It is of particular note that the Ajanta caves are carved in the rugged cliffs which form the bend in the canyon of the Waghore River - a distant tributary of the Godavari via the Purna [*1.03; 1.04*]. This flows towards the important Buddhist sites, in the 2-3rd centuries A.D., of Amaravati and Nagarjunakonda in the joint delta with the Kistna (Krishna) River far distant on the East Coast of India. The shape of the river canyon at Ajanta and the fact that there were originally only seven caves along with the evidence of the sky-band being virtually identical to that of Mesoamerica suggests that Ajanta was the model for the "Seven Sacred Caves" or "Caves of Origin" in Mexico known as Chicomotzoc [*1.01*], and this is a subject expanded in "Mayan Genesis"[4]. It is clear from the Ajanta "sky-bands" that those still readily and clearly to be seen there are the last of a long development and appear to form no apparent scheme reflected in terms of the Western zodiac. In other words they had become corrupted into decorative patterning although they still retained in the circular sky-band in the ceiling of Cave 2 [*3.31*] an apparent order which is clearly related to the ancient Vedic zodiac. There is much more of the sky band surviving in other caves which appear repeated in one direction only consisting of parallel strips clearly indicating the rafters of a timber roofed temple or building. It is likely therefore that there was a coherent symbolic pattern applied to what are intended to be represented roof rafters in the ceiling [*3.38-3.40*] apparently determined by a preconceived cosmic construct. These painted bands were almost certainly the origin for the Polynesian stellar constructs relating to the "vault of heaven" represented in the roof structure of their sacred temples and have a similar reflection in the Popol Vuh[5].

It appears, therefore that cultural influences were transferred from India to Mesoamerica and to Palenque and Copan in particular which later incorporating aspects of cosmology including the sky band concept. Traders would have been the first to make contact and formed, or were adopted into local clans which achieved power and influence. Later in the late first millennium B.C., and after the traders, missionaries would soon follow from Buddhist India and spread their influence throughout Mesoamerica evident in their iconography being assimilated into the indigenous civil and religious organisations rather than developing as a separate religious movement. In considering Mayans visiting India it is noted that other Buddhist contacts or missions outside India resulted in a counter-flow of pilgrims from the countries contacted being probably restricted only to those of religious occupations, artisans and perhaps those of elite birth. In practical terms, however, local mariners would be recruited as relief crews to replace the incoming crew-members who succumbed or decamped along the sea route to Mesoamerica from India, and these also would have more local influences in the ports of India on the return journey.

It is clear that none of these contacts from India with Mesoamerica were primary migrations since the distance was far too great and too dangerous for a large number of people to survive. It is likely therefore that there would be little or no evidence of migrant peoples and those who did survive the journey are likely to have intermarried with local women resulting in descendants who would be absorbed with very limited traces of their paternal origins except in local legend. Those later generations whose initiative and circumstances allowed them to make the return journey to the land of their paternal ancestors would therefore have been physically different from the predominantly Caucasian peoples of early Buddhist, Hindu and Jain India. The mixed origins and traditions, particularly their blood rites, would hardly have endeared themselves to the peoples of the high cultures in the main ceremonial and civic centres of India at that time. It is likely that they would have found more empathy among some of the aboriginal peoples nearer the coasts of India whose rites so resembled some of those of the Maya and Mexicans.

Whatever the Mayans made of the incoming influences from India it is clear that it was welcomed since their ceremonial sites clearly indicate that it permeated every part of their religious and civic, and even their calendrical iconography. This deserves more exhaustive consideration and comparison although the subject is hotly contested by the Americanists who are determined to hold with an exclusively indigenous origin for the development of all aspects of Mayan, and Mexican, culture.

Palenque:

The origins of the name Palenque is not known for sure but Professor David Kelley has suggested that it may derive from the name of one of the Hero Twins of the Popol Vuh, Xbalanque, the other being Hunaphu earlier noted. It is thought that one of the Emblem Glyphs for Palenque displays a bone or an animal skull as a component part and this may refer to Xbalanque. He and his twin brother are considered rulers of the dead having defeated the Lords of the Underworld in a celebrated ballgame[6]. However it may be worth considering that at Izapa, a site which appears to have close antecedent ties with Palenque, a palanquin is shown as an element a background on a stela [*1.02*] and this site reflects many iconographical aspects which appear to derive from India. It may be significant that in Sanskrit, the ancient literary language of India, one of the derivative terms for palanquin is "palanque".

The Pacific coastal site of Izapa is now seen as crucial to the development of the Maya since it appears to be a close link between the fading greatness of the Olmecs and the development of the early Maya. Of particular interest is the evolution of the "Long-lipped" deity who appears to be the prototype of God G1 at Palenque. This deity appears to have been widely spread to become the Chac, or rain or lightning god of the Maya. A second element prominent in the public bas-reliefs at Palenque is the "serpent-footed" god, usually shown as a child held in the arms, but is found earliest also at Izapa as God K[7].

A third important element of Mayan mythology is the "Principal Bird" deity detected for the first known time at Izapa and later illustrated among the Maya of Belize and Central Lowland Guatemala, but also at Palenque. This deity is usually identified with the god of the age of the former Sun, Vucub Caquix. Certain aspects of the Sky Band are also found at Izapa and later this reached its highest surviving development at Palenque and it will be shown that this Mayan sky band is closely related to that of India. It is surely significant that Izapa therefore is located a short distance from the Pacific Coast of Southern Mexico and that the sea currents that wash its beaches are the Pacific Counter Current direct from South East Asia. It is of particular note that an "old god", one of the "Lords of the Underworld", is seen smoking a cigar depicted in a relief carved on one of the exterior pilasters of the Temple of the Cross at Palenque. It has been suggested that the narcotic effects of tobacco and other substances was used by mariners to suppress the effects of hunger and thirst during long sea journies and this "old god" may represent those ancient mariners or perhaps one of their deities[8].

The three temples at Palenque which exhibit the finest reliefs and many inscriptions are known as the Temples of the Cross, the Sun and the Foliated Cross and are constructed around a plaza with a small central ceremonial platform. It is now known that these were constructed by the ruler known as Sun Lord Chan-Bahlum - this name meaning "Snake Jaguar", and dated to his accession in 683 AD[9]. The inscriptions and reliefs are now seen as a declaration of his right to rule as successor to his father Pacal.

Atop the main pyramid at Palenque facing the palace building complex with its tower, is the Temple of the Inscriptions which reflects the same architectural style as the three temples already mentioned and is so called because it contains 620 hieroglyphs on its walls inscribed on its characteristically plastered walls. The latest date recorded is 692 AD but this does not necessarily date the building exactly since the plaster inscriptions are likely to have been included some time after the construction of the building, the structure probably being commenced by Pacal himself. It is likely that Pacal ordered the construction of this, his own funerary temple and it is probable that it was complete in his own time since it is now believed that he ascended the throne at the age of twelve years and died in 683 A.D. aged eighty.

In 1952 the Mexican archaeologist Alberto Ruz removed one of the slabs of the temple floor at the top of the pyramid and discovered the entrance to a blocked stairway which he cleared to reveal a tomb chamber, unique in the Americas, about 80 feet, 24 metres, below. In a large sepulchral chamber, 30 feet long and 23 feet high (9 metres long by 7 metres high) the great sarcophagus of the ruler Pacal ("Hand Shield")[10], was found with its stone slab measuring over 12 feet long (3.8 metres) [*1.04*]. This was carved with a relief of the ruler himself descending into the Underworld after his death. A large number of precious objects were recovered from the sarcophagus including a mosaic mask but of particular interest was that in his mouth and hands was placed a jade obolos, a practise known in China and preserved by the Aztecs as well as among the Maya[11]. These jade masks resemble the jade works found in the more sophisticated full body

1.04 Pacal's funerary slab shown in the sepuchral chamber. Palenque, Chiapas, Southern Mexico, 8th., century, AD.

burial suits of China. Reflected in many aspects of the ceramics of the Teotihuanacos and similarly in the Mayan Highlands at Kaminaljuyu designs appearing to derive from Chinese sources are evident and it is significant that Palenque had apparently close ties with Izapa on the Pacific Coast, a logical entreport for the cultural import of ideas from Asia. This Asian influence tends to be emphasised since the underground tomb of Pacal resembles much more the Asian, or even Egyptian model, rather than any found in the Americas.

Of particular interest, and noted by the earliest European explorers in Palenque, is the accession panel showing Pacal sitting on a ceremonial platform representing a throne composed of addorsed "lions" or jaguars[12]. This has always intrigued interested researchers because the array of the ruler is identical to that shown in the earliest depictions of the Buddha. This regal array was adopted throughout South and East Asia as a symbol of rulership and was one of the panels which early explorers considered to be influenced from India[13]. In this panel the crown is being handed to the ruler as part of the act of succession and this appears to be an elaborated form of those still to be found into the last century in Borneo but identical to those of the Dongson two thousand years ago.

The inscription panels in the corridors of the Temple of Inscriptions, the structure erected by Pacal as his funerary monument, reveal the king list of Pacal's dynasty surviving for posterity[14]. Importantly this long inscription records the mythical ancestors who are recorded as divinities and were believed to have been instrumental in establishing the world order[15]. This family history records that a mythical founder was born in 993 BC and a divine pair, or First Mother and First Father initiated the dynasty from whom three children were born. These divinities or demi-gods became immortalised as the so-called Palenque Triad[16]. The close similarity of the early sections of the Palenque ancestry with that known from the Belize ceremonial centre of Cerros suggests that the former has plagerised the latter or were a collateral branch from Belize. The early part of this dynastic history claiming descent from the gods originates from one inception date of 3113 BC[17]. As noted in "Mayan Genesis" this date appears to coincide too closely to that of the Kali Yuga in India, 3102 B.C. to be called coincidental.

The "Palenque Triad" of gods appears to have extended beyond the ceremonial centre of Palenque itself and they are identified with the birth dates of the first Mayan gods all falling within an 18-day period echoes in the importance of their contemporary representative at any one time in the person of the ruler. This birth date was the most important that the ruler, and indeed the commoner, was identified with since it was believed that the deities who presided over that day and the omens associated with it, good or bad, set the life pattern and influenced the individual in a fateful way for their life-span. This birth date was encapsulated in the "initial date indicator" which was pictured as the glyph form of a frog with an upturned head[18]. At Palenque this Triad of deities was finally identified and are now known as gods G1, G11 and G111 and their mythical birth was recorded during the time of Pacal's successor, Chan Bahlum. Their birth dates are given across a three-week period in 2360 BC and the first of these, G1, is named as his own father who was said to have been born in 3122 BC.[19]. These deities appear to have been associated with the rain god Chac and it is interesting to note that other symbols suggest a sea origin. These appear to indicate ancestral connections with the sea this being evidenced in the many imported artefacts having fish or sea shells associated with them and often appearing to relate particularly to God G1 at Palenque[20].

A glyph of particular importance among the Maya was that denoting rulership - "Ahau". The term is frequently applied in association with rulers and distinction of birth or achievement and of particular interest is the fact that the same term exists, as well as a number of others, among the Polynesians and used in similar ways. As has been noted in "Mayan Genesis" the hero canoeists of the Polynesians, and particularly notable in the Tongan myths, are found often in pairs and have close similarities to the Paddler Gods of the Maya. Modern scholarship has identified the Mayan Paddler Gods with the Ballgame Hero Twins, Hunaphu also called Hun-Ahau and Xbalanque, and pectorals depicting Hunaphu displaying this glyph was worn by the ruler to display his authority[21].

Also associated with birth dates is a glyph depicting a representation of the God K or the Maize God emerging from what is considered by some to be a snail's shell[22]. The God K appears to be closely similar to the representations of the Pauahtuns and it is shown in "Mayan Genesis"[23] that this exact depiction of deities or demons emerging from a shell is found across the Pacific Ocean to India and is also associated with the wind deities Quetzalcoatl and Kulkulcan. This would suggest that these gods, at the heart of Mexican and Mayan myths and religion, were in fact associated with or were probably mariners or those who migrated from across the Pacific.

Writing - Hieroglyphs - Logograms:

The so-called hieroglyphs of the Maya have long been of interest to scholars and much effort has been expended in "breaking the code". Considerable progress has been made and it is now known that many of the inscriptions at Palenque relate to historical events and personages, particularly declarations of the "right-to-rule". The inscriptions are logographic which indicates that the hieroglyph or pictogram represents occasionally a whole word but more usually is linked to another to form a complete word[24]. These logograms are then developed further for their phonetic value alone or extended to link with others to produce more complex meanings. It is clear, however, that many of the logograms were in fact small cameos or pictures of particular mythical events which have become encapsulated through loss of original context and the redaction of cursive handwriting after transfer from India to Mesoamerica.

The phonetic aspect of the Mayan hieroglyphs is notable in the name of Pacal which means "Hand-Shield" and could be written in their contemporary system either as a picture or logogram or as a hand-shield but also phonetically[25]. The known Emblem Glyphs for the main Mayan ceremonial sites include those for Palenque and Copan and other specific glyphs relating to accession of a ruler or birth glyphs[26]. It is of interest to note that in the writing in the Temple of the Cross at Palenque which celebrating the accession of Lord Chan-Bahlum, it is inscribed that his father Pacal was born on 8 Ahau 683 AD. This is of special interest since this is the date on which a mythical ancestress was said to have been born and suggests that Pacal's birth date may have been adjusted to intentionally identify with her in an attempt to justify his right to rule through a claimed descent from her[27]. The date of the birth of this ancestress is too close to that of the date of the Kali Yuga, or beginning of the present World Cycle in India religious belief, 3102 BC, to be coincidental. Interesting also is the fact that the Mayan ancestress is called Lady Beastie, suggesting a fearful side to her nature, and Kali of India is the wrathful goddess whom the Hindus and Aboriginal peoples propitiate through fear of the havoc and disease she might wreak upon them.

Many learned expositions on these glyphs and the Mayan writing system have been written and it is not useful to include any further references here except to note where applicable the iconography associated with glyphs which are clearly derived from India. These connections and derivations from India are reflected in cameos or picture plaques and are more easily indicated graphically and comparisons are shown in the sky-bands of Ajanta and the temple portals of Orissa and Aihole within this work.

Copan:

Copan is located in one of the most isolated and remote of the Mayan sites on the very periphery of the epicentre in the Mayan Highlands and Lowlands to the north. It is here also that influences deriving from the Guatemalan and El Salvadorean Pacific coast were pronounced in the pre-Classic phases around two thousand years ago. Here were to be found links to the "pot-bellied" sculptures[28] found so widely on the coast, and at Kaminaljuyu now largely covered by the urban development of Guatemala City. These "pot-bellies" are clearly related to the early cultures exhibiting similar stonework in Sumatra and nearby islands in Indonesia on the other side of the Pacific Ocean[29].

Copan appeared also to have had early contacts with the site of Tazumal in modern-day Chalchuapa in western El Salvador which is itself located near the Pacific Coast and reveals Olmec settlements into the late first millennium BC. This was a major settlement among the others on this coast, Bilboa and El Baul at Santa Lucia Cotzumalguapa and Abaj Tajalik further to the west in Guatemala, with Izapa beyond in the southern-western corner of Mexico. However, with the violent eruption of the volcano Ilopango in 250 A.D.,[30] Chalchuapa was abandoned never to return to its former greatness or influence some centuries later when it was resettled.

After the Ilopango episode Copan began to expand, perhaps as a result of the resettled refugees from Chalchuapa. References in its inscriptions indicate that the first recorded dynasty dated the first founding ancestor, Yax Kuk Mo', or Green Quetzal-Macaw, to the beginning of the fifth century A.D., quite late for one of the premier ceremonial centres of the Maya[31]. It is interesting to note that it is believed that the mother of the last ruler of Copan, Yax-Pac, came from Palenque since one of the belts found near Copan carried an inscription with the name of a lord at Palenque.

This belt is now thought to have been an item associated with the marriage - perhaps as part of a dowry for Yax-Pac's mother at the time of her marriage[32]. Another apparent connection is that both centres spoke the same Cholan language where Copan was the eastern boundary and Palenque the western[33].

Copan is remarkable for its proliferation of sculpted stone images and its surviving inscriptions and there are more of these aspects of Mayan culture than at any other site among the ceremonial sites or in the Americas as a whole[34]. The ancient name of the ceremonial site is unknown and its present name has been adopted from the nearby post-Conquest town[35]. The earliest human evidence in the Copan valley dates back 11,000 years and agricultural settlements are detectable from about 1000 B.C.[36]. The artefacts displaying Olmec imagery are evident from that time and indicate that their settlements were established for the most part as a result of their trading for obsidian and jade. These Olmec artefacts and designs became locally modified as a result of their assimilation into local styles which forms the basis of the early formative Mayan style up until the early Pre-Classic.

The earliest date recorded in Mayan kingship descent is 160 AD being the time the state forming Copan as a polity was founded[37]. It was in the determination to record their own divine right to rule that some of the most famous carving in all of Mayan art was created at Copan. This particularly applies to large carved monoliths which represent the ruler as the World Tree and these spectacular monuments still survive in remarkable condition with some traces of the original colouring still evident on some of them. Most notable of these is the so-called "elephant stela" because of the two apparent elephant heads, originally complete with mahouts or guides perched on their heads[38] (see "Mayan Genesis" p 172-6 for comparative illustrations with representations in India). These are reflected in even larger monoliths in the short era of glory at the nearby site of Quirigua whose ruler so treacherously betrayed and executed Copan's contemporary king.

Of special interest among the carved works in stone and stucco at Copan are those depicting Pauahtuns - sky-bearers - these being identical to those in India and South East Asia. These are particularly well presented in their Asian forms [5.49; 5.50] in the ceremonial bench located at Structure 9N-82 [see illustration 5.52]. These are paralleled by those of the Mayan "monkey god" which are identical to Hanuman, the monkey god of India exhibiting the same stance as those exhibited at Copan - the so-called "torchbearer" flanking the stairway facing the West Plaza dated to 762 A.D. Hanuman as this monkey deity is shown as door guardians in pairs in India as well as at Copan [5.53; 5.61; 5.62]. In Copan this monkey god is thought to have presided over the sacrifice of war victims[39] and is usually identified with the scribal brothers Hun Batz and Hun Chuen who were damned to live as monkeys in Mayan myth while the Han-uman, or Hun-uman, is also the god of writing in India.

Most important in the theme of this book are the representations of the Cauac and double-headed serpent ubiquitous throughout Mayan culture being clearly derived from the ceremonial bars originally developed in early Buddhist iconography but adopted throughout in Hindu and Jain carvings. The philosophic construct of the cosmos was perceived either as a "large wheel", seemingly to have close similarities to the Buddhist "Wheel" [*3.37*], or a squarish lotus as the carapace of a large saurian or caiman-like form. This carapace was divided into four lobes or petals[40], which so closely resembles crocodilian creatures, or Makaras, in the myths of India.

Rosalila Structure:

In the last decade excavations beneath the structures at Copan, famous for its Hieroglyphic Stairway, have revealed an early ceremonial building useful as a marker set up in the fourth century A.D. This structure had also revealed a fifth century building with the remains of a giant crocodile in bas-relief at higher level modelled in stucco[41]. However, of special interest to the study of this book and cross-Pacific contacts is that in 1991 a remarkable building now called the Rosalila Structure was uncovered [*4.71-4.73*]. It had been built over, in the Mayan custom, by a later temple construction but is dated to the end of the early Classic period. The very fact that it had been hidden by this later building meant that it had actually preserved remarkably its original colours and surface sculptures. A prominent feature is the Principal Bird Deity, Vucub Caquix, facing west towards the dying Sun - that is toward the Pacific Ocean.

For the purpose of this study equally important as this Bird Deity are the 6 caiman heads with upturned gaping mouths displayed as the ends of ceremonial bars since these correspond so exactly to surviving images of the makaras or crocodile (caiman) deities originally deriving from the Ganges River that this cannot be a coincidence. This iconographical importation is explored graphically in this work but also previously in "Mayan Genesis"[42]. It is at Copan that there is the most obvious iconography which originates in India than any other Mesoamerican centre and only Palenque comes near it. Interestingly also is the fact that at Copan the sculptors worked with a stone which was a green-coloured volcanic material[43]. In India, but also in Polynesia, greenstones had sacred connotations and were utilised particularly in the important carved panels incorporated in early Buddhist and later Hindu temples in Orissa [*3.56; 3.57*]. At Copan also are to be found paired door guardians, both Monkey Gods and Makaras, known as Dvarrapalas in India [*5.63; 5.64*], and these are so closely similar to those of India that there could hardly be any coincidence in their identical appearance and location in the building[44].

Calendrical References and the Wind Deity Vay:

It is of interest to note that the Mayan calendar "round" at Copan was 365 days long comprising an "Uayeb" of 18 months each of 20 days. The term Uayeb appears to have a common origin with the term for the unlucky five days at the end of the Mayan year recorded by Bishop Landa as "u-vayey-ab"[45]. As noted in "Mayan Genesis" this term appears to derive from the sky deity Vayu, a sky and wind deity of India who originated in Ancient Iran[46]. In more recent examination of the Mayan glyphs it has been discovered that the term "Uay" is the term for the soul or "alter-ego spirit" and these among the ancient Mayan rulers were often depicted in animal forms[47]. However this is exactly the use and meaning of the term of "vay" among the early Iranians and certainly remained so for the early peoples who adopted these early religious terms in Ancient India and is reflected in the identification of the soul with the wind[48].

At Copan it appears that an accurate system of lunation of 149 moon cycles equating to a period of 4400 days dates from 682 AD and this astronomical reference spread to the rest of the Mayan ceremonial centres[49]. The eclipse cycles, resulting through a close astronomical interest developed by the Maya, appeared to be of great interest and concern to the Mayans. It is important to note in the iconography, which appears adopted into the Mayan system from India, are the references related to the ecliptic and the eclipse deities Rahu and Ketu - the Moon's North Node or Dragon's Head and the Moon's South Node or Dragon's Tail representing the ecliptic and eclipse cycles. The general adoption of the luni-solar year, after being utilised widely among the Maya, lost its appeal after 756 A.D. which suggests that it may have been introduced from outside but after those who proselytised it died out it could not be sustained because of the lack of a long history of local development.

It is of interest to note that another calendar which was adopted more widely by the Maya is that found at Palenque which was based on the 405 lunations over 11,960 days and it is this one which appears to be the forerunner of the calendrical tables in the later Dresden Codex[50]. Interestingly also, therefore, is that at the two Mayan ceremonial centres which exhibit iconography more completely similar to that of India are speculations preserved similar in calendrical studies to those found also in India. In India, however, these were the product of an apparently much longer period of development with initiatives and new theories being introduced from Iran and Greece from the Vedic age in the first millennium B.C. through to the middle of the first millennium A.D.

In recent times it has been noted that the Chorti, who appear to have retained ancestral knowledge from ancient times and who live near Copan, celebrated the first passage of the Sun across the zenith on the evening of April 30th heralded by the location of Orion's Belt, the Southern Cross and the Pleiades[51]. It is therefore intersting that both Orion's Belt and the Southern Cross are of particular note to mariners but of less apparent interest to supposedly land-based peoples. It is also of note that the calendrical studies in Vedic India in the first millennium B.C. and early into the first millennium A.D. began with the appearance of the Pleiades and this is also the case for many of the Pacific Island cultures suggesting its spread from India into the Pacific region at that period through to the Americas.

Symbolism and Cultural Events:

Both Mayan and less well-known cultures such as the Huichols of North West Mexico have remarkable elements of similar or identical cultural expressions to those of India. These similarities, particularly in myth and iconography, have never been hidden or occluded, or so esoteric that they have never been available to the serious, or even casual researcher. Many aspects of culture between Asia and Mesoamerica have been compared by earlier researchers well-known in their field and they have submitted papers which have been presented in the main outlets in their respective fields two to three generations ago. Overall research since then has progressed little to confirm cross-Pacific contacts between Asia and the Americas except for a few more notable studies. This present study is mainly concerned with the contacts between India and the Maya, and Palenque and Copan in particular, but a brief general review of connections between these major cultural zones is therefore not out of place.

Aspects Of Mai Or Maya:

In India and notably in the Ganges region the term Maya is associated with the great early goddess of India, Mai, who is also associated with the ills of mankind as Mari Mai (or Mari Maya) - the "Mother of Death"[52]. Mai may have been the origin of the mother of Buddha, Maya[53], and the iconography of Buddhism in particular appears prominent at Palenque and Copan. This mother of Buddha was said to be magically impregnated by the celestial Gadja, or elephant[54], and it may not be a coincidence that Stela 13 at Copan appears to exhibit the head of the elephant at high level on two of the monoliths "shoulders" so closely similar to depictions in India[55]. The Buddhist deity Tara, associated, or as an emanation of the deity Avalokitesvara, may have evolved from the Sumerian goddess Ishtar. She is seen as a counterpart of the fierce Hindu goddess but in Buddhism was seen as an epithet for the mother of Buddha, Maya[56]. It is of interest that she was particularly referred to as the deity and "saviouress" of mariners. The mantra HRIM, or the hrim-mantra, is called the mayabija or saktibija and is dedicated among Tantric sects of all religions to the deity Maya[57]. Maya, the Danava, or anti-god was the great architect who was said to have built the three great cities, one on each level of the divine spheres, in the Upper World or Heaven, in the Air (probably meant as Ether), and Earth[58]. He was said to have been associated with the Nagas and Danavas who were said to live in the sea - a probable reference to a sea-borne immigrant influence.

Disgorging Siva - Makara:

Central to the iconography of Mesoamerica is that of a disgorging demon or deity. This is true also for India and this aspect is found widely spread particularly associated with what was the god of the Ganges River, the Makara. This element of mythology appears earliest in Buddhism but the reasons behind its development are lost, only the later, sparse, Hindu references are available to research apart from its ubiquitous iconography throughout India and South East Asia. In Hindu mythology the element of disgorging is associated with the emanation of Siva named Vira-Bhadra. This incarnation of Siva, the Lord of Time or World Cycles, was said to have been born from Siva's sweat or came forth from his mouth. This disgorging motif is found earlier in the Vedic texts where the Lord of Creation was said to have disgorged the components of the world and later Vira-Bhadra's function, to some degree, is usurped by Siva. Interestingly Vira-Bhadra is sometimes depicted standing or dancing on a human form called Daksa, a characteristic "trampled" figure found in Mayan stele. Of particular note is that the mudra or handpose attributed to him, varada-mudra, is of two types, one with the hand hanging loose with the fingers extended and the palm outward and the other raised upwards with the palm outward[59]. This is clearly copied from some of the mudras attributed to Buddha and is identical to that shown on the famous bust of the Maize God brought back to the British Museum from Copan by Maudslay over a century ago[60]. The motif of gods or heroes being born from the sweat of a deity is widely found in the mythology of Polynesia and Melanesia through to the Americas.

Architecture - Cardinal Directions - Respective Colours:

The architectural principles displayed in Mayan architecture seem to have been adopted, at least in some degree, from India. The ceremonial plazas in some of the sites among the Maya, such as at Tikal and Quirigua, indicate that there appears to have been a stricture preventing building of ceremonial buildings in the South or South East. This principle known for many centuries in India from Vedic times is still visible at the sacred cities of India such as Varansi (Benares) where the north bank is heavily built upon but the opposite bank has no permanent structures since the South was the region of the god of death, Yama. The belief that the South was the region of death is in fact the Hindu variant of the Vedic original in the South East, and later than that of the original stricture. It is likely that the North West, the region of the gods and the direction from which the ancestral Aryan migrations had entered the Sub-continent, was the locational planning stricture imposed in settlements nearest to their homeland on the Indus and Saraswati Rivers. The original settlements were located on the North West bank traditionally out of practicality. The bank generally ran from the North East to the South West and this earlier tradition was probably transferred in the initial settlement on the Ganges at Varanasi (Benares). Among the Maya an interesting variant of this type occurs at Tikal where the traditional steam bath is situated in the South East where no other ceremonial building was located.

The orientation of building to the cardinal points is noted in both the cultures of India and those of the Maya. Even more convincing of contact between the two cultural regions is the fact that the colours and symbolism of the trees associated with the cardinal points or four quarters is virtually identical and this is broached in more depth in "Mayan Genesis"[61]. The worship of the phallic image embodied in monoliths, often carved with the face or head of Siva was a feature of Hindu and similar monoliths are known at Jain temples throughout India[62]. This monolith was placed in front of the temple entrance and memorial stelae are also known with some fine examples surviving from Central and South India. Similarly among the Maya monoliths, often phallic, were centrally placed in front of the temple entrance along with memorial stelae these having survived in the enveloping jungles which have given them such protection over centuries.

Ritual Use of Paper for Prayers:

Among the Maya the surviving ceramic illustrations, murals and reliefs record interesting rituals involving paper. It has been interpreted from the available evidence that paper, sometimes with writing on it, was spattered in ritually shed blood either from the elite supplicants, or their victims, and then applied or fixed to the supplicant or burnt in censers. This ritual, however, is certainly not exclusive to the ancient Mayans but is found, and probably derives, from the ancient Buddhists. R.V. Russell noted almost a century ago: ".... Words were considered to have concrete force, so that their repetition of words produced an effect analogous to their sense. The purely mechanical repetition of prayers was held to be a virtuous act, and this idea was carried to the most absurd length in the Buddhist's prayer-wheel, where merit was acquired by causing the wheel with prayers inscribed on its surface to revolve in a waterfall. The wearing of strips of paper, containing sacred texts, as amulets on the body is based on this belief ...."[63]. Similar beliefs and rituals, probably originating in India, were found among the Chinese.

Cosmic Myth - Waterlily - Makara - Turtle:

In the early beliefs of India it was said that Brahma was born from the divine lotus born from the navel of Vishnu the sky god. Other earlier beliefs which predate Hinduism preserved in simple myths from the Aboriginal tribes of India, the Baiga, state that before the world existed there was only water and sky. On a great lotus-leaf Bhagavan (God) sat and drifted across the waters. Another myth, from the Chero, states that there was only water in the beginning with a lotus flower blooming over its surface. In time Bhagavan who was living in the Underworld, arose to the surface on the back of the primal Tortoise[64]. These myths are closely similar to those of the Maya where the counterpart of the lotus, the waterlily, is of major importance to their cosmic construct[65].

Grain - Sacred - Human Creation:

Ground grain was considered sacred and recorded in the most ancient records in India and consumption of it was considered a sacred act among the Hindu inherited in rituals from the early Brahmans. This grain was cooked in the sacred hearth in the house called the "chauka" and this area was sometimes marked out with crushed quartz powder. Before approaching the grain meal the higher caste men would bathe and wear only a waistband of silk or wool, but not cotton as a mark of respect. In the most ancient records preserved in the Satapatha Brahmana it was the belief that from the cakes made with ground grain and water the gods created the human being[66]. R.V. Russell noted: "when grain came to be the sacrificial food, it was often held that an animal or human being must be sacrificed in the character of the corn-god or spirit, whether his own flesh was eaten or the sacred grain was imagined to be his flesh ..." [67]. This parallels the identical belief of the ancient Mesoamericans and the Maya in particular[68].

CHAPTER 2
GARUDA the PRINCIPAL BIRD
and RAHU the ECLIPSE DEMON

In "Mayan Genesis" it is posited that the Principal Bird, or Vucub Caquix, of the Maya is the Garuda of the Hindus of India not only because they occupy parallel positions in their respective pantheons but because the associated mythology with each is so similar. In this work it is intended that this assertion should be extended to indicate that not only the mythology of each is similar but also the aspects of the eagle displayed in Mayan iconography indicates that they must have known of the Garuda bird and adapted it in recognisable ways to its mythical display in India.

The Principal Bird is clearly evident in the iconography of Palenque and this deity is shown sitting atop the World Tree which appears to emerge from the centre of Pacal's body carved in relief on his funerary slab or from the monster skull on which he appears to recline [4.02]. Mythology incorporating the motifs of sacred trees emerging from a skull or the body is widely known across the Pacific from Asia to the Americas. Frequently associated with these mythologies is the "soul" bird or tribal bird which is fundamental to the myth cycle and particularly aspects related to birth and death. The motif of the tribal or World Tree is more often found preserved by the noble or dynastic lines since it was often believed that they alone had access to their version of heaven while the common people were condemned to extinction after death. The Garuda bird was perceived in India as the guardian of the inner sanctum of the temple and the portal it defended, usually only one, was considered the transition or doorway to heaven. The Garuda was the eagle and was therefore ruler of the sky. This winged predator directed its fierce forays against snakes and therefore the renown symbolism of the eagle with a serpent in its beak was as well-known in South and West Asia as it was in Mexico. In the iconography of India the opposition of good against evil was perceived as a battle between the denizens of earth and sky and is particularly well represented on the lintel over the temple doorways known from the late Gupta period in the middle of the first millennium A.D. These reliefs appear always fully formed and suggests they were the result of a period of development in temple structures which no longer survives. This development in iconography probably occurred in North or North West India which was the most vulnerable region for devastating invasions from the region of Iran across the North West border. The Kushans in the first centuries A.D. followed all too soon in the middle of the first millennium A.D. by the invaders of Islam saw almost the total destruction of Vedic, Hindu and Buddhist achievement and culture for the previous 1500 years in North and Central India.

In cosmic myths Garuda represented the creator in his sky element and the serpent, usually depicted as the deadly cobra, or naga, represented the earth and by extension the physical elemental sphere. The Garuda was the "vehicle" (vahana) or carrier of the sky deity Vishnu who was the supreme Hindu sky god[1]. It is no accident that the serpent became identified with the ecliptic since this was considered in philosophic speculation to be the entry vortice through which the gods acted upon the earth and for the individual soul to enter, and leave as a discarnate entity after incarnation upon the earth at the end of its life. It appears that the identification of the serpent with the ecliptic may have developed in ancient Iranian mythology and references to this are found in "Mayan Genesis"[2] and this motif found its way into the Vedic myths of India. It is in the mythology of India that Rahu as the ecliptic demon is more certainly identified with the Nagas, serpent worshippers, and this will be addressed further in due course.

The Eagle of India as Garuda:

In "Mayan Genesis" it is noted that the reinvention and definition of the Aryan religions developed from the Vedic period in the first millennium resulted in hybrid deities. In expansion into the Sub-continent from North West Asia the religious ceremonies of Brahmanism, Buddhism and Hinduism became tainted with the blood rites of the aboriginal peoples in more isolated regions. The compromised rites associated with one of these more prominent hybrids Hindu deities, Bhairava, found its parallel in that of Heruka in Buddhist Tantricism. These rites were celebrated away from the main ceremonial centres of India in the North East and South of India but eventually modified versions seeped back into the mainstream of Hinduism and these deities are still regaled with offerings and prayers by the faithful.

Siva, the Lord-of-Time in Hindu mythology, appears to have been a deity which predated the latest Aryan invasions in the first millennium B.C. and there is some evidence to support the view that he was a major deity in the Indus civilisation in the second millennium B.C. The gradual, and often uneasy assimilation of the indigenous deities to the later Aryan religion of Brahmanism resulted in Hinduism although this was, and is a far from uniform in development. Siva shared supremacy with Vishnu the Sky God and he is associated with an Aryan import, Soma - or Iranian Homa, the divine ambrosia. Soma is related to the essence of the Moon and is represented by a crescent moon in the hair above the forehead of Siva. This symbolism when transferred to the human body was believed to manifest as the prana - the life energy or libido - being represented by the naga or serpent while the male seminal fluid was represented by Garuda, the eagle[3]. It can be seen therefore that the Garuda or Principal Bird at the top of the World Tree was representative of its divine sap or life transmitting fluid in both India and among the Maya. The Soma is of major importance since this immortality-bestowing beverage is fundamental to the myth of Rahu or the eclipse demon. This identification with the tree is emphasised in some texts extolling Krishna, believed to have been the incarnation of Vishnu on earth, where the Garuda bird entitled "Wing-of-Speech", declares[4] that he is the "pippala tree" - the sacred banyan. The banyan is almost certainly the "upside-down-tree" of such note in Mayan iconography as indicated in "Mayan Genesis"[5].

The wrathful form of Siva - Bhairava, is of particular note since he is seen regaled by serpents and appears in the role of a naked mendicant with matted hair. He is almost invariably shown accompanied by a dog upon which he seats himself ceremonially and his other vehicle is the Garuda where he is identified with the wrathful form of Vishnu[6]. The blood rites associated with Bhairava in remote areas bear striking resemblances to those of Indonesia and Mesoamerica and are described in "Mayan Genesis"[7].

Garuda is most usually portrayed as half-man (upper half) and half-eagle (lower half) and was said to represent the sacred "utterances of the Vedas"[8], although in China he was often depicted fully as an eagle. It is said that the various parts of his wings, perhaps because they had to flap rhythmically in flight, represented the various parts of the gayatric hymns of the Vedas[9] which were uttered as a poem and were thought to soar upwards as flight to the ancestors or gods. In the Paramesvara Samhiti he is said to have the "head of an eagle, a red beak .... And two arms like a man"[10]. Here the only anthropomorphic attribute are the two arms. Extraordinarily the depictions among the Maya seem to have been influenced by this attribution since some of the reliefs seem to indicate the reptilian legs and talons more in the display posture of a human [*4.72*].

Garuda is perceived as the natural enemy of all snakes but it is clear in the mythology of India that in fact the snake-people or snake-worshippers, called Nagas, were in fact tribes who retained the pre-Vedic Aryan religion of snake or serpent worship. They may in fact have been the descendants of the Indus people who were for the most part themselves descendants of earlier migrations from the Iranian plateau to the North West. The first tenets of Buddhism in the mid-first millennium B.C. scathingly derided the serpent worshipers but by the reign of Asoka in the 3rd., century B.C. the established religion had become saturated with Naga symbolism.

It is clear that serpent worship had formed the basis for the indigenous religions in all their diverse forms before permeating both Buddhism and Hinduism. The Garuda appears to be the transfer of the Simburgh, the Iranian eagle, which the Aryans brought with them in their migration from their homeland into India in the early first millennium B.C. identified there with their sky deity. The naturalised serpent-worshippers, already long resident in the Indian Sub-continent, in being invaded by the Aryans were the defeated and suppressed objects of contempt encapsulated in the myths recording Garuda's triumph over their serpent deities. The intimate relationship of Garuda as the eagle, who required wind currents to enable flight but also perceived to be able to master the air, with serpents is emphasised here and this relationship is extended in the myths of India to designating Garuda the "Master-of-Speech".

The importance of the wind deity, Vayu, is noted in several sections and appears to have survived almost intact in his transfer to the Maya as Uayeb, the five unlucky days at the end of the Mayan calendar[11]. This appears related to the Mayan term U-vayey-ab similarly associated[12] which appears to have derived from "vyapya" in India meaning "pervading"[13]. The name Vayu derives from the root "va" which means "to blow" hence the relation to wind. The origin of this deity from ancient Iran is emphasised by one of his titles Pavana or "cleanser", this term clearly relates to that of the Mandaean terms referred to in "Mayan Genesis" where Pawan is the name of their sacred mountain[14] and Parwaniia refers to the last unlucky five days of the year[15] which is so closely emulated by the Ancient Mesoamericans. Also of interest is the fact that Vayu was considered the father of the monkey deity Hanuman, also a scribe and of such note in this work, who is probably the origin for the scribal monkey gods of the Maya, Hun Batz and Hun Chuen. Hunaman, or Hanuman, appears in his characteristic running-kneeling pose [*5.54*] widely throughout India, singularly and as a pair of door guardians, as one of the most popular deities but in the same pose at Copan as a pair of guardians [*5.53*; *5.61*; *5.62*].

Vayu is said to be the son of the "four quarters of space" and therefore has a special relationship with the compass points and because of his incorporeal nature as air or wind there was nothing that could restrict or contain him. It is this inability to inhibit or contain the wind that he was also called Vata or "wanderer". Because of the need for wind in the sails of boats to propel them it may be that the ancient name for a sail canoe, waka, was originally derived in the ancient Middle East from Vata. Waka, and its derivatives, is also the name for canoe throughout Polynesia[16]. He was seen as the pervader of the three divine spheres of existence but his strength as a hurricane or cyclone could only be defended successfully by the wings of the Garuda[17].

The intimate relationship of the wind deity, the Principal Bird as Garuda in India and sea travel appears to be well established in South Asia. Of particular interest is that Vayu was depicted as a powerful white man riding a deer holding bow and arrows with all his attributes being coloured white[18]. It is also of interest that there are several deities throughout Mesoamerica who are shown holding arrows. Of note, however, is the depiction in some of the surviving codices of a deer "hanging" from a sky-band. These may originally have derived from the stories associated with the wind deity of India, Vayu, particularly as deity terms among the Maya such as Uayeb and U-vayey-ab appear to be directly related as already noted.

In the mythology of India Garuda, as a sky god, was the younger brother of the Sun's charioteer, Aruna, who was the deity of the dawn. Interestingly the associated records indicate that the chariot clearly derived from Iran. Some versions, however, indicate that the Sun's chariot was drawn by a naga, or dragon[19], suggesting an assimilation of the earlier naturalised, or tribal myths in India or that this was no other than the eclipse serpent - Rahu. Garuda was the vehicle of Vishnu, the sky god, and the two earrings were said to be shaped as Makaras[20] the sea or river "monster" so common in the iconography of India. These clearly represent the two halves of the ecliptic recorded in the most ancient myths of India and Iran as a serpent which was cut into two by Vishnu hurling his discus at it and these two halves became Rahu[21] - the Moon's North Node, and Ketu - the Moon's South Node. Rahu was said to be the brother of Maya - the great mythical architect of ancient India who was said to have arrived in India from the Underworld or from across or under the sea along with the other danavas or "antigods"[22]. This suggests that he personifies a foreign people or cultural intrusion from abroad - from "over the sea".

The Principal Bird:

The Principal Bird or the "heaven-bird" of the Ao Nagas in Assam called the Kotak Waya was said to protect the most precious of all stones on top of a mountain called Japvo. This was the most illustrious form of a type of stone associated with power and good luck called the Awalung and these stones were said to be found in bird's nests or the python's stomach[23]. This has clear parallels and probably has the same origin as the precious stones said to be found in the hood of cobras or the forehead of serpent or Nagas. There is much in the culture of the Nagas of Assam which is reminiscent of the Maya of Central America and interestingly these warring people wore pectorals or breastplates reflecting the same ceremonial display. Of particular interest was a form of pectoral worn by old men on festival dance days - those who had taken human heads and sacrificed the native mithan (wild ox) in the late nineteenth century - which was the head of the Great Indian Hornbill suspended on their chest[24].

In Polynesia - the last island group in the Pacific eastwards of Asia before reaching the mainland of Central America - a deified bird was crafted to be placed on the ridgepole of their priest's sacred house. In Polynesia, and India, as well as among the Maya the ridgepole was of special significance in the cosmic construct associated with sacred buildings and the structure of the roof and its supports were likened to that of the World Tree or Axis Mundae. In the Marquesas Islands this bird was called "manu ku'a" or Red Bird[25]. Craighill Handy records from the notes of Pere Pierre: "There were three orders of gods - gods of the sky, gods of the land and sea, and gods of the underworld. The chief gods of the sky were three. In their honor the three cries (hono) were uttered by the ceremonial priest when human sacrifices were brought, and the three bundles of "fau" stems were erected upon the me-ae on the occasions of funerals of inspirational and ceremonial priests. Upon the occasion of such funeral rites the third of the gods of the sky, Te-hiti-kaupeka, was represented by coconut leaves braided, or by pieces of wood cut roughly, in the form of a bird, this emblem being the embodiment (or perhaps the messenger) of this god, which received the spirit of the deceased priest and conducted it to the sky. The manu ku'a would seem, then, to represent this bird messenger; and the hukihuki to be identified with the bundle of fau stems mentioned by Pere Pierre"[26].

This Polynesian "underworld" bird, the manu ku'a, appears to be very similar to that of the Principal Bird of the Mayans and it is probably no coincidence that it appears early at Izapa on the Pacific Coast of Southern Mexico. Among the Maya the Principal or Celestial Bird is associated with death and sometimes the only grave object to be recovered is one depicting this deity[27].

The Principal Bird deity is usually considered to be identified with the god known as Vucub Caquix in the Quiche-Mayan sacred book the Popol Vuh. He appears first at the early sites from Monte Alban to the Pacific Coast at Izapa in the last centuries B.C.[28] reaching the ultimate expression in his depictions in the Mayan Classic period from about 600-800 A.D. At Izapa on Stela 25 the Principal Bird as Vucub Caquix is seen above a hero figure believed to be Hunaphu[29], one of the Hero Twins, whose arm he has torn off[30]. The myth notes that Hunaphu, however, shot an arrow at Vucub Caquix and wounded him in the mouth and he fell from the tree-top. It is also of interest that the sons of Vucub Caquix were giants and the myths associated with the elder, Zipacna, bear close similarities to those in Polynesia and Indonesia with elements suggesting that he is a Mayan assimilation of elements of both the Orion and

Atlas myths from Eurasia. Similar myths extend from Polynesia and Indonesia to India and Iran[31].

In a myth of India one early tribal hero named Lingo, and his brothers, was said to have raised the clouds into the sky to allow mankind room to stand up erect but in a time before the Sun and Moon arose in the sky. There also existed at that time a great tree called the Huppe Piyer and it was day when it blossomed and night when it dried up. Lingo and his brothers decided that the tree could be cut down and brought back to their own territory, to provide some light and with the thirteen Bhimal brothers they set about felling it. When they rested the deep cuts in the trunk could accommodate all of them for their food preparation and rest. When the tree had been cut through it still would not fall and they discovered that there was a great bird called Gara-surial-pite (Garaman or Garuda) and Lingo told his brother to kill it with his axe, and then the tree fell to the ground[32]. The myth indicates an early reference to the Garuda bird and its association with the World Tree which for the most part is identified with the banyan or another of the ficus family. The "upside-down" tree in which Vucub Caquix is represented at Izapa is undoubtedly the banyan whose propagating roots extend to the ground from its branches.

The ceiba tree is the Central America cotton-tree of the Bombax family[33] and is closely similar to that found in India and called the Sema or Seyba, a name virtually identical to that of the Central American and revered also as the Yaxche or "green" tree by the Mayan. It was believed by the Maya that there was one of these sacred trees at each of the four cardinal directions and a Principal Bird was associated with each one[34].

The term for the high god of the Maya was Ahau-lil which meant "lord". This illustrious title was usually applied to Itzamna, a reptilian form of the Principal or Celestial Bird, and during the month of Uo the screenfold books were presented before his image by the priests since he is often depicted as a scribe. Uo the month of scribes relates it to the monkey gods, Hun Batz and Hun Chuen, where in India the scribal god was Hun-aman, also a monkey god and son of Vayu, the wind deity, and therefore consistently relating Vayu to Uo and Uayeb earlier noted. Itzamna is also identified with the great caiman deity and the term Itzam is the term also for caiman, lizard or large fish[35]. The Principal Bird Deity is sometimes depicted with a snake in its mouth and in large reliefs at Cerros and Nakbe is surrounded by serpents. Extraordinarily it is believed that the Principal Bird was the companion of the reptilian Itzamna and in this guise is thought to be called Vay[36], the same term as the wind deity of India and so closely associated with the eagle of India, Garuda, the master and subduer of serpents.

The Naga or Serpent Worshippers of India:
Although the serpent worshippers are depicted by the victors as primitive and unworthy to be considered as humans surviving references of a less prejudicial nature indicate that they were far from barbaric. The cities of the nagas were extolled for their beauty and their king was said to be named Airavata[37]. This suggests that the nagas

were connected with an earlier Aryan migration since Airavata derives from Aryan and was a Vedic parallel of the name of a sacred mountain of the gods. A hero of one of the sagas involving a visit to the Naga kingdom was named Uttanka and there he is attributed with the following record: "...And he saw a twelve-spoked wheel which was being turned round by six youths. And he saw a man and a horse beautiful to behold". These he extolled with the following sacred stanzas:-

"Here three-hundred-and-sixty are attached to the fixed, yet ever moving wheel of four-and-twenty knots, and six youths turn it round. This multiform warp two women are weaving, while constantly turning the threads black and white, unwearily turning all creatures and the created worlds. [Hail to Indra] who is the bearer of the thunderbolt and the protector of the world, who hath slain Vitra and Namuchi, the great god who donneth his black garments and who severeth truth from untruth in the world, who bestrideth his vehicle - which is the ancient steed Vaisvanara (Agni the fire god) born of the waters - hail to him, the Lord of Creation, the Lord of the Triple World, the Destroyer of Castles". This was explained as follows: "The two women were Dhatar and Vidhata. The black and white threads which they were weaving were the night and days. The twelve-spoked wheel was the year with its three-hundred-and-sixty days, and the six youths who were turning it round were the six seasons. The man was Parjanya, and his horse the Fire-god Agni. The giant whom Uttanka had met first was Indra, and the bull on which he was seated was Airavata, the lord of the Nagas. The ordure of the bull which he had eaten was nectar, and it was owing to the virtue of this food that he escaped alive from the World of Snakes"[38].

These references to the Nagas clearly illustrates these serpent worshippers as a people well-versed in the astronomical arts since the twelve-spoked wheel is a direct reference to the 12 signs of the zodiac (ecliptic subdivisions). The imagery of the twelve-spoked wheel appears to be directly antecedent to, or adopted from that of the early Buddhists who considered the zodiac, the symbolic divisions along the ecliptic, as the Wheel of Law through which the individual soul passed as the doorway to earthly existence. The zodiac of 12 signs as a wheel turned by 6 youths suggests again the pairing or half cycles so fundamental to the philosophical speculations of India. This aspect is clearly indicated in the twenty-four divisions of the Ajanta sky-band indicating a paired system of 12 units originally composed of a light and dark half - in the text the "black and white threads".

The vehicle on which Indra sits is noted as Airavata, here represented as a bull, indicating his origins among cattle-herding tribes in ancient Iran. That a Naga or serpent king should also be identified with a bull is remarkable but is understandable only if the serpent worshipers had also entered Northern India from Iran. In fact there is much in the mythology of India relating to that of the Ancient Middle East and as noted in "Mayan Genesis" there are very close parallels with that of the Nagas among some of the Aboriginal myths which clearly derives from Ancient Sumeria and the Mandaean peoples of the Middle East. From what little is known of the Nagas in pre-Buddhist India there appears reason to believe that they inherited their serpent worship, in part at least, from the Elamites in Western Iran, but further examination of this possibility will have to be deferred for a later publication.

The Nagas as a mythical people were believed to guard the sacred jewels in their fabulous underworld or underground palace. This is the equivalent of the "pearl of great price" and Jean Phillipe Vogel noted: "In the Bhuridatta-jataka we have noticed the same trait; here the jewels which originate from the Nagas, vanish when they touch the ground and disappear into the Nagaloka. Plainly the earth is considered to be the depository of jewels and precious metals and the snakes which are the sons of the earth are the rightful owners of treasures concealed in the wombs of their mother"[39].

"Here we may also mention the curious belief that the hooded serpent carries a priceless jewel in its hood. Says Varahamihira: 'The snakes of the lineage of Takshka and Vasuki, and the snakes roaming at will (kamaga) have bright blue-tinged pearls in their hoods".

The jewel here is specifically referred to as a blue pearl and this suggests Tibetan influence but many other references are to precious stones which naturally shine more brightly. Vogel further notes: "Spence Hardy, after quoting this aphorism (from Chanakya) as belonging to a collection of a hundred proverbs current in Ceylon, adds the following: 'This jewel is thought by the natives to be formed in the throat of the naya (naga). It emits a light more brilliant than the purest diamond, and when the serpent wishes to discover anything in the dark it disgorges the substance, swallowing it again when its work is done. It is thought to be possible to obtain the jewel by throwing dust upon it when out of the serpent's mouth; but if the reptile were to be killed to obtain it, misfortune would certainly follow"[40]. It is notable that similar beliefs were found among the Ancient Greeks.

These references to the valuable jewels guarded by the Nagas indicates that they were a relatively advanced and wealthy group of tribes at the time the Aryan invaders confronted them and grudgingly admired or envied their achievements. Of special note is that virtually identical myths related to the serpent's jewelled neck are found in Japan and on the North Pacific Coast of North America[41]. It is clear that this path indicated is that along the sea routes from India to the North American continent as further recorded in "Mayan Genesis". The pearl associated with the serpent, however, appears to be of a much older provenance and appears to have remarkably preserved origins in the Ancient Middle East. The archaeologist Geoffrey Bibby uncovered a sacred dish on the island of Bahrein revealing the remains of serpents with pearls indicating a very special religious or mythical association. This association appears to be have dispersed not only into India but may be the origin, or have a common origin with the great serpent mound at Louden, Ohio in Eastern U.S.A. following the same oceanic path as the serpent jewel myth more commonly found.

The entrance to the Nagas world, or kingdom, was believed to be either through a cave, underwater in the middle of the ocean, or through the bottom of an ant-mound. The favourite haunt of the cobra in India was noted by the people to be an ant-hill and this factor is found repeatedly in the mythical references to serpents and folklore of India. In some of the ancient epics it is recorded that the arrow piercing the body of the enemy is compared to a snake entering an ant-hill. It is stated in the Meghaduta written by Kalidasa that the "bow of Indra" issued forth from the top of an ant-hill. Another ancient record states that the rays beaming from the jewels embedded in the head of the great Naga Vassuli penetrate and reflect into the sky from the Underworld through the fissure of the ant-hill, and coming into contact with the rain cloud, they assume the form of Indra's bow[42].

The association of serpents with the sky and rain and clouds in particular is further emphasised by the ancient identification of the ant-hill and the rainbow. Other references were believed to have been the exhalations of the serpents of Ananta's family. A further commentator notes that the divine bow in the rainy season is the ant-hill because "it is pregnant with snakes"[43].

"The ant-hill itself is utilised as an altar by those who perform their rituals by serpent-worshippers"[44]. Serpents are depicted in many elementary tribal contexts and even in the most sophisticated carvings of Amaravati emerging or entwining ant-hills or omphalli. It is of particular interest that closely similar depictions and associated mythology are found in Mexico and recorded in "Mayan Genesis"[45].

The ruler of the Nagas was said to be Varuna, a counterpart of the Greek Ouranos. He was the ruler of the seas and "knew the paths of ships"[46] suggesting a close association with mariners and was the "owner of magic power" - "maya"[47]. Varuna, in this association with the sea, was said to know the "track of the birds of the sky" and the "course of the far-travelling winds" and this undoubtedly refers to long distance mariners who used the known flight of migrating birds during the day when the stars were not available for navigation. He is one of the earliest known of deities and who in fact derives from Anatolia in the Hittite period where he is mentioned in inscriptions in the 2nd., millennium B.C. In India he is identified with the west, no doubt indicating his geographic origins to the North West of India, but was also ruler of the "oceanic girdle" believed to encircle the world[48]. Although Varuna is considered the ruler of the Nagas he was in fact subordinate to Indra, the storm god, another Iranian deity already noted. The Asuras or anti-gods, the demonised form of the Iranian Ahuras or deities of light, were said to live with Varuna. They were believed to reside in other distant regions, such as the Underworld or to live in the middle of the sea (naga-loka) where they occupied opulent palaces in fabulous cities built by their kinsman Maya the architect[49].

The coiled Nagas in the mythical speculations of India represented, when in motion, the cycles of time and Sesa was the king of the Nagas who lay under the earth and supported its weight[50]. It was believed that at the end of time he would belch forth the blazing all-consuming fires of destruction to bring the world cycles of existence to an end. Interestingly he is said to be the half-brother of the Garuda and therefore intimately associated with the fiercest enemy of the Nagas and his brother Vayu the wind deity[51].

Indra - Serpents and Lightning and Rivers:
Indra was considered the ruler of heaven and was of greater prominence in the Vedic period of India before the development of modified Brahmanism into Hinduism when

Vishnu became the supreme sky deity. It is now believed that the Vedic deities, recorded as early as the 2nd millennium B.C. during the Hittite empire in Anatolia, were neighbouring Mitanni deities and these were Mitra, Varuna, Indra, Brhaspati and Aryaman, the last of these indicating the origins of this Aryan kingdom[52].

There were considered to be three spheres of manifestation, Earth, Space and Time, and it was the fire deity, Agni, who was believed to a special relationship with these since all things were believed to manifest through fire, Agni and Soma (offering) and manifesting in each of these regions[53]. The lord of fire was recorded in the Brhaddevata declaring that "His names are Fire (Agni) in this World, Thunderbolt (Indra) or Wind (Vayu) in the intermediary sphere, and Sun (Surya) in the sky"[54]. In some texts Indra and Vayu ride as equals in the divine chariot while in others Vayu is the servant[55], but the intimate relationship between Indra, Vayu, Agni, Varuna and Garuda is very evident. Many references to Indra guarding or protecting the Soma are made in the surviving texts of ancient India and of particular interest is that he placed the bowl of precious ambrosia in the care of the sons of the wind deity Vayu, the Maruts[56].

In Vedic thought it is recorded that the Soma, the ambrosia, or elixir of life, was brought to earth by a large hawk or by the thunderbolt personified by Indra[57]. Indra was a storm god and gave rain which was of critical importance in his original habitat on the arid Iranian plateau and was perceived therefore the "giver-of-life"[58]. By extension it is believed that that there was a parallel between the rain and the male seminal fluid, both being life-giving, and the Soma itself was considered this fluid. It is interesting to note that among the Mesoamerican Olmecs there are depictions of rain as tiny phalli. Indra's fiercest enemies were Namuci who attempts to prevent the heavenly waters from flowing, and the sons of Diti who were anti-gods, and he used his thunderbolt to defeat them and the god of drought Ahi[59].

Cosmically Indra rules the Eastern Quarter and the lords of the Wind, the Maruts in the northwest, Fire or Agni in the south east and the Sun in the South West[60]. His ancient Iranian or Mitanni origin is preserved particularly in the regions of North West India where these Aryan gods first entered India. There can be little doubt that Nagas are associated with him because of the serpent-like form of the bolt of lightning and this usually presages the desired for rain in the dry climates of Iran and North West India. Of particular note is that the rivers resulting from downpours and those more permanently availed of their life-giving water were also seen to reflect the shape of the serpent. It is of little surprise that these, along with springs, lakes and waterholes, were of great importance and were propitiated in the belief that this would ensure a constant supply of water. It was considered to be inhabiting deities who took the sympathetic form of snakes, the shape of the river and streams which supplied them, and these are of great importance in the myths of India and almost identical beliefs are found among the Huichols of North West Mexico.

Since Indra, as storm god, entered India via the North West his worship was adopted in the Indus River Valley before moving into the Ganges region of the Subcontinent. Clearly the Indus was the life-line in this arid region and the origin of this beneficence must have been sought out early and known for several millennia. It is therefore in the Kashmiri foothills of the Himalayas that the Nagas were thought to have originated and the entrance to their Underworld kingdom was long reputed to be there. The kingdom of the Nagas was called Patala and beside the Sikander River there was said to be a deep waterhole and this extended downwards to this kingdom[61]. Other later myths associated the Nagas with the headwaters of the Ganges River in the Himalayas and the hero Arjuna was said to have married a Naga nymph from this river[62].

In Buddhist myths Varuna and the Nagas are really sea divinities and became Naga-rajas, and it is interesting to note that this term is found in the Pacific Ocean myths (Maori). In Buddhist cosmology the guardians of the four cardinal points, or Lokapalas, are depicted as Nagas or serpent deities and their ruler, Viru-paksha, rules over the West as does Varuna in Hindu mythology[63]. The Nagas are also associated with Ravan the demon king of Sri Lanka[64] and it has been shown elsewhere[65] that there is a close connection between this island and the coast of Guatemala[66].

It is clear in the mythology of India that there is an obvious perceived link between the serpentine form of the thunderbolt presaging the coming storm to the rain that falls from the same clouds enfolding mountains from which it issues as rivers or streams resembling the form of serpents. This appears to parallel exactly similar perceptions and beliefs in Mesoamerica but the imagery used in Mexico and among the Maya appears to be too similar to that of India to be coincidence. This is emphasised by the fact that the eclipse demon or serpent, Rahu, is so closely paralleled not only among the Maya and Mexicans but in the rest of the Americas. The associated belief regarding the solar eclipse as a giant serpent or dragon attempting to swallow the Sun was held on the Asian and American continents and the Pacific Islands between and, as among the Chinese also, the whole population joined in to make as much noise as possible in attempt to scare the monster away[67].

In Melanesia the association of the bow with the sky, as it is in India, is found in some pointed myths which are of some interest. On the north of the island of Mala there is a tradition that the bow originally fell from the sky but these are also associated more particularly with the ancient stone-using peoples on Malaita in the New Hebrides. As in the myths of India there are mythical links with serpents which almost certainly representing the ecliptic and derive from India itself. On nearby San Cristoval the "figona" serpent cult was again associated with megalithic or stone-using peoples and a people known as the Araha. The myth surrounding the figona snake named Walutahanga is also known in South Malaita and Ulawa islands. The story of this serpent deity, or demon, follows closely that of Hatuibwari, of some interest in a previous work[68], whose actual name appears to be recorded among the Huichols of the West of Mexico along with many other references. The figona wanders from island to island and in some cases is cut to pieces or into two and rejoins again. When well-treated the figona guards the children of those so disposed and rewards them for their respect and this serpent myth closely resembles the myth of the Mundas called Pundariki in India[69]. It is most likely that this serpent myth had been derived from the eclipse demon of India - Rahu. The severing of the serpent into two or several parts appears to be a reference to the two halves of the ecliptic which was depicted as the serpent in ancient Hindu myths. This is especially so as the figona, and Hatuibwari in particular, are associated with the sacred mountain which is usually also a symbol of the Axis Mundae or World Tree.

The World Tree as Centre of the Cosmos:

Pacal's sarcophagus slab exhibits one of the finest depictions in symbolic terms of the perception of the philosophic constructs picturing the transition of the soul from its earthly life to its heavenly, or Underworld, abode of any people. The World Tree carved on the slab is paralleled by that depicted as the focus of the bas-relief carved in the Temple of the Cross, dated 692 A.D.[70] [4.07]. The funerary illustration from Pacal's slab has been of great interest and study for some while it has aroused wild speculations in others. However, it is necessary to detach from the passions of the Americanists who consider that it is arguably the finest, wholly indigenous artefact that has survived from the ancient cultures of the Americas and those who believe that it is the product of aliens. The iconography represented by the tree and the associated imagery is clearly reflected in the myths and legends not only of the Mesoamericans but also those along the oceanic routes from the Central American Pacific Coast to Asia.

The World Tree illustrated carved into the sarcophagus slab of Pacal is one of the most famous known but others exist at Palenque in the Temples of the Cross and the Temple of the Foliated Cross. The surviving Mesoamerican codices also illustrate the World Tree and the philosophic constructs attached to them are closely similar to those of India and its sphere of influence. The World Tree of the Buddhists was frequently illustrated by a tree depicted behind the Buddha [5.94] but the Tree was often also identified with, and pictured as a parasol. In the Pacific Islands, appearing to be the stepping stones from Asia to Mesoamerica and used as such by ancient mariners, traders and missionaries, it is probable that this contact was in both directions.

The myths of these Pacific Islands or Australia and their common cultural heritage evidenced through myths transferred by mariners is recorded in "Mayan Genesis". There are a plethora of interesting myths relating to trees considered sacred or are associated with this myth motif of the World Tree. In South Eastern Australia the Yuin tribe maintained a sacred mound with a path associated with it. From a tree nearby the men stripped off from a tree "a spiral piece of bark" from the branches to around the bole at the ground which was said to represent the path from the sky to the earth. A ground design is marked out considered to represent the mythical boy known as Daramulen, the son of Baiame[71]. It has been noted in "Mayan Genesis" that there is evidence that these deities are related to those of the tribal peoples of India, a fact which was perceived and recorded over a century and a half ago by the first British researchers in Australia. The deity Baiame was thought by some to be the Indonesian form of Buddha but there is probably also here a confusion with the earlier Indian deity in Indonesia, Brahma. Names or titles related to Baiame are found throughout South and Eastern Aboriginal Australia and in Melanesia.

Among the early British in Australia on-site researches recorded among the tribes of Central Australia indicate that an identifiable World Tree was less frequently found among the Aboriginals than among the myths of many other peoples. One which illustrating the possibility of a probable introduced cosmic tradition among the Kaitish people of South Central Australia was recorded by Baldwin Spencer and F.J. Gillan: "The Kaitish people have a belief that the sun, who is regarded as having originally been a woman, arose in the east and travelled away to the west to a place called Allumba. Here there arose a great tree which must not be destroyed. If any one were to kill it, then every native would be burnt up. Nothing on it may be touched. If a native were to kill and eat an opposum caught on the tree, then the magic from the latter, which is imparted to everything on it, would pass from the opossum into him and burn up all of his insides"[72].

The Sun being conceived originally as a woman has parallels with some Asian mythical beliefs. But the tree being identified with the intense energy of the Sun and an embodiment of its life force clearly indicates that this is a World Tree. The mythical place where it grew - Allumba - suggest that this name has a common origin with those found elsewhere in Australia such as the Northern Australian terms for the Moon, Alinda or Aluna[73]. Similar terms are found in India[74], and among the Kogi in Northern Colombia in South America[75] suggesting distribution by mariners and traders across the Pacific Ocean.

The Kaitish myth does not have a mythical bird associated with it but one from the Mara people associates what is clearly intended to be a World Tree with the mythical hawk hero (in this case two of them). Spencer and Gillan again record: "In the Alcheringa (the mythical time) there was a Kakan or eagle-hawk man who discovered how to make fire by rubbing two sticks on one another. He was a black Kakan, and belonged to the Murrugan class. He wanted to keep the fire for the Murrugan and Mumbali people, and not allow the Purdal and Quial to have any, but a white Kakan came along and objected to his being so greedy. The two had a long discussion, and finally the white Kakan took a fire-stick and gave it to the Purdal and Quial men, though the black Kakan covered the fire over with his wings and tried to prevent him from getting any. Close by where the two hawks were disputing there was a big pine-tree which was so tall that its top reached right up into the sky. Up and down this the natives used to climb. The hawk unfortunately set the grass on fire, and the pine-tree was burnt, so that the natives, who happened to be up in the sky at that particular time, could not get down, and have remained there ever since. The fire spread as far north as what is now called the Roper River, where the white hawk threw his fire-stick away to Mungatjarra. The black hawk stayed behind, and died on the spot at which he first made fire...."[76].

The Mara myth has many aspects similar to those of Melanesia and indeed myths among the peoples on the North West Coast of North America. It is less usual in Australia to find the pine tree, a rarity compared to the native eucalypts, denoted as a sacred tree, and here clearly identified with the World Tree reaching to the sky. Here also the hawk, so often the soul or totem bird of a tribe, is associated with it and of particular note there are two opposing hawks of opposite natures. In numerous other myths in Australia, and in Melanesia, the Hawk is usually opposed by the black crow which has some elements of the struggle between darkness and light and good and evil known in the mythology of the Middle East. As in the Kaitish myth the Mara myth illustrates the importance of fire and its believed source the Sun with the World Tree which so commonly are found associated in one form or another from Asia across the Pacific to the Americas.

2.01 Banyan trees. Chikka-guda, near Badami, South Central India.

Of special note in Mayan iconography is the so-called "upside-down tree" which was of particular interest in "Mayan Genesis"[77]. In this last book evidence is presented that the Izapan crocodilian tree, depicted upside-down, derives from the banyan tree so sacred in India and found as far east as the Eastern Polynesian islands and associated, as in India, with the sacred ritual platform or temple. It was also proposed that the reptilian figure of the tree may have been a mythical mutation of the banyan and the Komodo dragon or giant monitor lizard still existing in a small group of the Indonesian Islands. In Central to North Eastern Australia, a ceremony called the Bora was widespread among the native tribes and among the Chepara an interesting focus of the ceremonies was a tree planted upside down as A.W. Howitt recorded: "In the middle of the cleared space in which the ceremonies take place, a small tree is taken up and placed with its roots in the air, and around it saplings, peeled of their bark, are placed, the whole thing tied together with strips of bark, thus making a sort of small enclosure. The saplings are painted with ochre. On this structure one of the medicine-men stands with a cord hanging out of his mouth. He is said to represent a supernatural being called Maamba. The medicine-men are called Bunjeram, and the one spoken of is the principal one of the tribe, and is believed to ascend at night to the sky to see Maamba about the welfare of the tribes-people..."[78].

The Bora is a ceremony found from Polynesia in the Central Pacific through some islands of Melanesia to the East Coast of Australia. It is clear that placing the tree upside-down in this Chepara ceremony has central significance in the ceremony although it was not explained in the record and it is unlikely that the participants knew the traditions behind it. The Bora in fact is most readily associated with the Polynesian cultures and it is likely that it was transferred by them to Melanesia and Australia, particularly as the ocean currents wash from the Central Pacific onto the East Coast of Australia. The deity Maamba is in fact another name for Baiame, already mentioned, and Bunjeram is another name for Bunjil which will be shown to have close references to the cultures of Eastern India in a following publication. It is not surprising therefore to find this representation of the "upside-down tree" arriving in Australia from Polynesia which is on the oceanic currents from Central America to South Asia.

In the Bora ceremony it was also recorded that the tribal men who have been previously initiated into the Bora ceremonies stand around the boys to receive initiation with cord hanging out of his mouth[79]. The cord was said to represent the sky cord which the medicine man was believed to ascend and down which the sky being Maamba could visit the earth. Such beliefs that ascent to and, or descent from the sky world could be made were frequent in the past and are held throughout the Pacific Ocean islands, around the Pacific Rim in both the Americas and Asia, and was no doubt transferred by mariners in past millennia, probably from India where the myth motif is also known.

A more subtle reference to the sacred "upside-down tree" is recorded from Melanesia from the islands which flank the sea currents in the opposite direction from Asia to Central America. Magical spells were of extreme importance in the daily life of the peoples of the islands of many tribes of Melanesia and those in the archipelagos north of Papua New Guinea were no exception. Most spells displayed the three-part construction which purposefully were identified with the sections of a tree or post. The first part was known as the u'ula which means the bottom section or foundation of the tree or post. In the understanding of the spell this means the "reason", "cause" or "beginning" and this initiates the power of the spell. The intermediate section of the spell is called tapwana which means, "surface", "skin", "body" or "trunk" or "middle part" of a tree and therefore indicates the central section of the spell. The last section of the spell is called the dogina which literally means the "end" or "tip" which indicates the final, closure or end of the spell. This was sometimes called the "top" or dabwana of the spell, that is its culmination[80]. The image of the spell is that of a tree turned upside-down where the beginning at the base and the tip or end at the top. This might have some origin in an unknown connection with the actual imagery of the "upside-down tree" depicted at Izapa, but in reality it probably also originates from the banyan of India, the roots of which propagates itself by their descent from its branches [2.01; 4.04]. It is probable therefore that the spell was originally associated with the banyan and imported over long centuries by traders from India into the Pacific.

Of special interest in terms of the World Tree is that preserved in the Popol Vuh since the myths and their deities recorded are paralleled by those shown in the funerary monuments and artefacts at Palenque. It is related in this sacred book of the Quiche-Maya that there existed a tree upon which was hung the decapitated head of

Hun-Hunaphu the father of the future Hero Twins Hunaphu and Xbalanque. The tree had never before borne fruit but the instant that the Lords of the Underworld had the head placed in its branches it suddenly burst into fruit - these fruit were said to resemble gourds. The tradition of placing the trophy head of a victim in a tree was known anciently, and also into more recent centuries, in the Indonesian islands and among the Nagas of Assam. The Mayan myth goes on to record that a maiden named Xquic heard the story of this tree from her father and she resolved to visit it although all were forbidden to approach it. Arriving at the tree the skull in the tree spoke to her and the result was that spittle dropped from the skull into her hand and by this she became pregnant[81]. From this magical act the Hero Twins were to be born from her to defeat the Lords of the Underworld. On finding out his daughter was pregnant he condemned Xquic to have her heart cut out and brought back in a vessel. She convinced her four guards on the way to execution to make a substitute heart and allow her to flee. This ruse worked when they saw that the tree from which she directed them to create the heart poured forth sap which looked so much like blood that, when the guards later presented the arteficial heart to her father, he did not detect the deceit[82].

In Melanesia, on the large island of New Guinea, a story recording the origins of the coconut, often considered a substitute for the head from India to Polynesia, related that a woman used to go down to the shore from the mountain on which she lived to catch fish. It was said that she used to take off her head and place it on the sandy base of a shallow area of the water. After a short time a small fish would swim into her detached head and she would shake it out of her head and place it back on her shoulders, then take the fish home to eat. A man from another village noticed the fish bones outside the woman's house and decided to follow her discretely to find out how she managed to obtain the fish. When he saw how the fish was caught in the detached head he threw the head away and when the woman returned she could not find her head and died. After some time the head sprouted where it had been thrown and grew into a coconut palm. The man who had thrown the head away returned and picked up the coconuts which had fallen from the tree, husked them, and opened them to find that they were full of blood. He then climbed the tree to pick the younger nuts, and husking those, found they were also full of blood. He then sprinkled them with lime and left them to dry in the sun and the blood disappeared as it did so. He then took half a nut and shredded the "meat" inside it and, squeezing it with water, took it home to add the juice to his wife's cooking. This greatly improved the taste of their food and since then the people have always used the coconut oil in this way. It is further said that the bird named Pwakua smelt the scraped coconut and when he saw the man preparing the coconut he flew back to the place of the coconut tree and stole a nut and took it home to Nada. There he planted it secretly and it too grew into a coconut tree and fruited and from there he distributed the coconut so others could plant and eat it[83].

The coconut in rituals and sacrifice was frequently perceived as a substitute for a human head and it can be seen from these examples of myths that the World or sacred tree emerging from the skulls of sacrificial victims or ancestors was a central element in the cosmology of many peoples. The same peoples often record that these beliefs were transferred, rather than were indigenous, from a common origin by mariners or traders.

The high religions of India focus on the World Tree being an analogy of the cosmic structure and particularly related to the zodiac and this is emphasised by the religious rituals inherited from the Vedic period. In sacrificial rites to the god of fire, Agni, a mantram is repeated which illustrates this analogy and is paraphrased as follows:

> "I adore Bharma (Brahma) in the roots;
> Vishnu who is the trunk,
> Rudra (Mahadev) pervading the branches;
> And the Devas (Angels) in every leaf".

In the Bhagavad-gita, one of the earliest recorded texts of India, the most sacred tree, the Asvat'tha or Pipal is of special mention. Many of the early British writers a century or two ago noted the close similarity of the beliefs relating to Sacred Trees of the major religions of India to that of the Scandinavian World Tree, Iggdrasil[84].

The World Tree or sacred tribal tree of the more remote tribal peoples of India are closely similar to those of Mesoamerica. Among the Tottiyans of Southern India there is a class of beggars attached to them (occurring also among many other tribes and castes) known as the Pichiga vadu. An origin myth recorded a century ago notes: "There were, ..., seven brothers and a sister belonging to the Irrivaru exogamous sept (clan). The brothers went on a pilgrimage to Benares, leaving their sister behind. One day, while she was bathing, a sacred bull (Nandi) left its sperm on a cloth, and she conceived. Her condition was noticed by her brothers on their return, and, suspecting her of immorality, they were about to excommunicate her. But they discovered some cows in calf as the result of parthenogenesis and the six brothers were satisfied as to the girl's innocence. The seventh, however, required further proof. After the child was born, it was tied to a branch of a dead chilla tree (Strychos potatorum), which at once burst into leaf and flower. The doubting brother became a cripple, and his descendants are called Pichiga varu, and those of the baby Chilla varu."[85].

This Tottiyan myth has several elements which are of interest since they resemble so closely those in the Popol Vuh myth. The miraculous conception of the virgin sister by a deity or hero and her being outcast is the main theme although in this story the decision is rescinded. Most important of all, however, is the fact that the baby rather than the skull of Hunaphu in the Popol Vuh, is tied to a tree which, in the Tottiyan myth dead, or in the Popol Vuh myth, never fruited and it either flowers or fruits immediately. This would suggest that, along with so many other myth motifs so very similar from India to Mesoamerica that they were from a common origin. It is interesting to note that it is the characteristic association of the Divine Bull's fluid which takes the place of Hunaphu's spittle in the Popol Vuh myth causing the impregnation. In India the celestial tree is common to all three major religions and the image of this, or "Kalpa-Uriksha", are frequently carried in festivals in South India often together with that of the "celestial cow" - Kamadhenu[86]. The fierce aspect of Siva,

Bhairava, referred to elsewhere, is sometimes shown seated under the World Tree which is called Mandara and is probably influenced by Buddhist beliefs and iconography[87].

The Nagas of Assam residing in the Himalayan foothills north of the Bay of Bengal have frequently been considered to have cultural connections with the ancient peoples of the Americas. A myth recorded from the Sema Nagas tells of a woman called Muchapile who loved a man married to another woman. She kills the man's wife and assumes her identity. From the hidden body of the deceased wife a bamboo grows which becomes an orange tree. While Muchapile is in the fields the deceased wife comes back to life and appears before her husband to inform him of the deceit and as a result he kills Machupile. However, both husband and wife later touch Machupile's bones and they die[88]. The bamboo growing from the body is a substitute for the sacred tree and corresponds to this tree appearing to emerge from Pacal and the skull on his funerary slab.

On the Melanesian island of Guaua a legend recorded suggests that people who were so far antecedent to the populations existing there in the nineteenth century to the present day established traditions which could not be accounted for by the later inhabitants. Dr. Felix Speiser noted in the early twentieth century: "I obtained a good number of skulls, which were thrown into the roots of a fig tree, where I was allowed to pick them up as I pleased."

"The Suque is supposed to have originated here; and here certainly it has produced its greatest monuments, large altar-like walls, dams and ramparts. The gamals too, are always on a foundation of masonry, and on either side there are high pedestals on which pigs are sacrificed. Among the stones used for building we often find great boulders hollowed out to the shape of a bowl. No one knows anything about these stones or their purpose; possibly they are relics of an earlier population that has entirely disappeared"[89].

The placing of skulls in the base of a ficus or banyan was known widely in the Pacific Islands and many times recorded and photographed by early anthropologists having clear parallels to the Mayan Popol Vuh account of Hunaphu's head being ritually hung on the tree in the Underworld, and known also among the Nagas of Assam. The gamals mentioned were the sacred men's houses known also in the New Hebrides and which are certainly connected to the ghotuls of the Maria and other tribes of India. The Suque is a ritual considered as having the same origin as the Maki of the New Hebrides and a ceremony with a similar name is found among the same tribes and castes in India[90].

The skull identifying with or being the origin of the sacred tree is found also where that of a mythical serpent is the substitute for the skull of a hero or deity sacrificed or a trophy head planted by him. In the New Hebrides it was believed that the coconut grew from the head of a snake[91]. On the island of Tanna in the New Hebrides it is said that Tangalua, a local form of the great Polynesian deity, Tangaroa, had an Anwian woman named Seimata as his wife and a son. Tangalua was eel- or serpent-shaped and the other Anwians hated him and conspired to kill him when he drank kava. Before he died he told his wife to keep watch over his grave for a tree would grow there which would be useful for them. Eventually from the grave a coconut grew from his two eyes and the fruit ripened into nuts good to eat which Semiata kept secret to provide food for herself and her son. The boy eventually revealed the secret to other boys he spent time with and when his mother heard of this she was so angry she pulled up the tree tearing it into fragments and threw them into the wind. These scattered to all the other islands and grew into coconut trees so that all the islanders were able to benefit[92]. In another myth the coconut tree sprang from the skull of a woman[93] but in a further example a dugong (manatee) named Chima was said to have sent his sister's son out fishing. He speared a stringray which dislodged the arrow and killed and devoured all but the head of the young man. This Chima retrieved and placed it in the house and there it sprouted as the coconut tree and when it fruited he distributed them to his friends[94].

The human, serpent or dugong skull along with coconut tree clearly implies a modified if less expansive cosmic structure which the local islanders on Melanesia have appeared to have accepted at face value without any incisive philosophic speculation attached. In some myths on a few islands there are references which suggest that the coconut tree had been considered a "World Tree" or "Axis Mundae" in the sense developed in the speculations of India or Mesoamerica. This tends to indicate that these myths have been assimilated less than completely from some other source and the local versions are therefore diminished excerpts from more acculturated lands. From the Admiralty Islands near New Guinea in the late nineteenth or early twentieth century Meier recorded the main protagonists of a myth as a woman named Hi Pipiu and her two sons: "Once, when they went fishing there came a spirit which devoured the elder brother leaving only his head. The spirit then went back to his country, the sky. The younger brother brought the skull to his mother. They buried it, and five days later a coconut palm sprang from it, growing so high that it reached the sky. Now the younger brother took dog's teeth and on the coconut palm climbed to the sky to see the spirit. He hid the dog's teeth near the door. When the spirit took a stone axe to kill the man, the dog's teeth sprang up and bit the spirit so he died. Then the man took all things (the myth does not state what these things were) and descended to the earth on the coconut palm. He descended to the earth, he fell to the earth and died. If he had not fallen down the coconut palm would still be reaching to the sky, and we would be able to ascend to the sky. He fell and the coconut palm shrunk"[95].

In a myth cycle centred on a hero named Nazr one section features a sky cord which was used to take stone into the sky by the Thunder demon named Manimbu. The cycle continues with Nazr killing a female demon named Mongorn after which he eats her body throwing her intestines into a swamp, where they became reed grasses and sugarcane, and then planted her head. From the head grew a banana tree. Nazr met Mahu who taught him the skill of modelling skulls, painting them red and placing shells into the eyes. The sky cord is again featured as the means by which the sacred Polynesian beverage called Kava was taken up to the sky. Of particular interest is that in the same region of Melanesia a deity called Uar chiselled a face into stone and from this sprang Geb - a deity who was said to be black. This rock deity was associated with another serpent hero named Sido and from Geb's neck a banana tree sprang and it was planted, and it is said that he eventually climbed the tendril's of the yam to become the Moon.

The name of the hero Nazr's name bears striking resemblances to those in the Middle East as does the name Geb which was the earth deity in ancient Egypt. The name Uar suggests that it is derived from the Wind deity in India, Vayu, finding its parallel in the Mayan deities Uo; Uayeb and U-vayay-ab associated with the Mayan calendar. In Mesoamerica sky ropes are common in the mythologies of both North and South America and of particular interest in those of Mexico. Needless to say in India there are many recorded examples and it would appear that most of the Pacific Ocean examples and in the Americas derives from there and have been previously expanded upon[96].

In South Eastern Australia the Kurnai were of considerable interest to the first Victorian researchers and the ceremonies recorded have much in common with India and Polynesia. A.E. Howitt a century and a half ago recorded a ceremony called the "Bunjil-barn" which was performed to bring about the death of a pre-determined victim. Howitt in describing the creation of the ceremonial site notes: "They chose a young He-oak, lopped the branches and pointed the stem, then drawing the outline (Yambog inni) of a man as if the tree-stump grew out of his chest, they also cleared the space of the ground for a space round the tree, making a sort of magic circle. Then they stripped themselves naked, rubbed themselves over with charcoal and grease, a common garb of magic, and danced and chanted the Barn song"[97].

The tree in each case in India, Melanesia and in this relation among the Kurnai in Australia, appear to have a similar origin each either specifically stated as growing from a grave or it is implied. It is interesting to note that the hero Geb in Melanesia was considered black and in this Kurnai ritual the men are also painted black. In a number of depictions on ceramics and murals in Mesoamerica the participants are clearly depicted painted black.

Myths have been recorded where trees and their fruit are associated with transformation, or are portrayed as an analogy. This is exemplified by a myth from the Bhuiyas, a tribe of considerable interest and linked to the origin of the Mayan Pauahtuns in India. A myth of this type was recorded a century ago: "An old woman had domesticated a favourite parrot. The parrot once flew out on a pilgrimage and returned with a nectarial fruit (amrita phal) reputed to avert death and old age. The woman kept it carefully in the house. A cobra saw the fruit and stung it with its fangs and it rolled down. A cat saw it falling down, and, taking it to be a rat, devoured it and instantly died. The woman thought that it was poisonous fruit with which the parrot wanted to kill her. She buried the cat, and out of the grave sprang a tree which bore beautiful fruits. Another old woman who was living with her seven sons and their wives was disgusted with her because her daughters-in-law slighted her. She listlessly plucked one of the fruits and ate it, and lo and behold, she was forthwith transformed into a young woman of exquisite beauty. The other woman who owned the parrot and the fruit saw this wonderful metamorphosis and she too plucked and ate a fruit from the tree and was similarly transformed into a maiden with eternal youth"[98].

If these myths were perceived to have any didactic content then it must be that it was the mystical life-giving rejuvenation, acquired from the coconut or other fruit-bearing trees which emerged from the death of a hero, deity, or other important person to the subject of the story, extending life or immortality is gained through the sacrifice of another person or hero. Of particular note in so many of these myths is the total lack of emotion displayed at the loss of those whose lives seemed to be terminated so prematurely. Indeed the underlying message appears to be that it is necessary to die, either accidentally or purposefully, to bring about these beneficent acts or gifts for oneself and for the rest of humanity. This leaves only one step to the seeking of appropriate victims for sacrifice in order to gain the benefits associated or believed to be endowed by the often demanding ancestors or deities.

In terms of the theme of this book it is clear that the widespread belief that life-giving or World Trees could emerge in mythical times from the skulls, or chests of slain heroes was endemic to India from Aryan Brahman to Aboriginal tribes-people. This belief can be traced through into Melanesia which can be perceived as a connecting link to Mesoamerica and the depiction of the World Tree emerging from either Pacal himself or the skull on which he is seated. In myth the fruit of the sacred tree was also thought to be able to regenerate and this by extension was related to rebirth since the leaves of the World Tree were considered the souls of those who had departed this life and remained as such until rebirth. The fundamental principles of these myths whether from India, Melanesia, or Mesoamerica are the same suggesting a common origin.

Sun God and Serpents:

The association of the serpent with the ecliptic and as Rahu personifying the eclipse demon in India finds its parallel, although less coherently, in the myths of Indonesia and Melanesia. The Nagas in India and serpents generally are considered antipathetical to the sky and its sky deities such as the Sun since the serpents represent and are associated with water, such as rivers and streams which reflect their shape, as well as lakes and springs. The Sun and sky represent air and fire and water extinguishes these elements. However, it is in the equilibrium of the solar system centred on the Sun that it was considered that there is a balance of these elements. The Sun was considered as supreme deity and the ecliptic, represented by the serpent as the encompassing "girdle", against which the location and orbits of the planetary bodies and constellations are measured. Since these symbolic representations are the product of geocentric cultures where the Moon is particularly associated with water, the ecliptic demon was believed to have a special relationship with this body and the earth. As Rahu in India the eclipse demon was said to be the Moon's North Node and after the sky deity, Vishnu, cut off its head with his discus, the tail was defined as Ketu, the Moon's South Node, although it is often depicted also having a head. This may have been the origin of the two-headed serpent so common in the Pacific and along the Pacific Rim where eclipses were greatly feared. In India it was common to believe that there existed a snake with two mouths, called a Domunha -believed to be quite fierce, and it probably has its origins in the double-headed ecliptic serpent[99]. In describing the serpent ceremonial bars of the Maya it is considered that this item of regalia was representative of the ecliptic and defined as the "path of communication" or "interface between the supernatural world and human world"[100]. This corresponds perfectly with the traditional interpretation of the ecliptic symbolism in the philosophic speculations of India as well as being virtually identical in their physical appearance and symbolic elements [*4.74-4.78*].

Sun Holds Serpents Tails:

In a myth from the text of the Adi-parvan the Naga or half-human, half-serpent Padmanabha, who lived by the banks of the Gomati River, was employed to drag the chariot of the Sun-god Surya[101] in its orbit. Clearly there were no half-serpent people as such but the Nagas were in fact earlier assimilated peoples from the Iranian plateau who were serpent worshippers. In the symbolism of the myths, and through long ages of recounting, those who worshipped serpents became identified with the objects of their worship. In the Drona-parvan the divine bow and arrows appear as two fiery serpents, suggesting that in symbolic terms fire is not always considered inimical to water and the great serpent king Sesha was associated with the gods themselves.

The symbolism of a Naga pulling the divine chariot is of interest since this appears to be directly related to the sky deity - the Garuda bird - clasping the tails of two cobras which is do frequently depicted in India [*5.08-5.11*; *5.12-5.16*]. The depiction clearly indicates the belief in the supremacy of the Garuda over the two halves of the ecliptic represented by the two serpents, undoubtedly Rahu and Ketu, the eclipse demons. Garuda as the divine eagle has already been noted as being the opponent of the Naga deities and their worshippers but here surmounting and framing the portal to the temple the ecliptic is in fact illustrated as the entry from the divine world - the inner sanctum, from the outer world.

The projection of the ecliptic is illustrated perfectly in the intention of the temple portal as the "vortice" from the earthly, outer dimension to the sacred inner divine sphere, and many temples did not allow any other than the priest to enter that doorway. The inner sanctum was in fact meant to be the restricted precinct into which the divine entities from the Upper World or Heaven interfaced with the sanctified medium in the person of the priest and with whom they communicated. This is clearly the intention in the temples of India, and is also an aspect of the early Christian religion where the profane did not enter further than what is known as the "rood screen" in the cathedrals of England. This symbolic division was known elsewhere in Europe where the section devoted to the altar and choir was considered sacred and accessible only to those who had been sanctified. The depiction on Pacal's sarcophagus is clearly illustrating the descent into the Underworld by his soul but visualised as if seen through their idea of the sky-band as portal. This sky-band undoubtedly represents the ecliptic which is exactly that indicated in the portals of India and in particular the ecliptic divisions or sky-band shown on the ceiling of Cave 2 at Ajanta [*3.31*] - and in Orissa.

At Palenque also are depictions illustrating a connection of the sacred door with serpents [*5.18*] suggesting that this is a free interpretation of the original depictions in India and Indonesia. The serpent depictions at Palenque were in fact numerous and appeared to have been created in stucco on some, if not all of the mansard roofs. Little is left but those that have survived sufficiently to allow some reconstruction show that they are clearly derived from prototypes of serpents and makaras in India, and Paharpur in particular [*4.83*; *4.84*].

Serpents in Mesoamerica:

The symbolic usage of the serpent is ubiquitous in Central America and possibly indicates the similar adoration of the serpent in India before the incursions of the Aryan peoples from the Iranian plateau in the first millennium B.C. into the Sub-continent. In Mexico the "coatepantli" was an architectural feature in Late Classic Mexico displaying a walled enclosure faced with the sculptured heads and sometimes bodies of serpents[102]. This is reminiscent of stupas depicted in Buddhist reliefs where the dome is depicted as omphalli entwined with serpents appearing to define geomantic energies believed to "energise and vitalise" the subtle zones of creation[103]. Among the later Mayans Chichen Itza appears to be largely focused on the great serpent temple which is clearly also related to the solar calendar[104].

An important ceremonial location among the Aztecs was the "serpent mountain" - Coatepec, said to be the birthplace of Huitzilopochtli[105], and virtually identical representations of this in Mexican "books" occur among the Buddhists[106]. The mother of this Aztec deity was said to be Coatlicue[107] (Co-at-lee-kay), and this has already been considered as a direct inflection among the Mexicans of the term for the fierce goddess of India, Kali.

The derivation of the serpent deities appears to be easily proven since the similarities are so close that many of the earlier explorers and researchers were in no doubt of the connection. A further element of reference is the serpent rod or sceptre which was recorded as being held by images of both the Mexican rain god, Tlaloc, and the Mayan counterpart Chac[108]. These are determined to represent thunderbolts of lightning in exactly the same way as those of Siva in India already noted but which he assumed from the original Iranian prototype transferred into India in the Vedic period associated with Indra. These appear to directly relate to the Mayan ceremonial bars which are so clearly identical to those of India.

There are references to elements of illness being magically diagnosed and treated both with magical amulets and herbal remedies where the illness is considered to be caused by, or visualised as a serpent, often a rattlesnake[109]. Closely similar mythologies existing in India are ubiquitous among the tribal peoples of India. They are often associated with so-called "vagina-dentata" myths[110] where man is threatened in many tribulations associated with sexual problems and personal relationships and virtually identical myths occur among the Huichols of Western Mexico[111].

In Mexican mythology and symbolism the double-headed serpent deity Xiuhcoatl is known as the fire-serpent and this appears to be the counterpart of the Mayan Vision Serpent, associated with clouds, lightning bolts, storms and fire[112]. The waterlily, paralleling the lotus in India, was of major importance to the Mayan nobility and a major symbol of kingship. The serpent is also identified with this regal symbol as the water-lily serpent and is particularly associated with the number thirteen and the 360-day period in the calendar[113]. This appears to be paralleled in later Aztec myths relating to the thirteenth levels of heaven and their respective gods being deprived of their "great serpent"[114].

There can be little doubt that for anyone professing a serious interest in the mythology and iconography of Central America that many aspects have been introduced from India. The many parallels evident between the available surviving elements from the Mayan sites in particular and the long history of traditional imagery covering so many existing temples in India must militate for cross-Pacific contacts. The imagery and elements of iconography are displayed in similar contexts on both continents and there had to have been transfers from Asia to Mexico and the Maya over many generations and were not simply as a result of one-off voyages.

CHAPTER 3
ICONOGRAPHY - SKY BANDS
and SACRED PORTALS

The presence of the calendar among the early peoples of Central America - the cultural zone now usually referred as Mesoamerica - is considered pictorially evident in the "Sky-Band" which is exhibited on a number of the Pacific Coast sculptures of the Pre-Classic Mayan sites along the Pacific Coast of South Mexico and Guatemala. These sites are more recently considered a late occupation of the Olmecs who were transcendent from the second millennium B.C. This sky-band appears to be a later development after their expansion from their Caribbean coast sites across the Gulf of Tehuantepec to the Pacific Coast. However it is also thought that the Olmecs may have founded trading sites on the Pacific Coast and evidence at the sites in El Salvador suggests that they were early on this coast if not originating from there.

The coastal centre of Izapa is one of these sites in the far south western corner of Mexico and is ideally located to have been involved in a Pacific marine trade. Izapa is a partially excavated site which has revealed platforms and especially interesting are the carved reliefs on a number of stelae. It has been noted in "Mayan Genesis" that there are many apparent cross-Pacific connections in the iconography, and contemporary in development with those in Indonesia and India. The Izapan stelae have references to other early Mayan sites accessible to the Pacific Coast such as Kaminaljuyu in the Guatemalan Highlands but some modern day archaeologists draw parallels between Izapa and Palenque[1]. This suggests that the iconographical influences so obviously transferred from Asia, and India in particular, were probably introduced by mariners, traders and missions through Izapa. It is also likely that this was so for the sites of Abaj Takalik, El Baul, and Bilbao further east in Guatemala, and it must certainly be true for Copan.

Palenque - City of the Underworld Twins or of the Lordly Palanquin:
One of the stelae at Izapa, Stela 21, depicts prominently in the background an elite person, perhaps foreign trader or priest, being transported in a palanquin while a decapitation scene is rendered as the main theme in the foreground [3.03]. This interesting survival from about the first century A.D. records that the palanquin was a form of conveyance for rulers and high-born people was known among the Maya and probably so for Central America generally. This of course resembles the same mode of transport in India and long known in Asia generally over millennia into recent centuries.

The surviving emblem glyphs relating to the place names of the ceremonial sites appear not to reveal the name of the ceremonial site itself but means "the place of ...." which is reflected in the similar traditions being retained by the Chol Indians to this day[2]. It has been suggested that the origin of the name Palenque derives from that of the hero twin Xbalanque. On the evidence available in the Popol Vuh, the sacred book of the Quiche-Maya, it is suggested that the Hero Twins, Hunaphu and Xbalanque were identified with the Moon and the Sun. Those most closely associated with the archaeology of Palenque agree with Prof. David. H. Kelley's hypothesis that the original name of the site was Balan-ke (Palenque) which meant that this was the place where rituals for the evening or dying Sun were celebrated. Palenque is one of the most westerly of the Mayan sites, hence the theory, and that Copan as one of the most easterly, correspondingly, was related to the rising Sun.

The original name of Copan is not known and the theory cannot be checked for consistency but it is curious that there is so little surviving iconographical evidence for either of the Twins being the tutelary deities of the ceremonial centre at Palenque, or indeed Copan. Whatever the final name given to the site by the Maya it does not undermine the fact that there is considerable evidence that they received major cultural infusions from India and integrated them into their traditions in their own very identifiable way. This suggests that the name for Palenque may indeed have originated from a foreign word which became adapted, inevitably, into the Maya dialects, deviated from its original meaning as time passed in the recognised characteristic manner of language divergence. Interestingly a palanquin was used to convey a Don Pilos princess, Lady Wac-Chanil-Ahau, to Naranjo to marry into the local dynasty. She is associated with the rites of opening the portal to the Other World with the intention of re-establishing contact with the ancestors on 30th., August, 682[3].

In India the Sanskrit term for palanquin is "Palyanka" (bed; couch) and "palanque" is one of its derivatives. In Java the term "palangi" means a "litter" or "sedan" clearly deriving from the Sanskrit original. These terms for "bench"; "litter" or "sedan" appear to have been confused or extended from the pole used for carrying burdens by a porter at each end which is also named "palanque". The Kahar were palanquin-bearers as was the caste known as the Dhimer[4] in India. These may have been related to the Khadal, another palanquin-bearing caste, who were descended from the Bauri caste of Bengal. These people were totemistic and their septs (clans) appear to have been tree and serpent worshippers, the Kilasi, where the Julsi and Kandnaki septs had the snake-hole as their totem while others such as the Balunasi had a stone or the Sun[5]. The Khadals have a tradition on the death of one of their tribe, which may be a copy of that of the Hindus, after the corpse has been cremated each takes a twig of the mango tree and beats the grass to force a grasshopper out of its hiding place. This, when found, is wrapped in a new cloth and taken home to place beside the family deity. The deity's name is then intonated in the belief that this will endow the soul of the recently deceased person with immortality, thought then to reside in the grasshopper. Closely similar beliefs are found as far east in the Pacific as Samoa and these no doubt were transferred by mariners and traders many centuries ago following the oceanic route from Asia to Central America.

In "Mayan Genesis" the Bhuiya tribes of Orissa and North East India were noted to be of major importance since the Mayan term for sky-bearers, "Pauahtun", appears to have derived from their wind god "Pawa-Ban"[6]. Among these same people it was traditional for a bridegroom to be taken to the marriage in a palanquin[7]. This is also true for some other peoples and the Kamsala - the Telugu equivalent of the Tamil Kammalans - are also known for this custom. There are examples of some lower castes such as the Madigas of South India having adopted the custom but this was considered a privilege of the higher castes and caused some resentment[8]. In some of the rituals of the Madiga Asadis they use a "toddy", normally of palm wine, and the pot in which it was contained was called the "pallakki" or palanquin[9]. There is a curious deviation from the normal Mayan traditions of hereditary in the Palenque records and that is that the women appear more prominent than elsewhere. The depiction of a palanquin on the Izapa stela might suggest that there may have been foreign suitors on their way to consolidate family or other alliances. An interesting reflection on the male line at Palenque and that it may not have all been indigenous, is reflected in the portrait of Pacal 1, an ancestor of Pacal 2 ("the Great") depicted on the side of Pacal 2's sarcophagus.

The portraiture so evident at Palenque and so limited at other Mayan sites has long been commented upon. The numerous surviving examples have been eulogised because of their believed life-like quality and if this is so then the portrait of Pacal 1 [4.09] must be of some significance. Of special note are the artificial nose-pieces which appear to have been applied to portraits to bridge the nose, perhaps in real-life only for ceremonial purposes, to achieve the clearly desired ideal profile. Just why this should be is open to conjecture but the extraordinarily large one applied to Pacal 1 deserves comment. Clearly this exaggerated Roman, or Semitic, profile was an ideal aspired to for either religious or ancestral reasons, but that one of the first ancestors to the Palenque throne should be depicted as exceptionally deficient suggests that he was of foreign or perhaps of a less acceptable local origin requiring enhancement.

If the portraiture was of such a high standard and the memory of Pacal 1's profile accurately remembered then the relief as drawn suggests that their might have been dwarfism in the line since the depiction suggests a very flat-faced individual. There are references to dwarfs being maintained as the jesters, perhaps scribes or even as religious mediums or priests at the courts of the Mayan nobles. Equally there are many artefacts which reflect designs virtually identical to those in China particularly centred at Kaminaljuyu. This suggests a possibility that Pacal 1 may have been in fact from China. In "Mayan Genesis" the close connections between the peoples such as the Bhuiyas and Nagas of the Ganges through to the Bhramaputra Delta in India with peoples in Southern China[10] is noted as being of some importance. The many references to the South Chinese iconography and that of the Maya has been recorded not only in "Mayan Genesis" but in articles more than two generations ago by Robert Heine-Geldern and others.

The Gadabas in India were a caste of palanquin-bearers who were believed to have originated in the Godavari Delta on the east coast of India[11]. They migrated to Orissa and it may be significant that both regions are associated with the early Buddhists who appear to have had such an influence in Mesoamerica. It is interesting to also note that among the Zapotecs the term Golaba is found and the name of a tribe with the same name are associated with the Savaras who are identified with the Bhuyias whose wind deity Pawa-ban is probably the prototype of the Mayan Pauahtun earlier noted.

The occupational term applied to the palanquin-bearers in South India was Sivyan or Sivala[12]. Also in South India a sub-caste of the Idaiyans, the Pondan or Pogandan, were palanquin-bearers to the Zamorin, the ruler Calicut on the Malabar coast[13]. The term Zamorin and this region will be of greater interest in a following publication. Associated with these former South East Indian states Tulu fishermen known as the Mogers also acted as palanquin-bearers[14]. Fishermen also on the Malabar coast were the Mukkuvans as well as coconut growers and palanquin-bearers[15]. Their chiefs were called Arayan and this appears to have descended from the term "Aryan" and it is probable that these were in fact sea traders or mariners from either Northern India or the Middle East. The Mutracha Karans were the defenders of the later Mysore state in South India but they appear to have descended from the former rulers before being overrun and became, beside warriors, palanquin-bearers to the ruler[16].

The Dravidian Nayars were the renowned warriors of South India and in status were considered second only to the Brahmans. They reflected a large proportion of Aryan blood and were palanquin-bearers only to the rulers[17]. Palanquins were particularly associated with certain claims of status in South India. The Sanans, a Tamil palm-wine producing caste, claimed higher status and riots in the 19th., century resulted from their demand for the right to Kshatriya (warrior) caste and the associated benefit of high status to ride in palanquins[18]. In another state called Travancore the sons of the sovereign were called Tambi and were exclusively allowed to be carried in palanquins before their father - the ruler[19]. This palanquin and its exclusive use indicated the special rules associated with status in India and this is probably in some way connected with the Izapa stelae.

In other castes the privilege of carrying palanquins was sometimes associated with other, usually related, occupations. The Tsakals, Sakalas or Chakalas were palanquin-bearers and also torch-bearers[20] while others were also Sank or Chank (conch-shell) bearers and blowers. Associated with the revenue officers of the local sovereign the Vellalas considered themselves as Brahmans and were noted as a scribal class. In the first half of the twentieth century over two generations ago a Vallala was remembered being seen carrying out his scribal occupation associated with his caste as Edgar Thurston noted: "As accountants they are unsurpassed, and the facility with which, in by-gone days, they used to write on "cadjan" or Palmyra leaves with iron styles, and pick up any information on any given points from a mass of these leaves, by lamp-light no less than daylight, was most remarkable. Running by the side of the Tahsildar's (native revenue officer) palanquin they could write to dictation, and even make arithmetical calculations with strictest accuracy"[21]. It is interesting to note that writing is always associated with status and the ruling classes both in the Old World and the New and particularly among the Maya where scribes were believed to have been selected from the ruling families.

Whatever the origin of the name of Palenque nothing is certain at this time as to whether it derives from the mythology of the Maya or their forebears or whether imported or evolved from an external source. At Palenque itself imagery of six-toed babies, as serpent footed deities, depicted being held during a ceremonial rite have been identified with the ruling family [*5.113*; *5.116*]. There are suggestions that Pacal 2 himself may have been club-footed and the depiction of Pacal 1, appearing possibly to reflect aspects of dwarfism on the side of his tomb may be evidence of a history of deformity in the family. Equally, and perhaps more likely is that some of these depictions are symbolic and the serpent-footed deities were intended to identify the ruler at birth with aspects of divinity expressed in forms of imagery rather than eulogising limiting factors of deformity. This would then suggest that Pacal 1 was not necessarily deformed but may have been foreign or simply lacking the ideal profile associated with ruling dynasties. The association with the serpent-footed deity (God K) is the more likely since this exists independently of personalities as a deity in Mayan script [*5.114*] and this god form appears to be directly derived from similar imagery found

3.01 Tiger cave. Udaigiri, Bhubanesvar, Orissa, India, 4-3rd., century, A.D.

3.02 Monster mask sky band. Izapa, Southern Mexico, Late Pre-Classic.

3.03 Monster mask sky band with Palanquin in back -ground. Izapa, Southern Mexico, Late Pre-Classic.

3.04 Monster Mask (Kirtimukha). Nalanda, North Central India, 6th., century, A.D.

3.05 Monster Mask Tiger Cave. Udaigiri, Bhubanesvar, Orissa, India, 4-3rd., century, B.C.

at Nagarjunakonda in the Krishna and Godavari deltas near the east coast of India [*5.115*].

The Monster Mask or Sky Demon:

After the diversion to consider the name of Palenque and its probable association with the Mayan Pacific Coast ceremonial sites, Izapa in particular, it should be further noted that the sky-bands depicted at this latter site indicate that they were usually represented as anthropomorphic in that they depict the upper jaw of a fanged sky "monster" or demon [*3.02*]. In some cases other representations depict the upper and lowest register as the upper and lower jaws of this creature [*3.04*]. Of particular note is that the fangs extend down from the "lip" representing the sky-band itself but towards their ends curl away to the left for the one on the left, and to the right for the one on the right. This peculiarity is found in stelae dating from the Pre-Classic in the late first millennium B.C. into the first millennium A.D. It is interesting to note therefore that a closely similar development was known in Ancient India. The curved fangs are depicted either as the primary pair or as separate extrusions emanating beside the fangs [*3.03*]. In Mexico and among the Maya there are clay figurines which depict these "fangs" as labrets inserted in their mouth probably for ceremonial occasions only. This mid-first millennium B.C. depiction from Nalanda, the great Buddhist university in Northern India shows a so-called demon's face most usually called "Kirtimukha". This is a late development, frequently depicted surviving into the present from the centuries of the first millennium, in a tradition which had originated almost a millennium earlier and still evident in the sculpted rock-faces adjacent to the cave temples of India shown in *3.01*; and *3.05*. These two illustrations were taken a century apart depicting the same rock temple or shrine. This is the so-called "Tiger Cave" at Udaigiri on the outskirts of modern-day Bhubanesvar in Orissa, North West India. It dates to the 4-3rd., century B.C. and indicates the probable origin or at least association of the tiger's or monster's jaw and the "sky-band". This will be amplified in later sections dealing with the caiman of Mayan myths and iconography or that of the makara of India but it is clear that there are too many parallels for there to be no connection between the two developments. The succeeding sky band found at Palenque in particular parallels the identical development in portal panels found in Orissa and the cave sky bands at Ajanta. The identical earlier panels and later development of the sky band in India and among the late Maya cannot be a coincidence.

Hieroglyphs - Origins and Imports:

The beginnings of the Mayan script has received a great deal of attention from scholars in the last decades. This has resulted from the break-throughs in the latter half of the twentieth century revealing some of the keys by which a more accurate interpretation of the surviving inscriptions could be made.

The earliest script in the Americas appears in the Valley of Oaxaca in Southern Mexico near the Isthmus of Tehuantepec by about 600 B.C. The earliest example is preserved in a script on an Olmec stela known from La Mojarra near

3.06 Olmec stela. La Mojarra, Oaxaca, Southern Mexico, 1st century, AD.

3.07 Detail (above) from the Olmec stela showing earliest known writing in Mesoamerica. La Mojarra, Southern Mexico, 1st., century, AD.

Oaxaca, now housed in the Anthroplogical Museum in Jalapa in Veracruz and is usually considered an example of the Mixe-Zoque script [*3.06; 3.07*] At least one other appears on the Pacific Coast which suggests that it was developed on the ceremonial sites between Izapa in Southern Mexico and those on the Gautemalan Coastal region. The more easterly sites include Abaj Takalik, El Baul, Bilbao and Monte Alto, through to Chalchuapa further east along the same coast in El Salvador. This script has yet to be interpreted since the surviving examples are extremely eroded and some have suggested that it is on this coast where the Mayan script was invented and developed before diffusing to the rest of the Mayan states[22].

The means by which the remarkably cursive style preserved on the ceramic examples of hieroglyphs and painting have led some researchers to suggest that it is too similar to that of the Chinese for their not to have been some influence from Asia. This, compounded with the close similarity of ceramic body styles on which this cursive style was applied and the almost identical brush types and a predilection for black and red, confirms a more than a probablel influence from contemporary China. It is unlikely to be an accident therefore that the Southern Chinese people known as the Na-Khi, a division of the No-Su, developed an independent script resembling some of the imagery and symbols among the Maya[23].

It is clear, however, that these were influences assimilated into a developing society and not a full importation of language and script. Clearly the earlier scripts, of which the only surviving examples appear at Oaxaca and are possibly detectable in embryonic form in earlier Olmec symbolism, had some influence upon the early Mayan script. But the believed evolution of this script on the Pacific Coast must leave the question as to why such a localised, apparently peripheral section of the Mayan homeland would need to develop a script at all.

It may have been that the Olmecs had an original system of symbols which was reserved for ceremonial purposes and therefore could still be found on some surviving monuments. The proximity on the major trade route of the Oaxaca Valley adjacent the Isthmus of Tehuantepec between the Caribbean Sea and the Pacific Ocean suggests that imported means of recording trade or foreign religious imagery by scribal means may have been introduced from the Pacific Ocean. It is likely that this gave impulse to any existing scripts however simple and become mutated with or assimilated by them. Such a possibility would suggest that the most likely region for the first and more progressive display of such imported scripts assimilated to those locally known would be at the port(s) of entry. This would highlight the coastal sites much more than the inland centres and this is exactly what is indicated in the surviving archaeological monuments and records. In other words writing was developed at the Pacific coastal sites washed by the Equatorial Current from Asia directly to Central America delivering any mariners to these coastal sites and Izapa in particular.

The many apparent associations that Izapa had with Asian cultures has been broached in "Mayan Genesis" and need not be considered here. The fact that this appears to be the site where the Mayan script is recognised early, if not first, suggests Pacific contacts and is the most likely coastal region where any contemporary influences from China, Indonesia or India, or indeed Polynesia would come ashore. Many of the earliest and therefore simplest pictograms associated with the Mayan script, or

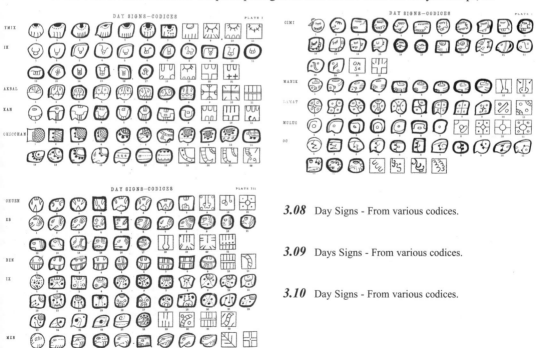

3.08 Day Signs - From various codices.

3.09 Days Signs - From various codices.

3.10 Day Signs - From various codices.

those from which they have recognisably developed, have been considered by earlier scholars and their work is readily accessible. Several aggregates of these symbols in developmental order have been presented by the earliest researchers in this field and they are briefly of interest and included in the illustrations here.

In considering these signs it must be remembered that only the glyphs surviving well over a millennium of decay and destruction are available to be categorised and therefore represent only the remnants and not the full development sequence of Mayan glyphs. What is available indicates from the simplest glyphs similar design structures to those found among the symbols and basic design structures of India. Of particular note are glyphs, such as the most basic of the "Day Signs", [*3.08*; *3.09*], which appear to relate to similar designs of the cardinal points and temple layouts which reflect the four quarters. These in turn correspond to day signs since the day was also considered structured (philosophically) to the cardinal points. The Mayan glyphs therefore appear to be influenced from several sources and integrated into already naturalised practices in the recording of symbols and images as picture glyphs.

The more complex development of the glyphs themselves retained many references from pictoglyphs and some which are clearly identifiable with imagery derived from India. In the many glyphs relating to "Grand Cycles" those numbered 32 to 36 [*3.11*] retain their origins in the mythical caiman of the Maya. This caiman symbol was itself closely similar to depictions of the Ganges crocodile or makara absorbing elements from the characteristics ascribed to lion deities and elephants and will be of more interest in later sections of this book. This is also true of the "Periods-Face Signs" where trefoil disks behind the ears mimic the trilobes found on images of the makara from the first centuries A.D. in India[24]. This is particularly demonstrated in the image of a "frog" deity denoting the Uinal - number 36 [*3.12*]. A great deal has

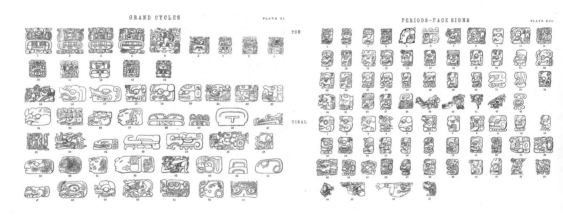

GRAND CYCLES   PLATE XI   PERIODS—FACE SIGNS   PLATE XII

3.11 Glyphs developed for the Grand Calendrical Cycles. Mayan, Classic Periods.

3.12 Glyphs developed for the calendrical Periods - Face Signs. Mayan, Classic Periods.

ONE   TWO   THREE

FOUR   FIVE

SIX   SEVEN

EIGHT   NINE

TEN   ELEVEN

TWELVE   THIRTEEN

FOURTEEN   FIFTEEN   SIXTEEN

SEVENTEEN   EIGHTEEN   NINETEEN

3.13 Normal Numbers from Inscriptions. Mayan Classic Periods.

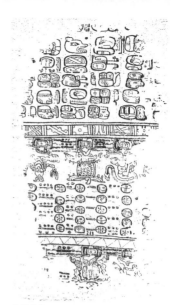

3.14 Sky band with panels identical in design structure to those found in India. Paris Codex, Pre- or Post Conquest Mexico.

3.18 Page from Mexican codex showing sky bands similar to India. Codex Tro-Cortesianus, Pre- or Post Conquest Mexico.

3.15 Sky loops denoting the sky. Sanchi, North Central India, 2-1st, century, AD.

3.16 Sky band with sky loop panel - see *3.17*. Paris Codex, Pre- or Post Conquest Mexico.

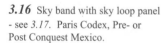

3.17 Sky loops denoting sky interface. Sanchi, North Central India, 2-1st, century, A.D.

been made of the numbering system developed by the Maya but there is much in their system reflecting elements known in the Middle East. The Mayan numbers are shown in illustration *3.13*.

Codex Sky-Bands:

Some of the most interesting depictions of sky-bands are recorded in the surviving few codices. Of special relevance are those depicted in the Paris Codex since they reflect design structures and aspects so completely corresponding to panel designs in India. Associated with these sky-bands are depictions of mythical serpents clearly derived from the makara of India. In the Paris Codex illustrated in *3.16* each of the sky-band elements can be approximated to similar images in a similar context in India. Of particular interest are the interlocking loops, less often depicted in the surviving examples of the Mayan sky-bands, appearing to derive from interlocking sky garlands in India [*3.15; 3.17*]. Of the panels most frequently depicted are the saltire crosses and those which appear to originate with a central "dot" with one in each corner reflecting the cardinal points in Buddhist and ancient Indian temple planning [*3.14; 3.16*].

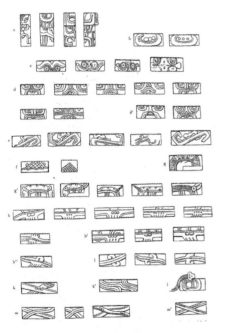

3.21 Sky band goddess. Codex Dresdenus, Mexico

3.20 Sky band panel. Nalanda, Bihar, India, 6th., century, AD.

3.19 Sky band panels - planet symbols? Mostly Copan and Palenque, Mexico and Honduras, 7-8th., centuries, AD.

Characteristically in almost all Mayan sky-bands there are two vertical bands separating each of the panels. This convention also derives from the sky-bands shown in India and will be of more interest in due course.

A particularly interesting group of glyphs are those believed to represent the planet Venus or are in some way associated with it. In illustration *3.19* the two shown in group "b" are now thought to relate to the Moon. Those shown in groups "c" and

3.22 Dado panels - proto
type sky band. Bhumara,
North Central India, 5th.,
century, AD.

3.23 Dado panels - proto
type sky band. Bhumara,
North Central India, 5th.,
century, AD.

3.24 Dado panels - proto
type sky band. Bhumara,
North Central India, 5th.,
century, AD.

3.25 Dado panels - proto
type sky band. Bhumara,
North Central India, 5th.,
century, AD.

"d" appear to have developed from the human face or a mask and are now more typi-cally thought to relate to the planet Venus itself. Those in group "f" clearly derive from a particular panel found in India - see *4.13-4.18b*. All panels "h" to "m2" are clearly variations of the glyph but of particular interest is that these clearly relate to a panel found at the ancient Buddhist university at Nalanda in Northern India shown in *3.20*. Remarkably this is the only stucco panel to have survived of its type in this group and the lotus petals above the panel denote the sacredness of the sign. The panel is so clearly identical to that depicted in so many of the Mayan glyphs that it is unlike-ly that they could have been developed independently. Transfer of these important cultural images is emphasised by the fact that so many other associated images from the same location or other Buddhist sites are so clearly apparent in similar contexts in Mayan imagery. Unfortunately there is little surviving in texts to indicate the intend-ed meanings of many of these panels of Buddhist imagery and this can only be guessed at.

Temple of Siva at Bhumara:

From the early Gupta dynasty, 4-6th., century A.D., and post-Gupta in India it was considered that this dynastic period was the formative foundation upon which Hindu temple planning and structure was established. This flourish of stone temple building owed much to, and saw the final development of, Buddhist architectural and sculptur-al excellence already supreme in the Sub-continent for six or seven hundred years. Three centuries earlier the Kushans had swept into the Ganges River region from the North West and created havoc for the Buddhist dynasties which were then predomi-nant throughout northern India. Four centuries later saw the great florescence under the first great Hindu dynasty of the Guptas. The cultural evolution from the close of the Indus civilisation to the great apogee of Buddhist achievement at the university of Nalanda had continued to peak under the Buddhist dynasties but who were now on the wane. These great Buddhist centres had been receiving pilgrims from racially diverse peoples far from India and records of life in India at that time have survived from Chinese devotees from the 5th., to the 8th., centuries A.D.

In terms of architectural style and prominence the temple of Siva at Bhumara is of little importance, and not of any great size. Dated to the late Gupta in the late 5th., century A.D. it reflects the culmination of the more direct and angular style which typified the Gupta and its inheritance. It very much reflects the finely chiselled Gupta style introducing more uniformly the building of temple structures in stone rather than using brick with finely carved stone relief panels and inset sculptures more typical of the Buddhist buildings.

Of special interest in this otherwise undistinguished temple building at Bhumara are the dado panels which, although fragmentary have survived in remark-ably fine condition. Even more important are the designs exhibited in these panels since they appear to be of great value in themselves as individual panels besides appearing to be the proto-types for those found a little later, but more florid in expres-sion, in Orissa. The clarity of the iconography is of special interest but also notable are the "dwarfs", known as "ganas" in India, which separate each panel. These sculpted dwarfs are flanked by two small pilasters there being miniature copies of columns used frequently in contemporary temples. This separation of each panel by the dwarfs is rare, at least among the surviving temples from this period, and in most other similar dado panels only the two columns are present. These columns are critical to the meaning of the dado since they indicate that they are intended to represent the columns which mythically were said to hold up the sky. In other words the dado represents the "sky band" as depicted in the local style in India and these elements of iconography appear to have been borrowed from Buddhism

It is known that the craftsmen who worked on the Buddhist temples were also employed on the Hindu structures. They introduced iconography only thinly disguised as Hindu but owing much of its origin to Buddhism. The vertical elements separating the panels as columns at Bhumara are also clearly seen as such in the sky-band, or ecliptic, at Ajanta dating to about the same period [3.31]. The reduction of the columns to two bands is clearly reflected almost universally in the Mayan sky bands [3.28; 3.32; 3.33]. It is interesting to note in the Ajanta sky-band that the panels throughout and even the cursively drawn columns are separated by two vertical strips emphasised by a broader black line in each from which the Mayans must have developed their version.

The dwarfs, such as those at Bhumara, are clearly the so-called Pauahtuns so widely depicted in Mayan iconography and literature. They are also depicted holding up the sky associating them with the sky band as they are also considered to do, and depicted, in Mayan iconography [5.52].

The most remarkable evidence for the transfer of cultural developments across the Pacific Ocean must be the sky band depicted on the ceiling of the portico to Cave 2 at Ajanta in Western India [3.31]. This superb tromphe-l'oeil of a domed sky is more reminiscent of Greek or Roman work but the wide belief in sky pillars holding up the heavens is clearly depicted here. The sky band itself clearly represents the ecliptic since there are twenty four panels in all including those in which the sky pillars are shown. These correspond to the twelve signs of the solar zodiac each considered to have a dark and light half, this being recorded also for the lunar monthly cycle, as noted also in the earliest records of the Vedic rites in India.

The solar traditions linked to calendrical speculations and constructs have a long history in India and it is remarkable that these have survived in pictorial form in this, perhaps last, great visual record of centuries of philosophic speculation and visual representation. The sky pillars are cursively expressed in three panels and it is interesting to perceive, as already noted, that each panel is separated by two vertical bands with a darker centre line. The two vertical bands are clearly a survival from the earlier representations where the separations were always miniature pillars or pilasters, such as at Bhumara. However, it is of critical interest to note that this is the identical means by which the Mayan panels forming a sky band are almost invariably separated [3.28; 4.15; 4.16; 4.19; 4.21] and must be an element of major evidence for the principle and design construct of the Mayan sky band having originated in India.

Many indicators in the early records note that the major Buddhist sites attracted pilgrims from all over India and it is known and recorded that they travelled from at least as far as China. It is from the surviving records by a few of the pilgrims themselves that the life and state of these pilgrimage centres is known in India, but which also reveal insights into the means of travel. This was usually by highly risky sea voyages which were broken by lengthy visits to other destinations at mission centres on the way to and from China to India such as in Indonesia. And yet they came risking their lives from pirates and typhoons on the high seas surviving on board voyages which lasted many months and with transit breaks which sometimes lasted years. If this is known to be true of Chinese pilgrims who were well aware of these risks then from what other destinations did pilgrims arrive who would not necessarily need any longer to achieve a round trip to their destination at the great Buddhist centres at Ajanta, Nalanda or Bodh Gaya in India and then return home?

In 1947 Thor Heyerdahl, in an attempt to prove that the traditional South American balsa rafts could have sailed to Polynesia, set out in one he had made by traditional methods by local Peruvians. He arrived in the Marquesas Islands 101 days after setting out from the Peruvian coast covering about one third of the way from the South American shore to the Asian mainland. This suggests that if trans-Pacific voyages did take place then a complete voyage from one side of the Pacific to the other could easily be achieved by experienced mariners in 12 months. This would certainly be true from Central America to Indonesia and then on to India where the prevailing winds and ocean currents combine so perfectly to assist such an undertaking. For experienced mariners, who for millennia plied the seas and oceans along the coasts of the Middle East, India, South East Asia and China, the journey would have been undertaken as a matter of course. There is, after all, the known ceramic evidence of cultures from the shores of Japan and China being found in New Guinea thousands of miles away from 5,000 B.C.[25]. The Lapita culture diffused from South East Asia into the Bismark archipelago and the Melanesian and Polynesian islands dating from about 1500 B.C. until its last flowering in Tonga about 500 A.D. These could only have been spread and even maintained long enough to take root by cultures with long mariner traditions.

Of importance is the consideration of the attitude and impressions gained by pilgrims to the already ancient Buddhist sites in the early and mid-first century A.D. The records left by the Chinese pilgrims Fa Hsien in the 5th., century, A.D. and Hsuan-Tsang in the 7th., century A.D. inform us in limited detail of the exotic life they noticed on their travels in India. In some instances they give descriptions of monastic centres and pilgrimage sites, and quote facts and figures. However, importantly, their reflections, attitude, perceptions or detailed descriptions, even in outline relating to iconography or specific symbolic references, are few. This suggests that, so similarly to modern-day tourists, they did not retain a clear picture of the images, murals or structures, except in certain circumstances, that they had seen but are left with a general impression becoming diminished and blurred with time after leaving India.

If a Mayan or Mexican had visited India it is clear that he would have experienced the same difficulty in remembering exactly the imagery and their contexts

3.26 Sky band drawn by Alfred Percival Maudslay. Palenque, 7-8th., century, AD

3.27 Altar stone with weave pattern. Tikal, Guatemala, Late Classic.

3.28 Cranked Sky band panels. Yaxchilan, Chiapas, Southern Mexico, 8th., century, AD.

3.29 Mayan sky band panels closely similar to those in India. Yaxchilan, Chiapas, Southern Mexico, 8th., century, AD.

3.30 Sky band detail - see *4.47*. Typical Mayan lotus matches that in India. Yaxchilan, Chiapas, Southern Mexico, 8th., century, AD.

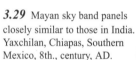

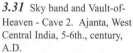

3.31 Sky band and Vault-of-Heaven - Cave 2. Ajanta, West Central India, 5-6th., century, A.D.

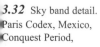

3.32 Sky band detail. Paris Codex, Mexico, Conquest Period,

3.34 Base detail from ritual vase. Usumacinta Valley, Tabasco, Southern Mexico, Late Classic Period

3.33 Makara sky band - flood myth. Codex Dresden, Mexico, Conquest Period.

from all the sites they would have visited. When visiting Ajanta they would certainly
have been impressed by the many representations of sky bands to be found in the
caves. There are, in fact, many circular ones similar to the example shown here in
Cave 2 but this is the only surviving one which exhibits the sky band deriving from its
original symbolic connection with the zodiac. In rooms off the portico of Cave 17
[*3.39*; *3.40*] and in other cave shrines and porticos (Cave 11) the sky band is shown
which is clearly of the same date and symbolic detailing as that of the main band in
Cave 2 [*3.31*]. The sky bands shown in the porticos of Cave 17 and painted to define
the corners of the room inside a perimeter band must certainly have had a symbolic
intent. The ceilings of Caves 11 [*3.35*; *3.38*] however show these bands running in
one direction only usually in the direction from the front of the cave temple to the back
wall - those in the opposite directions were clearly not intended to portray sky bands
as such. It must be obvious that these bands were intended to have special symbolic
references and it is likely that they were painted to represent rafters in a long held
philosophic construct. The rafters depicted as sky bands appear to represent the ridgepole of the temple reflecting the original timber framed temple structures depicted on
the walls of some of the caves. It is unlikely to be coincidental that the sacred timber
framed temples of Melanesia but particularly Polynesia were said to reflect the sky and
its symbolic construction where the rafters were of such symbolic importance.

In the symbolic constructs of some of the Polynesians the "vault-of-heaven"[26]
is depicted as a hemisphere supported by sky pillars[27] and this together with other
philosophic versions where the rafters and ridgepole are of such importance suggests
that these derived directly from Ajanta. The symbolic importance of the ridgepole

3.35 Ajanta Cave 2. Sky bands reflecting rafters in
ceiling decoration. Ajanta, West Central India, 5-6th.,
century AD.

3.36 Celestial disk divided into four quarters of thirteen elements totalling 52 reflecting the lunar calendar
- a number reflected in the Messoamerican calendars.
Jain, Ranakpur, Rajasthan, North West India, 13th.,
century, AD.

3.37 Underside of giant stone parasol showing Western zodiac - more than one survives - a few between 2.5 and 3.0 metres in diameter. Sarnath, near Varanasi, Bihar, North Central India, 2nd., century, AD.

appears not only in Polynesia but in adjacent Melanesia as well as found among the Maya recorded in the Popol Vuh.

It should be noted that the sky band exhibited in Cave 2 at Ajanta appears to be the end of a long development from the Vedic philosophic construct of light and dark half-cycles which had influenced the time cycles in India for well over a millennium before this was painted on the Cave ceiling. Its tendency to ornamentation obscuring the original intent suggests that it was reflective of the decay in tradition common to all traditions of long-standing. This appears certainly true of all the other circular sky bands in Cave 2 and perhaps they are examples of an earlier tradition over-painted where symbolic function becomes a vehicle for almost pure decoration.

From at least the beginning of the Mauryan dynasty (3rd., century B.C.) Northern India reflected the influences of Iran then Greece in stone carving and other associated building arts. It is clear in the first centuries of the first millennium A.D. that the Western calendar had been introduced and this solar-based zodiac is clearly seen with naturalised zodiacal monthly symbols in Buddhist carvings at that time [*3.37*]. As with all the great civilisations these foreign cultural influences were gradually assimilated and achieved supremacy after some generations while the earlier Vedic forms were still retained but diminished in the following centuries after. For this reason the half-cycles of the Vedic calendar were gradually devolving into elements of decorative work as the solar orientated foreign calendar gradually became more prominent.

The 24 panels at Ajanta were therefore undoubtedly intended originally to have represented the two halves, light and dark, in Indian philosophy. The 12 zodiacal panels divided into 24 units are clearly shown as the supporting ring or circle of the ecliptic in this tromphe l'oeil depiction with the dome of the "vault-of-heaven" springing from it [*3.31*]. At the centre and highest point of the vault is the painting of an eight-petalled lotus - a reference to the eight points of the compass, four cardinal and four secondary, with a lesser division indicated by intermediate petal points between each of these at the periphery.

The ecliptic sky band is subdivided in the same panel designs when numbered as follows:

1;7;14;   2;4;6;11;13;18;22;   3;9;12;15;17;23; 8;20;24;   + 21;

10;   5;   16;   19;

The sky band scheme does not immediately suggest a particular pattern but this may simply be unknown or the original Vedic system on which was based had become degenerate to the extent that it is now difficult to reconstruct. The latter is the most likely since astronomers and scholars in the nineteenth and early twentieth century spent a great deal of time in attempting to define Hindu astronomy and account for its origins. It is clearly stated by them that the Hindu system deriving from the Vedas, of which the most complete surviving records were available compared to the Buddhist or Jain, were inconsistent and the origins of the several systems they used were almost impossible to define. Their studies are epitomised by that undertaken by George R. Kaye in the early part of the 20th., century, and published in the Archaeological Survey of India.

It is of primary importance that this ceiling design in the ante-chamber to Cave 2 at Ajanta represents the philosophical construct of the "vault-of-heaven" and the outer circle patterns are clearly intended to convey the philosophic divisions of the ecliptic. Apart from this it is important for the theme of this work to indicate that the individual panel designs in this ecliptic are clearly identical in design structure to those found in the Mayan sky bands.

All of the wall paintings covering all the walls and ceilings of Caves 2, Cave 11 and Cave 17 are the apogee of Buddhist sophistication in conveying their history and mythological references through the technique and design pinnacle in the 5th., century A.D. In examining these surviving works it is clear that there has been over-painting of murals, also of high sophistication, which can still be seen in certain areas and therefore the originals may have been several generations older than those now existing. The first Caves at Ajanta date from at least as early as the 3rd., century B.C. and these were believed to have been originally seven including the five oldest Hinayana caves. Over the next centuries the number of caves extended to 30 in all by the fifth century A.D. - 27 of them being more or less adjacent on the outer rim around the horse-shoe gorge of the Waghore River [*1.02*; *1.03*]. The caves and setting cannot but powerfully impress the minds of visitors even today and for those who approach them in the more traditional attitude of reverential pilgrims the spectacular setting of the caves and the opulence of the cave structures and paintings would have undoubtedly sated their every expectations.

The mental and emotional reflection which any pilgrim would have experienced during and after a visit to Ajanta or any of the other main pilgrimage centre would have been of some importance. In attempting to do this the researchers can only draw on personal experience to evaluate the reactions and emotions of other people.

3.38 Ceiling to Ajanta
Cave 11. The imitation
underside of the rafters
reflect patterns appearing
to be the inspiration fpor
the Mayan sky bands.
Ajanta, West Central India,
5th., century, AD.

3.39 Ceiling of portico
rooms Ajanta Cave 17.
Sky band borders. Ajanta,
West Central India, 5th.,
century, AD.

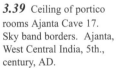

3.39 Ceiling of portico rooms
Ajanta Cave 17. Sky band borders.
Ajanta, West Central India, 5th., cen-
tury, AD.

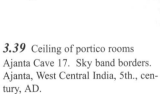

The added difficulty is that it is something of a presumption to attempt to gauge the state of the human faculties 1500 years ago in India. The elements of religious and social education from whichever system these pilgrims came would have affected greatly the way that they perceived and reacted to these sights and which of the memories predominated and survived after departure. Before photography the only means of providing accurate records was by painting or drawing, but because most people then, as now, had a limited time when on pilgrimage few would have been able to afford or had recourse to such means of memory joggers. The memories for all would have inevitably dimmed in time and only the most notable elements would have remained clear depending on the predilections of the individual observer.

If a Mayan or Mexican, or other pilgrim from the Americas did make the pilgrimage to Ajanta what would have been the memories he would have taken with him? Firstly, even though the "vault-of-heaven" appears in Cave 2 to be finely painted it is an import from another tradition thousands of miles away in the Mediterranean. The present day Westerner is able to discern the attempted depiction as a vault on a flat surface because there is a tradition in perspective training broadly included in traditional schooling. For a pilgrim from a culture where no such tradition of perception as part of their educational process it would be less than apparent even if it had been explained to him. The traditional four cherubs at each of the corners of this sky band ceiling painting in Cave 2 is immediately associates the ceiling mural with tromphe l'oeil painting[28], as vault supporters in the West, but the rest of the painting would not immediately suggest a three dimensional aspect. Indeed there are several other "vaults" which are circular patterns in other sections of the cave without cherubs which do not immediately indicate sky vaults even to Westerners. To have to explain the meaning and intent of perspective and the intended philosophical construct behind this particular ceiling painting therefore must have been very difficult and even more difficult to understand.

After having had the meanings of the sky vault and other paintings and murals explained and having then left what impression and memory would a pilgrim, particularly from Central America, have taken away to his homeland? Firstly the perspective attempting to represent a "dome" on the flat ceiling must have baffled him totally, having no background by which to interpret it. More importantly he would have even more difficulty in attempting to explain such a thing, even if he had understood the principles behind the sky vault depiction, when he returned at a minimum period of 12 months later to his home at one of the Central American ceremonial sites.

It would have taken at least 12 months to cross the Pacific even if he had left Ajanta immediately for his homeland. It is more likely that it would have taken longer with the resultant dimming of memory more or less proportional to the length of time that is inevitable without material aids such as detailed sketches or photographs. It is likely therefore that the memories which survived were of the basic colours and prominent design structures rather than for minute details and for this reason the sky band of Ajanta is doubly important. Not only does it record that the ecliptic, the representation of the path of the solar orbit, was known in India in terms closely relative to that known among the Maya but the basic design structures found in this example are also found together and similarly linked almost to the panel. If a Mayan pilgrim was to take some memory of the ecliptic back even after studying at the caves as a "chela", or religious student for some time, it is the basic structure behind these panel designs and their overall linkage in a band.

Virtually every single panel in the Ajanta sky band is found reflected in the more elementary design structures in the panels of the Maya. Several of these have been included in illustration section *3.26-3.34* linked to the relevant panels in the Ajanta sky band, or ecliptic. It is clear, however, that these later Mayan examples are linked with other panel designs not appearing in that at Ajanta and therefore had assimilated other designs. These other designs can be shown to have derived from Bhumara as one of the last surviving representations displaying this type of sky band or other contemporary sites with Ajanta, and Orissa in Eastern India which was a stronghold of Buddhism until about the 11th., century A.D. and perhaps later.

The fact that the concept of the sky band and virtually all of the panel designs depicted at Ajanta are recorded among the Maya suggests that it was from these caves in the rock faced chasm of the Waghore River that the principles for the Mayan system of iconography was derived. Also it cannot be outlandish to suggest that it was from the original seven caves in the Ajanta gorge in the second half of the first millennium B.C. that the myths of the legendary origins of the Mexican tribes and indeed the Maya - Vucub-Pec[29] - paralleling the name of the "Seven Caves" in Mexico - Chicomoztoc[30]. Interestingly, another term found in the Popol Vuh of the Maya is Vucub-Zivan meaning "Seven Ravines" and this perhaps is another memory of the Ajanta gorge[31]. It has been shown in "Mayan Genesis"[32] that the term Zuiva and Zivan almost certainly derive among others from the Mandaeans of the Middle East who have been shown to have close connections with early formative cultural influences in India.

3.41 Panorama of Palenque. Palace complex with tower to the right and the Temple of the Inscriptions to the left surmounting the pyramid under which Pacal's tomb was discovered. Palenque, Chiapas, Southern Mexico, 7-8th., century, AD.

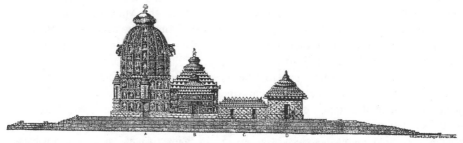

THE TEMPLE OF JAGANNATH AT PURI

3.42 Great temple of Jagannath at Puri. Built on the seashore it was seen far out to sea and the first view pilgrims from South East Asia would have of India. 7-8th., century, AD.

3.43 Panorama of Bhubanesvar - the pilgrim city of temples in Orissa depicted in the Victorian age and similar to that seen by pilgrims many centuries earlier from India and abroad

The finest of the Mayan sky bands are those surviving from Palenque and many of the pier panels are bounded by sky bands. Some of the most notable of these are located on the Temple of the Inscriptions dating from the late 7th., or early 8th., century, A.D. atop the pyramid under which Pacal's funerary chamber is located [*3.41*; *5.97*; *5.102*]. It cannot be a coincidence that one of the most complete examples also displays a central representation of the so-called Principal Bird [*3.26*] and that this is clearly derived from the Garuda sky bird so widely illustrated in India [*5.08-5.15*]. At its ends are fantasy examples based on the serpent head almost certainly derived from the makaras so typical of the sky bands in India.

Sky Pillars:

Although the basic visual elements associated with the sky band in India appear to have survived being transferred to Central America the graphic depiction of the sky pillars does not appear in the same way. However the mythology associated with the sky pillars is found widely across the Pacific Ocean cultures from India to Mesoamerica and these are clearly derived from the same Asian origin.

The architectural impulse for the columns introduced into the imagery of the sky band derives from the Mediterranean via the Middle East. The mythology behind the sky pillars in India appears to be related directly to that in ancient Iran. It has been posited in "Mayan Genesis"[33] that the Agaria tribe or Assurs in North Central India were in fact migrants from Anatolia and their skill in iron-working and the worship of deities related to the furnace has suggested to other researchers that they were of a north western origin from outside India. Verrier Elwin, whose researches and records of the indigenous myths among the tribal peoples of India has not been surpassed, suggested that these tribes may have been the much-feared ancient people known as the Asurs, or Asuras the anti-gods who were a division of the demonised Rakshasas[34].

In an Agaria creation myth recorded by Elwin it is said that God made the world of lac and it broke up into many pieces when he stepped upon it. From the sweat of his breast he made a crow which he suckled from his own breast milk two-and-one-half times. Because of this He told the crow that it would never have to want for food or drink and they went off to search for the earth. The crow flew off but after a long time grew weary and began to believe that God, her father, created her only to kill her. She flew down to rest on to the back of the great crab, Kekramal Chhatri, prompting it to descended into the depths of the primal waters. There the crab found Nal Raja and Nal Rani who had been sleeping for twelve years and awoke them. The crab asked where the earth was and Nal Raja stated that Nizam Raja had it not he. The crab, however, grabbed Nal Raja by the throat until he vomited out the earth in small balls. These the crow took back to God and from this the world was made. After five years Nanga Baiga and Nanga Baigin emerged from a fissure in the earth and asked Mother Earth, 'Where is my fiddle (baja)?' and she retorted that he was as yet only a navel and a cord and what possible need would he have for a fiddle? On the same day the Bamboo Maiden (Basin Kaniya) was also born so Nanga Baiga cut the bamboo one breadth long. He constructed from this a fiddle using his own hair for the strings and when he played it the vibrations shook the throne of God which alerted the deity that the first people had been born. God sent his messenger to Nanga Baiga who he found asleep in a winnowing fan but when woken Mother Earth told him not to go with the messenger. Nanga Baiga, however, took his fiddle and went off with the messenger to see the deity. The deity then instructed Nanga Baiga to drive nails into the earth to stabilise it but, having no nails, Nanga Baiga cut off the little finger of his right hand and drove it into the ground. This did not satisfy God and he demanded proper nails so Nanga Baiga called the god of the forge, Agyasur, worshipped him, and this deity then burst forth in flames and from this the Agaria were born. Under instruction from Nanga Baiga the Agaria made twelve pillars of Virgin Iron and placed them at the four corners of the world. This made the earth steady and God then sowed seeds across the earth[35].

The myth records the number five so important in the myths and philosophy of India and also Mesoamerica but also of importance is the number 2 and 1/2 related to suckling here. This is a prominent aspect in the philosophy of half cycles but in this myth relates to that of the five-year calendrical cycle. The motif of the crow being created from the sweat from the deity is found widely in India but also through into Oceania. The descent of the primal crab into the depths of the sea to find the earth is a myth motif found also in the rest of India.

Seeking earth from the bottom of the sea is a myth in principle found also throughout Oceania and among the tribes of the North Coast of North America although it is more usually the turtle or other sea creature that retrieves the first earth. The twelve years that Nal Raja and Nal Rana were asleep is clearly a reference to zodiacal cycles but also possibly the twelve year cycle of Jupiter. The twelve pillars created at the end of the myth clearly confirms the cosmic creation principles behind the myth particularly as they are placed in groups of three at each of the four corners, or cardinal points. The twelve is usually taken as a reference to the twelve zodiacal signs and this indicates a connection with Middle Eastern calendrical speculation as this solar orientated division is evident late in the philosophical systems of India [*3.37*]. The Agaria appear to be the ancient Asurs and therefore most likely to be the iron-workers from Anatolia as alluded to by Elwin. This would suggest that these calendrical references may have been brought with them perhaps after the sudden collapse of the Hittite dynasty late in the second millennium B.C. rather than being influenced by later imports in the early first millennium A.D. A similar myth cycle to that of the Agaria is found among the Gadabas in India, an Aboriginal tribe already noted, but in this myth there are four pillars nailed at each of the four corner. The Gadabas are connected with the Bhuiyas so noted in their connections with the Maya and their wind deities known as the Pauahtuns (this Gadaba myth is noted in "Mayan Genesis" p.197/8).

The panels depicted in the Ajanta sky band can almost all be related to those found among the Maya as indicated. The lack of the sky pillars in the Mayan panels and the fact that the surviving examples among the Maya are later than these in Cave 2 at Ajanta suggests that the principles and basic designs were adopted by the Mayans first from here but then adjusted by later introductions reflecting the more modified examples found in later Indian derivatives. Certainly in terms of dates the sky bands at Ajanta and Bhumara are earlier than those from the East Coast of India in Orissa, these latter appearing to have had a broader impact upon contemporary Mayan iconography. This is also true in the Pala dynasty, who were based in North East India from the early 7th., century A.D., where influences from the Ganges and Brahmaputra Delta on Indonesian iconography are detectable as well as from the South Indian dynasties of Pallava and Chola.

The declining influence of the Vedic through Brahmanic principles in iconography and the rise of the Buddhist was projected in the most central elements of philosophy displayed in their symbolic imagery in the late first millennium B.C. into the first millennium A.D. At the heart of Buddhist teaching was the association of the Buddha with the World Tree or Axis Mundae, which was believed to extend to the Pole Star in the north, being iconographically represented by the sacred banyan tree or the parasol but also the pillar. In later iconography the Buddha is seen shaded by this World Tree with one at each of the four cardinal points[36] [*5.93*]. The Ajanta sky band appears to depict an archaic representation of a multi-pillar philosophy which it shared with Brahmanism and its offshoot Hinduism. This was later replaced with the single pillar and this appears to have been broadcast as an element of diversified mythology

3.46 Sky belt with saltire plates or sections identical to those found in India and Tibet. Seibal, Guatemala, 9th., century, AD.

3.45 Sky belt with saltire plates similar to those of the Maya. Pala, North East India, 10-11th., century, AD.

3.44 Itzamna as the Old God or Pauahtun seated on the ecliptic sky band supported by a broad sky band representing the sky. Part outline of vase roll-out, Mayan Late Classic.

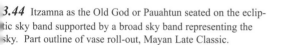

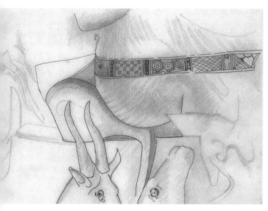

3.47 Remarkable sacred belt with designs which are found widely at Ajanta and other sites in India but also among the Maya. The original principle of the design probably derives fron the twelve signs of the zodiac. Ajanta, West Central India, c600-42 AD.

into Oceania and to the Americas. This mythical element was sometimes identified with the Orion myths where it was said to be located under the earth and was shaken by a great giant, turtle other mythical being. It is in this form that it is found in the mythology of the Maya into modern times among the Lacandon where the earth was believed to be supported by giant stone pillars in the Underworld and were said to be created by the god Hachayum[37].

In the exact form of the sacred Buddhist temple planning the Mayans laid out their ceremonial centres and towns on the principle of a sacred tree planted at each of the cardinal points on the outskirts of the settlement and a central one placed on the ceremonial site[38]. This layout was recorded by the first Spanish chroniclers and these sacred Ceiba trees were said to have atop them a symbolic bird usually identified with the Principal Bird and each had its own designated colour[39]. In a less usual reference to sky pillars among the Navaho in the South West United States their mythology records sky pillars which are associated with colours and precious stones which is too similar in principle to that of the Buddhists and Polynesians not to be connected[40].

Ecliptic - Sky Band - Sacred Girdle/Belt:

Of particular interest is the depiction of sacred belts or girdles found almost universally among the religions of India but prominent also in the iconography of the Maya.
In the mythology of India the surviving references indicate that the human form is considered symbolically to be made up of two halves - the upper and lower divided at the
waist. In myths considered in "Mayan Genesis" the symbolism evident in the "Half-
Human" myth cycles found widely in India, through Indonesia into Melanesia, and
apparent also in the iconography of the Maya, appears to derive from this original
philosophical construct from India, albeit somewhat debased[41].

The belt itself represented the ecliptic[42] and frequently this is identified with
the double-headed serpent[43] this in turn being identified with the eclipse demon Rahu[44].
From the Ajanta caves again an existing illustration appears to closely reflect the elements of the sky band panel design depicted as a loose belt around the hips of a young
attendant woman or goddess [*3.47*]. The panels illustrated on this belt appear to be
closely similar to those found among the Maya. It is of particular interest therefore to
note what appears to be a tasselled belt or girdle hanging from an altar before which a
"Pauahtun" or Old God associated with the cardinal points as a sky-bearer is seated
[*3.44*]. It is probably therefore no coincidence that the name Pauahtun can be traced
to the Ganges Delta as a derivative of the wind deity of the Bhuiyas and Asurs - a
region of North East India where so much of the Mayan imagery appears to derive[45].

The Pauahtun depicted in this illustration [*3.44*] sits on a sky band throne
with an eagle's (?) head at both end, and, as among the Maya and in India, the eagle
represented the sky and was therefore associated with the solar ecliptic. It is likely
therefore that this throne-like sky band was intended to represent the ecliptic. The
three elements of what appears to be the waist belt sky band, the Pauahtun and the sky-
band "ecliptic" throne, are clearly derived from the mythology and iconography of
India. All of these elements rests upon a supporting sky band which emphasises again
that mythological associations with the sky and the ecliptic are intended.

The two illustrations showing the identical sky band belt, one from North
East India [*3.45*] and a characteristic example from Mayan iconography [*3.46*] only
underline the close connections in iconography, mythology and intent. These cross-
cultural examples date from the 8th., century A.D. and suggest a simplification in the
imagery and perhaps decay in traditions over those from the Ajanta cave illustrations
2-4 centuries earlier. It is clear, however, the imagery surviving from the Mayan ceremonial sites was closely connected to, and reflecting iconography contemporary with
that half a world away in India in the same time bands.

3.48 Remarkable surviving inner shrine with red Buddha. The panelled architrave was probably the inspiration for the sky band representations among the Maya. Cave 2 Ajanta, West Central India, 5-6th., century, AD.

3.49 Pacal's funerary slab with colours derived from colour coding. The outer sky band panels appear inspired from the portals at Ajanta and Orissa in India. Palenque, Chiapas, Southern Mexico, 7-8th., century, AD.

3.50 Niche head cartouche in stucco - palace structure. Palenque, Chiapas, Southern Mexico, 7-8th., century, AD.

3.51 Cartouche panel in stucco based on Maudslay sketch. Sky band panel borders and makara (caiman) heads at each end. Palenque, Chiapas, Southern Mexico, 7-8th., century, AD.

3.52 + 3.53 Stone carved niche portraits in Chalukyan style. Durga Temple, Aihole, South Central India, 6th., century, AD.

3.54 Stucco larger than life-size portrait of a ruler or deity. Palace terrace facade, Palenque, Chiapas, Southern Mexico, 6th., century, A.D.

3.55 Hanuman displayed in characteristic half-sideways stance in torana style niche cartouche. Rock face relief, Badami, South Central India, 6-7th., century, AD.

3.56 Finely carved greenstone deity in characteristic Hanuman pose. Bhubanesvar, Orissa, North East India, c7th., century, AD.

3.57 Finely carved greenstone lotus portal. Note gelbai motif of figures entwined in a vine each side of the opening. Buddhist Vihara, Ratnagiri, Orissa, North East India, 8th., century, AD.

3.59 Masterly carving of a ceiling zodiacal "wheel" with lotuses instead of animal motifs representing signs. Durga Temple portico, Aihole, South Central India, 6th., century, AD.

3.58 Sema or cotton tree - the sacred flowering tree of India. The name is closely similar to the sacred cotton tree of the Maya - the Ceiba (Say-ba). Udayagiri, Orissa, North East India.

CHAPTER 4
PACAL'S FUNERARY SLAB and
the MAKARA TORANA

After the upheavel caused by the Kusan and the later Moghul invasion from North West India the repercussions lasted until about the 12th., century. The traditional balance of the religions of India, Brahmanism, Buddhism, Hinduism and Jainism, had greatly changed resulting in the Hindus ascendancy but decline of the Buddhists who were almost eclipsed. Their great university at Nalanda and pilgrimage sites were almost obliterated after a millennium of existence having acted as a cultural beacon to the Eastern World, and perhaps the West also, during the Moghuls advance across Northern and Central India. Only in Eastern India were the Buddhists able to survive to any great degree because the invasion ran out of energy before they reached the east coast of India and the Ganges Delta in the Bay of Bengal. Topographically the terrain was more difficult to penetrate particularly in the Chota Nagpur ranges protecting the region now known as Orissa across its boundary to the West and North West - the direction of the invaders thrust - while this protected region still retained dominion over a long coastline to the Bay of Bengal.

It was in this safe haven that some of the Buddhist shrines had survived including some of the most interesting caves from two thousand years ago. It is now known that many of the artisans who built the usually exceptionally finely-crafted Hindu shrines were in fact those whose forebears had been employed for generations earlier more or less exclusively on the remarkable Buddhist structures only remnants of these surviving into recent times. The building of Buddhist shrines and monasteries did not cease with the rise of Hinduism on the East Coast of India and later buildings display the finest craftsmanship of its time [3.57]. Although the Buddhist religion lost favour among the ruling dynasties it appears that their adherents did in fact retain control of powerful trading links extending far overseas into South East Asia and China and no doubt also across the Pacific to the Americas. Orissa remained therefore a major Buddhist centre in the second half of the first millennium A.D. and its location near the Ganges and Brahmaputra Deltas to the North confirmed it as a prominent region of cultural importance.

These links with the rest of Eastern India were apparently close as well as in South India where the Hindu dynasties had prevented the expansion of the Muslim incursions from North West India. Other historians have noted the remarkable variations and attributes of the early Chalukyans at Aihole, Pattadakal and Badami which some have considered the "nursery" of early Hindu stone-built architecture. This is because the Chalukyans displayed an apparently inventive approach to architectural temple layouts and towers found more developed in later decades or centuries in Orissa or some of the temple cities such as Kanchipuram in coastal South East India near Madras (Chennai). These three regions are critical to the theme of this work although not exclusively so and will be of more interest in future publications.

The early Hindu temples of Orissa vary from those of the Buddhists since these latter built in fine brickwork for the main body of the building and then inserted

4.01 Prototype sky band panels from Bhumara and Bhubanesvar in India. Almost identical panels make up the sky bands of the Maya. 5th., and 6th., centuries, AD.

4.04 Carved stone representing phallic omphallus and the banyan emerging from it. Buddhist, Lalitgiri, Orissa, North East India, 7-8th., century, AD.

4.02 Drawing of Pacal's funerary slab showing the sky band flanking both long sides depicting the overall design as being seen through a portal. Palenque, Chiapas, Southern Mexico, 7-8th., century, AD.

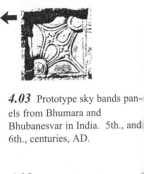

4.03 Prototype sky bands panels from Bhumara and Bhubanesvar in India. 5th., and 6th., centuries, AD.

4.05 Roundel depicting sacred banyan emerging from platform Buddhist, Barhut, Central North India, 2nd., century, BC.

4.06 Jambhala and Hariti seated beneath World Tree often identified with the banyan in India. Bihar, 9th., century, A.D

or faced this with the finest of stone-crafted dados, ashlar panels, portals, architraves and niches. Statues and stone carving of the highest quality were placed in these niches or on pedestals at prominent and symbolic locations. Hindu temple architecture was rarely built of brickwork except in delta regions where stonework was difficult to obtain. Their temples were usually built entirely of stone and much of the work was carved into the stone or applied as ashlar panels facing the stone superstructure. Statues and bas-reliefs were also carved into the stone face or were ashlar panels facing the stone but more and more the two forms merged and became high reliefs where the imagery was not quite free from the stone panel from which they were carved. In rarer examples the Buddhist tradition of incorporating greenstone panels into the façade in special architrave niches has survived [*3.56*] in Hindu work. This is unusual and no doubt stems from the fact that the craftsmen who were building the Hindu temples were usually the same as those erecting Buddhist buildings in the same time frame.

Much of the decorative detailing has been integrated into Hindu temple building from the Buddhist and it is because of this that the early Hindu temples of Orissa are of special interest. These earliest eastern Hindu temples are something of a curiosity since they are covered in carved stone panels depicting events or excerpts from the miracles attributed to the Hindu deities or heroes [*5.79; 5.81*]. These reflect the many examples of surviving "jatakas" or picture panels depicting similar events from the life of the Buddha.

Of special interest are the architraves of some of these early Hindu temples since they appear to preserve a record of the sky bands which are a transition from those of the Buddhists of Ajanta and the early Hindu preserved at Bhumara a century

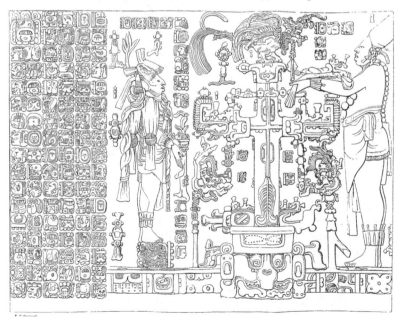

4.07 World Tree flanked by Pacal, left, and his succesor, Chan-Bahlum, his son. The Tree emerges from the sacred ancestral skull identical to myths and iconography of India and Melanesia. The whole is standing on the sky band extending from the skull. Temple of the Foliated Cross, Palenque, Chiapas, Southern Mexico, 7-8th., century, AD.

4.08 Kan-Bahlum-Mo', Pacal's father, reflecting the ideal nasal profile without a bridging piece. Pacal's sarcophagus end relief carving. Palenque, Chiapas, Southern Mexico, Late 8th., century, AD.

4.09 Pacal 1, Pacal 2's ancestor, whose facial features tend to indicate a dwarf or possibly an Oriental background. Note highly built-up nasal profile. Pacal's sarcophagus side relief carving. Palenque.

4.10 Chaacal 1, Pacal's ancestor, reflecting ideal nasal profile, note also beard. Palenque, Chiapas South Mexico, Late 8th., century, AD.

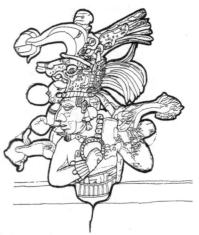

earlier. Importantly it can be shown that these must have influenced Mayan pilgrims to the Buddhist sites or were craftsmen working in these centres who were requested by the early dynasties of Indonesia to build their temples in the style of India. The design and iconographical styles of the Pala of North East India and the Chola and Pallava of Southern India are all evident in Indonesia - on the main islands of Sumatra and Java particular. It would also appear that these craftsmen continued from there with mariners and traders right across the Pacific to Central America.

The integration of these panel motifs from India into the Mayan sky band is epitomized by those depicted on Pacal's funerary slab [*4.01-4.03*]. The panels illustrated from both Orissa and Bhumara cannot be other than probabilities in influencing the Maya since they are among the few survivors from the great building traditions from the Gupta dynasty through to the apogee of the temple building efflorescence in Orissa. It is clear, however, that either these temples or others of the same period with similar panels were the inspiration for the Mayan and the surviving panels are juxta-posed with a sketch of Pacal's slab to indicate the close similarity in the design struc-ture of each panel. The inclusion of the World Tree growing either from Pacal's body or the skull below him is covered elsewhere in this volume but it is interesting to note the close similarity in principle of the Buddhist examples shown from the beginning of the first and second centuries B.C. through to the Orissan period compared to the Mayan example [*4.04-4.06*].

Most of the surviving older temples in Bhubanesvar, the main temple city in Orissa, where it is said that originally of over 600 temples stood, display references to aspects of the sky bands on the architraves of their portals or niche surrounds. Of spe-cial interest are those known as the Axamaneswar temple group and one of the three which form it called the Satrughesvara temple. These are located opposite another group known as the Rameshwar, one of these temples displaying the classic hipped mansard roof constructed from stone found throughout East and South India in vari-ous forms [*5.98-5.101*]. The Satrughesvara [*4.11*] survives largely in ruins but enough of its lower four faces remains to reveal the portals facing the cardinal directions being intact sufficiently to determine the sequence of panels related to the sky bands of Ajanta but also among the most likely to have been the inspiration for those of the Maya.

The temple door has been sealed off because of its ruinous condition but the northern portal is the best preserved and its central carved stone architrave reveal designs which are a transition between those of Ajanta and the sequences found among the Maya [*4.11*]. In rare surviving examples are some in Bhubanesvar reflecting the Buddhist tradition from which they appear to have originated. These depict also ele-ments of building construction which are probably the prototypes for the Maya. This portal from the Parasumesvara temple indicates two apparent sky bands adjacent on each side of the door opening [*5.101*]. Although surviving in a less well-preserved condition the north portal of the Satrughesvara [*4.11*] is more easily and simpler to consider as the Mayan prototype. The inner architrave for this portal is a foliated design which replaces the picture panels from the earlier Buddhists but even in some Hindu temples these are also much more florid and depict elements from mythology.

The most convenient means to examine the sky band portals from the Satrughesvara is by separating them and comparing each to those which parallel them so closely from the Mayan records - mostly from the surviving codices but also from the stucco friezes at Palenque [*4.12-4.23; 4.24-4.31*]. The effect of these sky band portal architraves upon a casual or even special interest observer must be considered and the memory which may be taken away by them, diminishing over a period of time, before they would be able to record it within their own traditions. The parallels between some of the imagery of the Maya and in India are so closely similar that it is valid to suggest that certain Mayan pilgrims were trained in the crafts of India while there or artisans who actually travelled to India to learn their skills. Alternately, just as the ruling dynasties of Java and Sumatra sent for teachers and craftsmen from India to instruct in religion and build temples[1], the earliest evidence dating to 5th., century

A.D., it is likely that the same principle was true for the Maya and the close similarities of some of the imagery and craftsmanship suggests that this may be so.

The simplifications, for the most part, can therefore easily be accounted for in the differences found in the surviving Mayan examples and those in India. It also accounts for the fact that the Mayan sky bands appear to form no discernable pattern specifically related to the zodiac. The examples in India from which they appear to have derived were clearly losing their originally intended Vedic relationship to the two half cycles in cosmic astronomical speculations still visible at Ajanta but virtually lost a century later in Orissa.

The sky bands at Ajanta [*3.31*] show that many of the Mayan panels retained the basic design structure of the panels while the almost rococo presentation, so much a part of the art and craft at that time in India, was lost since this relates to a large degree to personal or cultural taste or dictate. The strictures of distance and time ensured that only the essentials were retained in the Mayan mind and the resultant sky bands among the Mayan reflect their traditional craft skills developed through religious imperative and direction. In other words they made the sky band design panels their own and projected them in sky bands in their own way undoubtedly devising new designs and revising the assimilated ones to accommodate adjusted or reinvented meanings.

In detaching the architrave designs of the Satrughesvara they can be clearly seen to form a decorative pattern which does not immediately form a recognisable overall pattern. Its association with the entrance to the sacred portal of a temple, however, endows it with special associations in the eyes of religious devotees. Under the large fitted carved stones of the threshold the relief of continuous lotus petals is evident and this indicates that the whole of the building was to be considered the sacred precinct. In the strictest discipline of temple protocol no other than the priests were allowed to enter although in later times this has been modified. Since the portal itself was considered the entrance to heaven or the interface zone between heaven and earth the profane were not allowed to defile this sacred ceremonial area. Each vertical element of the architrave originally had specific meaning and those which were particularly important were the most elaborate. One example of particular note is the portals of the Siva temple at Lukkundi, near Gadag in South India being finely carved with nine vertical adjacent architraves, each having its own religious meaning. The association of the architraves of the Satrughesvara at Bhubanesvar in Orissa therefore endows the portal with special meaning even if the original intent of these panels had begun to degenerate into decoration. It appears that these must have been visited by Maya pilgrims since they are so completely similar to the contemporary versions of the sky bands among the Maya. If the Maya had been pilgrims to Buddhist India then Orissa would certainly have been one of the most likely ports of disembarkation into, and embarkation from India. Orissa had, and still has, its own places of pilgrimage and is relatively near the Ganges Delta further to the north and there other great pilgrim centres are known in the adjacent Brahmaputra Delta and these latter will be of more interest in a future publication.

4.11 North portal of the
Satrughesvara temple. The
carved architraves reflect the
sky band panels appearing to
have originated in the earlier
Buddhist temples and the
Ajanta caves. Bhubanesvar,
Orissa, North East india,
6th., century, AD.

The individual panels when simplified to their design structure per panel indicate the principle that memory will reduce the visual record to basic structures demonstrated and illustrated in the Mayan sky band panels. Of particular interest are the angular representations of the lotus - the supreme symbol of all three major religions of India and also among the tribal peoples [*4.13b*; *4.14b*]. The basic structure shows a four-lobed flower with a centre and four radial "creases" pointing to each corner. These are closely copied by the Maya [*4.16*; *4.21b*] and also evident on Pacal's slab [4.02; 4.03d] and on a ceramic design sky band podium [*3.44*].

Among the Mayan variations on the saltire, a diagonal cross, or more usually known as St Andrew's Cross, is found widely in sky band representations and is perhaps the most repetitive of all the panels. This panel was probably derived from what

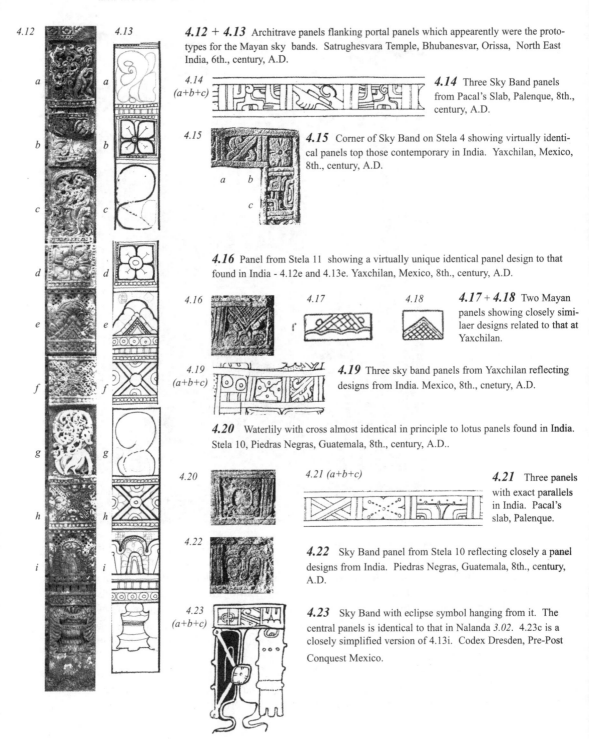

4.12

4.13

4.12 + 4.13 Architrave panels flanking portal panels which appearently were the proto-types for the Mayan sky bands. Satrughesvara Temple, Bhubanesvar, Orissa, North East India, 6th., century, A.D.

4.14
(a+b+c)

4.14 Three Sky Band panels from Pacal's Slab, Palenque, 8th., century, A.D.

4.15

4.15 Corner of Sky Band on Stela 4 showing virtually identical panels top those contemporary in India. Yaxchilan, Mexico, 8th., century, A.D.

a   b

c

4.16 Panel from Stela 11 showing a virtually unique identical panel design to that found in India - 4.12e and 4.13e. Yaxchilan, Mexico, 8th., century, A.D.

4.16   *4.17*   *4.18*

4.17 + 4.18 Two Mayan panels showing closely simi-laer designs related to that at Yaxchilan.

4.19
(a+b+c)

4.19 Three sky band panels from Yaxchilan reflecting designs from India. Mexico, 8th., cnetury, A.D.

4.20 Waterlily with cross almost identical in principle to lotus panels found in India. Stela 10, Piedras Negras, Guatemala, 8th., century, A.D..

4.20   *4.21 (a+b+c)*

4.21 Three panels with exact parallels in India. Pacal's slab, Palenque.

4.22

4.22 Sky Band panel from Stela 10 reflecting closely a panel designs from India. Piedras Negras, Guatemala, 8th., century, A.D.

4.23
(a+b+c)

4.23 Sky Band with eclipse symbol hanging from it. The central panels is identical to that in Nalanda *3.02*. 4.23c is a closely simplified version of 4.13i. Codex Dresden, Pre-Post Conquest Mexico.

appears to be a saltire with a central rosette [*4.01f; 4.02f*] in Orissa. In fact this is the representation of four half-lotuses back to back within the panels with their centres corresponding to the mid-point on each of the perimeter borders [*4.01a; 4.03a*]. This design is almost as popular among the panel representations in India as the full single panel. As a result of the design these half-lotuses, intentionally or otherwise, have been subjugated by the saltire separating them and the impression a casual observer is left with is that of the prominent saltire in the panel where the half-lotuses appear incidental or are not comprehended [*4.13f; 4.14h; 4.21a*]. In some less usual designs for sky bands among the Maya the saltire with a "dot" in each of the fields [*4.19b*] between the saltire arms may have developed from this Orissan panel but in fact this design also appears separately in India and China and is considered in "Mayan Genesis"[2].

Among the panels represented on the Satrughesvara sky band architrave is that depicted in the rarely found design, apparently a symbolic display of lotus petals being formed into a pyramidal design, shown in *4.12e* and simplified in *4.13e*. This design is so specific and rare in India that to discover it in the Mayan representations of their sky bands cannot be coincidental [*4.16; 4.17; 4.18*]. On the Satrughesvara architrave sky band panels it appears twice - once on each side of the door [see also *4.24a; 4.25a*]. The Mayan panel shown in *4.16* is a detail from that depicted in illustration *5.19* - a stela from Piedras Negras - and where the adjacent panels are also closely similar to those found in India. The lotus is a common theme in the panels of India and the half-lotuses separated by the saltire [*4.12f+h; 4.13f+h*] appear to be reflected or influenced, at least in part, in other Mayan panels. These reflect the "pearling" shown running along the centre of the saltire arms and is found in examples such as shown in *4.21b* which reflects that, in principle, of *4.12b+d* and *4.13b+d*. Other examples of the Mayan panels seem to show the lotus or waterlily which may also derive from the half-lotuses divided by the saltire such as shown in *4.20* as well as the simple saltires so common among the Maya [*4.21a*].

In India there are designs in some panels which are recognisably based on lotus or other leaves and these are variously treated. In some Mayan panels there are designs that are somewhat indeterminate and complex and these may well have originated from these lotus leaf panels at Bhumara or in Bhubanesvar in Orissa. The leaf panels shown in *4.12a, 4.13a* or *4.12c* and *4.13c* may well have been the prototype for the Mayan example in *4.15c*. Other leaf or bud forms such as *4.12i* and *4.13i* on the Satrughesvara architraves may have been the basis for the Mayan panel types shown in *4.21c* or *4.22*.

The right hand architrave at the Satrughesvara has survived to a lesser degree than the left and tends to repeat the panels of that side but in a different order suggesting the decline of meaning in favour of decoration by the 7th., century A.D. in Orissa. The topmost surviving panel again reflects the unusual design of a, most likely, lotus or other leaf in plan with three "rosettes" of lotuses flanked possibly by two half-lotuses [*4.24a; 4.26a*]. This appears to be closely copied as seen in the repeated example of the Mayan panel from Piedras Negras in *4.25* (also *4.16*).

A later Mayan panel at Chichen Itza shown in *4.28d* seems to have been derived from the original panel in India or from the later Mayan copies. The lotuses from this same sky band appear to relate to those in the left side of the Satrughesvara in panels *4.12b+d* and *4.13b+d*. The saltire based panels at Chichen Itza, 4.28b+c+i+k, all seem to be based on the half-lotuses separated by the satire cross in the Orissan examples, *4.24b+d; 4.26b+d*. The waterlily panel in *4.27a* appears to even more closely derived from the Orissan half-lotus saltire panels with the "rosette" of a lotus centrally placed as shown in panels *4.24b+d* and *4.26b+d*. The Mayan panels designs depicted in *4.27b*, *4.30a* (inverted) and at the base of *4.31* may all have originated in the leaf design shown on the right architrave of the Satrughesvara, panel *4.24e* and *4.26e*.

Finally the illustration of an "old god", a Pauahtun, seated on a sky band

4.24 + 4.26 Architrave panels flanking portal panels appearently the prototypes for the Mayan sky bands. Satrughesvara Temple, Bhubanesvar, Orissa, North East India, 6th., century, A.D.

4.25 Panel from Stela 10 showing a virtually unique identical panel design to that found in India - 4.12e and 4.13e. Piedras Negras, Guatemala, 8th., century, A.D.

4.27 Saltire cross from Sky Band identical to panels found in India. Stela 32, Piedras Negras, Guatemala, 8th., century, A.D.

4.31 Seated Old Deity/ Pauahtun seated on Sky Band. Uaxactun, Peten, Guatemala, Late Classic.

4.28 Late Classic Sky Band showing several panels identical to those in India. Chichen Itza, Yucatan Mexico, 10th., century, A.D.

4.29 Inverted lotus leaf pattern closely similar to Indian examples shown in 4.24e and 4.26e. Stela 10, Piedras Negras, Guatemala, 8th., century, A.D.

4.30 Three Mayan panels paralleling similar examples in India - *4.24*. Stela 4, Yaxchilan, Mexico, 8th., century, A.D.

4.32 Portal carving reflecting the "gelbai" motif depicting godlings intertwined with a vine close-ly similar to the identical motif in India. Mayan, West Face, Temple 22, Copan, Honduras, 8th., century, AD.

4.33 Gelbai motif depictin godlings intertwined with vines. Axamanesvar temple group, Bhubanevar, North East India. 6-7th., century, AD.

4.34 Detail of the Mayan "gelbai" motif from Temple 22. Copan, Honduras, 8th., century, AD.

shows his "throne" [*4.31*] being composed of panels seemingly having their close parallels in the Orissan temple architrave panels in India - here the Satrughesvara, apparently corresponding to the lotus and half-lotus saltire panels for the most part. This sky band is shown in a stepped form of platform throne which has probable references to the cranked sky-arch or "torana" of India but more widely surviving in Indonesia.

The Gelbai Motif:

For many the comparisons between the sky band panels displayed in the temple architraves at Orissa may not in themselves prove conclusively that contact existed between the Maya and India. However the accumulation of many aspects of Mayan iconography with close similarities to examples displayed in the same context and associated with many other apparently related aspects of culture must weigh heavily in favour of cross-Pacific contacts. Because of the natural isolation of Orissa from the rest of India its cultural imports and exports from across the sea, as a coastal state, were of great importance. There are many aspects of Orissan culture which reflect their mariners heritage and this extends all along the East Coast of India south to Sri Lanka and east to South East Asia, and Indonesia in particular. To the north influences from the

Ganges and Brahmaputra Deltas up into the Himalayas of Tibet are also evident introducing a cultural counterflow so clearly seen in Tantric Buddhist and Hindu sects which appear to have had a strong base in Orissa.

Many traditional tribal aspects of cultural myths and beliefs permeated the iconography of the Buddhist and Hindu religions and are evident in the temple building which still survives. Of particular interest to one earlier researcher, Professor Charles Louis Fabri, was an intrusive mythological element which he describes as the "famous Orissan motif of the Gelbai: a creeper intertwined with human beings"[3]. He particularly notes that this may not have been exclusively Orissan since he detected an earlier portrayal at Bharhut in Central North India, a site dating from late first millennium B.C. to the early second century A.D. A further development is found in Andra in Central India dating from 320-495 A.D. These elements he found are most likely to have been related to the "putti" - cherubs or dwarfs - who are depicted carrying garlands in the finely crafted friezes of the Greco-Buddhist art of Gandhara dating to about the first or second century A.D. The original inspiration for these putti was clearly Greek but as Fabri stated the original intention "has been changed considerably in order to express a typically Indian feeling about Life in Vegetation and the animation of all floral life"[4].

The gelbai motif of human or mythical figures intertwined with creepers is known in Orissa from surviving examples dating from the 8th., century, A.D.[5]. It is significant that some of the finest examples are those from the Axamaneswar temple complex. The example shown is clearly a replacement on one side only of an architrave which is itself flanked by panels which are similar to the stone-carved architraves [4.33] already considered flanking the north portal of the Satrughesvara - this being a temple in this same group. These figures intertwined with creepers or vines are characteristic of the Orissan style but more complete examples survive in other temples such as the Parasumesvara [5.101] where the intertwining "gelbai" design appears to have been an original part of the design and are more completely preserved as a mirrored pair flanking the sacred portal. This gelbai motif became a stock-in-trade for later artisans or silpins and very ornate versions are found at Lakkundi and elsewhere. The "gelbai" motif is found at its finest on the Parasumesvara temple and later at Ratnagiri maintaining the same tradition over two centuries.

Remarkably the same Orissan "gelbai" theme is found among the Maya at Copan where many other aspects of identical iconography are found and shared at this celebrated ceremonial site with India. The great doorway surround decoration on the West face of Temple 22 clearly derives its origin from the Orissan examples where mythical figures intertwine with "S"-shaped vines or creepers to form the overall shape of a great serpent[6][4.32]. The detail of this surround shows several of these intertwined figures [4.34]. It cannot be a coincidence that the Orissan "gelbai" motif and related sky panels are so closely similar to those of the Maya. These silpins or artisans transferred to the Hindu temples from the great Buddhist trading and monastic centres of Orissa which existed from the late first millennium B.C. through to about 1000 A.D. and were probably those who went to Indonesia and Mesopotamia.

F. Catherwood.   47. BAS-RELIEF IN STUCCO

4.35 - 4.38 Frederick Catherwood's drawings from
Stephens and Catherwood's expedition to Copan in the
Nineteenth century. They show the importance of the sky
band borders appearing to derive from portal architrave panels in India. Copan, Honduras, 8th., century, AD.

Sky Band Panels:

The remarkable, for their time, large pilaster panels drawn as they appeared to Frederick Catherwood of Palenque in the mid-nineteenth depict some of the best known of the sky bands in surviving Mayan stucco art [*4.35-4.38*]. The overall panels depict their perimeter sky bands suggesting portals through which the portrayal of the divine ancestors communicating with their priest-ruler descendants is intended to be displayed. This is probably derived from a memory of looking through the portal doorways into the single chamber shrines of early Orissa and other parts of India. This is particularly so of the inner shrines of the Buddhists where the great statues of the red-stuccoed Buddha are so prominent and memorable [*3.48; 5.04*]. Of special note is the beaded "magician's apron" and cape which are virtually identical to those of the Bon Po, and absorbed into later Buddhist ritual from the 7th., century A.D., in early Tibet, and these influences were accessible to the Ganges and Brahmaputra Delta [*5.118*]. Such a ceremonial apron is evident worn by Pacal in his carved funerary slab and other rulers or priests [*3.49; 4.37; 5.116; 5.117*].

Connections between Nalanda, the famous Buddhist university, and Orissa are evident from the middle of the first millennium B.C. but are certain from before that time. Buddhist sculpture from the 2nd., century A.D. in Orissa is similar to that of Mathura and North Central India far to the North West. Interesting also at Nalanda is stucco plastering less frequently found elsewhere in Buddhist work but appears to have been introduced from Orissa[7]. In early Buddhist temple and monastic building the Buddhists preferred brickwork and this predilection appears to have encouraged the skilled craftsmen to excel in the mastery of brick-construction so evident in their remarkable structures. In later times the taste for large areas of superb brickwork abated and a great deal of this was screeded over with plaster[8]. Stucco was also common on temples in ancient South India and particularly popular there to this day.

Although the Orissan dynasties were originally Buddhist by the seventh and eighth centuries A.D. they had, for the most part, changed their allegiance to the Brahmanic-Hindu religion. Buddhist patronage appears to have continued, however, since some of the most illustrious monasteries, such as at Ratnagiri, were constructed in this period [*3.57*]. These important institutions could only have been supported by wealthy merchants who appear to have remained faithful to their Buddhist roots. Their activities have been recorded intimating that the overseas trade was of major importance and documents such as those preserved in the Katha-Sarit-Sagara convey a record of the wealth resulting from the activities of these merchants. It was noted by Fabri that the depictions of this Buddhist goddess, Tara, the female counterpart of Avalokitesvara, the patroness of mariners and traders on the high seas, were prominent in Orissa[9]. Remarkable among the religious sects flourishing in Orissa was one which appeared to be linked to the Tantric forms of Buddhism and Hinduism influenced by the so-called "wrathful forms" - fierce aspects of the deities from North India and Tibet. Only two temples to this sect remain and referred to as the "64 Yoginis" since nothing is known of the rites carried on within the confines. These sects were probably a response to intrusive influences from abroad and although the ithyphallic image of Siva appears to have been the focus point of the circular temples there is little known of the rites held at these sites[10]. It is interesting to note that there were 64 aspects in the Chinese I-Ching cycle of "changes" and perhaps the 64 yoginis were in some way related or an assimilated form from the same cycle of belief and Prof. Fabri referred to other possibilities initiating this unusual temple constructed in the 9th., century A.D. These sects may have been as a result of overseas influences brought in by returning merchants and, or mariners from overseas or by pilgrims from far distant lands.

It is known that the Orissan merchants sailed as far afield as Burma, Thailand, Cambodia, Vietnam, Java and Sumatra and they were usually known by the name "Klings" which was a shortened version of Kalingans, after Kalinga the early name of coastal Orissa. Another name for the country was Ek-Amra particularly more local to Bhubanesvar and the term Ek Chauh, the trader's deity in Mexico, may have evolved from this association with overseas trade from that section of the east coast of India. In this context it is interesting to note that the rulers at the end of the first millennium A.D. claimed they were "emperor, kings of kings, lord of the three Kalingas, and often they add that they had conquered the whole world, nothing less"[11].

Sky Band - Cranked Arches; Toranas:

Some of the most remarkable sculptural forms are the Toranas or Sky Arch constructions found across India appearing from the earliest days of Buddhism through to the almost sublime representation of the ceremonial gateway to the Mukhtesvara temple at Bhubanesvar in Orissa [*4.49; 4.50*]. At Sanchi in Central North India the finest detached architectural representations survive virtually intact - the site dating from about the third century B.C. to the first century A.D.[12]. The Sanchi toranas, or sky arches, appear to have set the three-dimensional model for the "Vault of Heaven", as a vertical section through it. Another two-dimensional representation of this same "Vault of Heaven" is that as a view from underneath or earth view seen in the Ajanta sky band illustrated in *3.31*.

It is already noted that the temple doorways throughout Buddhist, Hindu and Jain temple architecture were considered as the ceremonial portal to an interface with Heaven or the Upper World. The sky bands carved around these portals were the equivalent of the toranas expressed in a different way but originating from the same religious and philosophic precepts. Sea connections between Orissa, and indeed all the seaboard enclaves along the east coast of India, had maintained close links with South East Asia but it is with the Indonesian islands that the most interesting of the cultural transfers took place throughout the first millennium A.D. The archaeological and sculptural remains in Java and Sumatra are some of the most revealing in South East Asia and are located supplanting earlier cultures which appear to have had common origins with those on the coasts of Guatemala, at Santa Lucia Cotzumalguapa among others and Southern Mexico at Izapa.

The great Buddhist sanctuary of Borobodur in the highlands of Java is one of the greatest of the archaeological sites in the world dated to the 8th., century A.D. Its overall stepped form resembles the pyramid structures of Central America rather than Asia, but its finished surfaces are pure Javan derived from the Buddhist traditions of India. Of particular interest to this study are several of the seated carved stone bas-reliefs which depict either the Buddha or rulers and, or their relatives seated under ceremonial canopies on a raised platform or stage (*4.43; 4.45*). These canopies are carved to represent the torana or sky arch so well-known in India and Orissa in particular. That shown in illustration *4.43* is designed in an angular form as a cranked arch rather than a semi-circle but it retains the makaras, or disgorging mythical Ganges deity based on the crocodile, each facing outward above each of the supporting, flanking pillars, in the fashion seen among the Maya. Faintly seen at the centre of the cranked arch is the disgorging lion head so widely favoured above portals in Indonesia but derived from similar depictions in Orissa and found in more extreme forms in Central America among the Maya. A simplified version of the cranked sky "arch" is shown in illustration *4.45*.

The seated Buddha or other divine deity or ruler seated on a padded throne or palanquin is found also seated or standing among the Maya and depicted very elaborately at Piedras Negras [*5.19*] and Naranjo [*5.20*]. The cranked sky arch is found not only in Orissa, in India, and Java in Indonesia but also in a clearly recognisable but assimilated form among the Maya. The Guatemalan site of Quirigua preserves two of the most interesting examples since they correspond so closely to the principles established in India. The great carved monolith, known as Stela K, dated 805 A.D. [*4.42*], shows a sky arch formed from the sky band panels which show a similar combined relationship of portal panels and sky arch so noted in Orissa but cranked to form a statue niche which appears to relate more closely to the Indonesian models. Stela K is considered to relate to the slightly earlier styles found at Piedras Negras dating from 608, 687, 731, and 761 A.D.[13] and this site shows many aspects which appears to derive from India.

At Quirigua also is found a monolithic "altar", Zoomorph O, dated to 790 A.D. [*4.39; 4.40*] and it depicts a cranked sky arch in the same outline as Stela K and Indonesian examples. This Mayan example is adapted to form a less usual design incorporating trefoils which have been shown in "Mayan Genesis" (p82-97) to be especially related to the iconography of Southern China among the No Su but which itself derives from early Buddhist iconography in India. The frontal view of this zoomorph depicts a deity, godling or the soul of a former ruler intertwined with a serpent which recalls the portal sculpture around Temple 22 at Copan [*4.32; 4.34*] and the apparent originals in India of the "gelbai" motif in Orissa [*4.33; 5.63*]. These aspects of Zoomorph O are depicted more clearly in the drawing in illustration *4.41*.

From Yaxchilan fine reliefs depict sky bands [*4.47*] which are related to those in the Piedras Negras style but reflect closely the example shown on Stela K at Quirigua [*4.42*]. This carving is depicted in *4.44* show a cranked sky band in the Indonesian style [*4.43; 4.45*] considered by some earlier American researches as the ecliptic in Mayan symbolism[15]. The ecliptic is here, therefore, represented by the sky band as it was in India and it is interesting to note in this example that there are three

4.39 + 4.40 Zoomorph O showing a cranked sky arch and associated deity shown from top and side. Monument 23, Quirigua, Guatemala, 8th., century, AD.

4.42 Stela K shows a cranked sky arch with a deity seated in the niche formed by it. This reflects the Buddhist cranked sky arches in India and Indonesia. Quirigua, Guatemala, 8th., century, A.D.

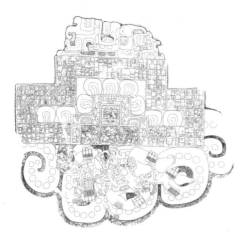

4.41 Drawing showing Zoomorph O "altar" clearing indicating the cranked sky arch. Quirigua, Guatemala, 8th., century, AD.

4.43 Cranked sky arch shown supported by columns enclosing the figure. At each end of the arch are makaras in the Indian style but also similar to caiman depictions among the Maya. Borobodur, Java, Indonesia, 8th., century, AD.

4.44 Sky arch supporting ancestral figures in the Upper World. This is closely similar to Mayan examples at Quirigua and in Indonesia. Yaxchilan, Chiapas, Southern Mexico, 8th., century, AD.

4.45 Cranked sky arch as canopy to ritual scene. Each end of the arch forms a makara closely similar to depictions of caimans forming the terminals of sky bands in Mayan iconography. Borobodur, Java, Indonesia, 8th., century, AD.

4.46 Original sky arches in India are both true arches and cranked. The trefoil niche centred over the sky arch is found in Mesoamerica as well as in Indonesia and China. Nalanda, Bihar, Central North India, 6th., century, AD.

4.47 Upper section of Stela 4 depicting carving of a cranked sky arch with two Venus signs under the highest part. Sections of this examples are used elsewhere in this work. Stela 4, Yaxchilan, Chiapas, Southerm Mexico, 8th., century, AD.

4.48 Cranked sky arch of this type became the prototype for those in Indonesia and among the Maya. Nalanda, Bihar, Central North India, 6th., century, AD.

"trophy" heads at each end which are connected to this sky band by Venus signs. In India and Indonesia the trophy head attached to the (ecliptic) belt appears to be related to the eclipse demon, Rahu, and this element of mythology is considered more extensively in "Mayan Genesis"[16].

More immediately it is the cranked shape of the Mayan sky band that is of interest and although the Indonesian examples in Java, at Borobodur, are the most similar to those of the Maya there are earlier examples in India appearing to be the prototypes. There are many sculpted depictions of gods, deities and godlings framed by what are clearly intended to be sky arches or portals deriving from the symbolism of the divine doorway as the entrance to the interface with the Upper World, or Heaven. It is at Nalanda again where many examples from a dado are still preserved in what is an otherwise ruined site dating to the 6-7th., century A.D. At Temple 2 a great number of finely carved stone panels have been reassembled on the lower register, in order where possible, almost completely surrounding the surviving less than complete ground floor storey. The representations are almost all deities or godlings and each is shown emerging or framed by a portal clearly reflecting a modified sky arch. One type of sky arch portal is surmounted by an arch proper [4.46] while others are of the cranked type [4.48]. Both of the examples shown here are of further interest since they also exhibit trefoils in the "gavaksa" or "bull's eye" niche above the sky arches. The trefoil is found throughout the symbolism of Buddhist and Hindu India and also widely detectable among the Maya and other regions of the Americas in similar contexts.

Further fine examples of the cranked sky arch have survived from Yaxchilan [4.47] and this one emphasises the Venus aspect since it is supported by two Venus glyphs with trophy heads hanging from them. Also of interest are the two ancestor figures holding ceremonial bars which are closely similar to those found in Buddhist iconography [4.74-4.78]. These two ancestor figures are shown seated in what appears to be crescent Moons. It is of interest to note that the myths associated with Rahu, the eclipse demon of India, are primarily about him becoming immortalised through consuming the Soma, the nectar of the gods - this being specifically associated with the Moon's essence. Rahu, the giant encircling serpent of the ecliptic, was said to have been discovered consuming the divine nectar, the Soma, by the Sun and the Moon. He was not entitled to do so since this was reserved for the gods so Indra seeing this and alerting the other gods resulted in Vishnu hurling his discus at Rahu splitting him into two[17]. The head of the serpent became the Moon's North Node, Rahu himself, and the tail became Ketu, the Moon's South Node. The double-headed serpent belts were considered a representation of Rahu since the belt in the symbology of India was said to represent the ecliptic dividing the individual self into the upper half representing divinity and the Upper World while the lower half represented the Earth and the Underworld. Rahu is of some interest since not only are double-headed serpent belts found throughout the Americas but his brother was said to be Maya, the semi-divine architect[18], but also an antigod who was believed in some myths to have come from (over) the sea to India.

The cranked sky arch in an example from Borobodur, *4.45*, varies from that shown in *4.43* in that the makaras extend down to the platform or dais on each side

4.49 + 4.50 Remarkable sky arch/free-standing portal of the Mukhtesvara temple. The identification of the sky arch with the World Tree is indicated by the foliated relief carving on top of the arch. The makaras, equating to the Mayan caiman are seen projecting from each end. Bhubanesvar, Orissa, North East India, 10th., century, AD.

4.51 Sky arch or torana with makara heads at each end similar to that depicted on Pacal's funerary slab *4.53*. Detail, Eastern Ganga, 13th., century, AD.

4.52 Surya the Sun god, standing in front of sky arch or torana with the makaras extending from the springing point at each end. Konarak, Orissa, North East India, 13th., century, AD.

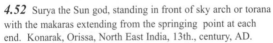

4.53 Details from Pacal's funerary slab show the cranked sky arch or torana closely similar to those found in India and Indonesia. Pacal is also wearing a "magician's " apron identical to those of the Buddhist and Bon Po Tibet. Palenque, Chiapas, Southern Mexico, 8th., century, AD.

and face outwards typical in the more characteristic Javan representations. The similar cranked sky arch is clearly represented at Quirigua, Piedras Negras and Yaxchilan in the form and styles found more typically in Javan representations but which ultimately derive from Buddhist India. Another, but older form of the sky arch or torana was retained in the ceremonial structures of India into later centuries in Orissa from the earliest known at Sanchi. This later torana form finds its finest expression in those of Orissa and in the sky arch of the Muktesvara temple in particular [4.49; 4.50]. Here the sky arch or torana as ceremonial gateway, repeating the long unchanging tradition from the earliest known Buddhist traditions, is still recognisable and assimilated into this finest of Hindu temples dating to the 9th., century A.D. in Bhubanesvar. This sky arch preserves the philosophic precepts of the merging of the torana as sky arch or "vault-of-heaven" and the ecliptic as sky band with the World Tree which is readily observed obvious in the foliated upper surfaces of the arch. Of particular interest are the two "makaras" or crocodilian heads projecting here outwards from the springing points on both sides of the arch base. Makaras are repeatedly found in the many sky arch representations from the earliest Buddhist ceremonial sites through to the present day in an unbroken tradition over the last two thousand three hundred years. These elements of iconography are of great importance since they are repeated in the crocodilian or serpent heads which are depicted in the identical way in Mayan codices, carved bas-reliefs and ceramic decoration.

The sky arch of the Muktesvara is in fact found in this type of representation throughout Orissa and it is this specific form that it is repeated faithfully in the same arched form on Pacal's funerary slab at Palenque [4.53] as a modification of the cranked sky arch and the torana in and around Bhubanesvar. As a torana or sky arch with the makaras heads extending from both ends the less complicated form of that shown in the depiction of what was thought to be a representation of Krishna but now thought to be Raja Narasimhadeva 1 [4.51] is undoubtedly related to the depiction of the ceremonial bar on Pacal's slab [4.53].

The ceremonial bar is found from the earliest Buddhist imagery into the present day assimilated into the Hindu and Jain traditions. It is usually shown supported by pillars or vertical supports behind the statue of the Buddha or other deity at about shoulder level, whether seated or standing. In the depiction shown here in 4.52 it is, apart from the style of the relief, identical in principle and placement to those recorded over many centuries of Indian religious art. This particular sculpture depicts the Sun deity, Surya, with the torana or sky band extending from shoulder level up behind his head in the characteristic Orissan manner. At the base each side the makaras extend outwards. This particular panel is of interest since the deity is shown wearing a pair of knee-length boots recognisably derived from Central Asia thousands of miles away. This element of imagery emphasises the long-distance connections that had influenced India from far beyond the foothills of the Himalayas and particularly from the Buddhist regions of Western Tibet, Khotan and the Takla Makan steppe through to, and beyond Zungaria in the Altai region of Siberia.

On Pacal's slab the ceremonial bar shown in a serpentine shape forming the cranked arch displays a makara's head at both end with a god head emerging from each. This corresponds to similar images known in early Buddhist iconography and assimilated into that of the Hindus for many centuries into recent times [*4.77*]. The makara was originally developed, as far as it could be traced, from the dolphin but most usually it is identified with the Ganges crocodile. It has been subject to a long history of development and it has evolved into many forms and sometimes, in the characteristic manner of imagery in India, the makara was merged with other mythical animals to form a composite image said to be endowed with all the various attributes of the animals incorporated. The fish body of the original dolphin was most often depicted with the head of a crocodile, an elephant [*4.62*; *4.64*], a lion, but usually displaying the characteristic gaping maw or jaws with a human head or form emerging or even a full figure. These hybrid figures were so common in the mythological life of India that they had their own term - "Ihamrga"[19], and was a speciality of the Mathura school in North Central India dating to the early centuries of the first millennium A.D. There are some examples suggesting that the inspiration was that of a hippopotamus - such as at Lakkundi in South India, indicating influences from Africa.

The early identification of the makara with the Ganges crocodile is not surprising but the makara as a symbol is also firmly identified with the serpent. This identification of a crocodile with the serpent undoubtedly derives from the Ganges being the ultimate serpentine form linking it to the very ancient serpent worshipping Nagas in North India. This mythological serpentine link of the life-giving waters of the Ganges with the crocodilian makara is clearly projected through the transferred imagery imported Central America among the Maya, epitomised through the design on Pacal's slab, was assimilated into their cultural context.

The surviving examples of torana arches found in India are quite special since they must represent aspects of Hindu mythology that were much more widely spread than is evident today. The free-standing torana arches represented the descent of the serpentine waters of the Ganges from the great deity Siva in his palatial abode, Kalaisa, in the Himalayas. The imagery of this belief is expressed through the wavy form of the arch where the makara heads at each end symbolised the disgorging aspect of the riverine symbol of the Ganges crocodile, located at each lower end of the arch [*4.55*]. The act of disgorging is expressed by the characteristic curved, raised upper jaw identically reproduced in virtually all the Mayan examples [*4.71-4.73*].

One of the most attractive examples of the torana is one found at Hirapur, near Bhubanesvar [*4.54*]. This arch is located in the centre of the village near the unusual circular temple of the 64 Yoginis and may be contemporary with it dated to about 800-820 A.D. being perhaps earlier or later. Three other sky arches of this exact type are also found on the stone platforms adjacent to the ceremonial tank a little way outside of Hirapur and reflect the mythological belief that the ceremonial tanks are filled with the divine water direct from the Himalayas [*4.56*]. A similar sky arch, or torana, to those found at Hirapur is located in the old centre of Bhubanesvar next to the great Lingaraja temple [*4.57*]. Finest of all is the sky arch located adjacent to the Baitel Deul, a remarkable, finely carved temple in the barrel-vaulted Dravidian style of South India dating from about the 7-8th., century A.D. This carved torana [*4.55*]

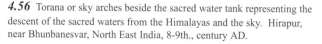

4.54 Freestanding sky arch or torana with makaras emerging from the springing points of the arch. Hirapur, near Bhubanesvar, Orissa, North East India, c8-9th., century A.D.

4.56 Torana or sky arches beside the sacred water tank representing the descent of the sacred waters from the Himalayas and the sky. Hirapur, near Bhunbanesvar, North East India, 8-9th., century AD.

4.55 Section of Torana/sky arch, depicting the makara-caiman projecting from the springing point. Bhubanesvar, Orissa, North East India, 8-10th, century, AD.

4.57 Torana showing the sky arch representing the flow of water from the sky identified with the River Ganges. Bhubanesvar, Orissa, North East India, 8-10th., century AD.

exhibits all the classical indicators of the traditional Orissan sky arch including the "gavaksa" niche heads, the makara with its up-raised upper jaw, reflecting a similar one shown incorporated into the later walled enclosure of the Baitel Duel itself.

Makara - Origins; Myths:
The sky arch of Orissa has its roots in the Buddhist torana many centuries earlier and

was probably borrowed directly from the Buddhist monasteries and temples in Orissa itself. Undoubtedly for the Mayan pilgrims this region of India would have been one of the first in arriving, one of the last in leaving, and therefore would have left a more lasting impression than some of the other sites. Although so many bas-reliefs throughout India in Buddhist imagery include the makara either as disgorger of the Sky Vault or facing outwards from its ends or at either end of a ceremonial bar little exists in their literature which indicates the purpose and origin of this element of iconography. This must be deduced from the reliefs themselves and from parallels in existing Hindu references.

The earliest apparent indicators are the reliefs and sculptures originating from Greek incursions via Parthia and Bactria and ultimately deriving from the dolphin so well-known in Aegean art. Interestingly in Hindu myths the makara was the vehicle of Kama the god of lust or desire[20], an aspect associated in Greek myths with Eros and Venus (in Greek - Aphrodite) who is also associated with the dolphin. The cranked sky band from Piedras Negras [*4.47*] is depicted being supported by two Venus Glyphs. In other Hindu myths the earrings of the sky god Vishnu were said to be "shaped like sea monsters" - the makaras[21]. The earrings in this case are considered the supporters of the "dome" of the skull - some higher cultures equating the cranium with the symbolic equivalent or microcosm of the "Vault of Heaven". The arched sky band at Piedras Negras is therefore repeated in this parallel with the disgorging makaras on either side similarly found so widely in Hindu and Buddhist iconography. This hybrid of dolphin or sea monster, the Ganges crocodile, serpent, elephant and lion is particularly associated with the sign of Capricorn or the New Year in the philosophic constructs of India[22]. No doubt this has much to do with its cosmic associations as disgorger of the Ganges - the River of Life, and with the vault being depicted as an almost watery or vaporous arch emitted from their mouths [*4.58*]. In Hindu mythology the ancient goddess of the River Ganges is Ganga and her two vehicles (vahanas) are the Ganges crocodile and Matsya, the fish deity. It is possible therefore that the two merged to form the fish-tailed crocodile or makara in very ancient times before being identified with the dolphin as sea monster.

In other Hindu myths the god of the West, Varuna, first referred to in the Hittite period in Anatolia in the second half of the second millennium B.C., is said to be carried on his vehicle, the Makara[23]. This emphasises his association with West Asia and migrations from the headwaters of the Tigris and Euphrates far to the north west of India and possibly also with Greek incursions a millennium later.

The disgorging aspect of the makara is known as Makara-Mukha - "mouth of the makara" which is associated with the emergence of divine aspects or attributes of heroes or deities from the makara's mouth, an act known as "pabhavali"[24]. In Brahmanic mythology, inheritor of Vedic lore but pre-dating the Hindu, it was said that the four castes were born from the body of Brahma but the Brahmans themselves were born from His mouth[25]. This belief appears to be the forerunner, or to have common origins with the myths associated with the makara. Where a sky arch displays these makaras as supporters it is known as the Makara-Torana[26].

4.58 Superb relief carving in the chaitya halls of the Ajanta cave shrines. The carving depicts makaras disgorging the torana or sky arch from their mouths - a motif found in the Americas. Ajanta Cave 26, West Central India, 5-6th., centuries, AD.

4.59 Elaborate relief carving depicting facing makaras with foliated tails. The makaras are disgorging the sky arch or torana and the godlings riding on their backs is found identically among Mayan reliefs at Palenque - *4.63.* Pattadakal, South Central India, 7-8th., century, AD.

The crocodile myths which were retained among the Aboriginal tribes of India were considered in "Mayan Genesis" and these no doubt were assimilated into the Buddhist and Hindu religions over many centuries and identified with the makara. However in ancient America the Vision Serpent among the Maya was clearly identified with the World Tree and the Cosmic structure of the Vault-of-Heaven in the same way as that of the Buddhists and Hindus. At Copan a conspicuous attempt to identify the rulers with the World Tree resulted in some of the finest sculpted monoliths in the Americas [*4.39-4.42*] and these resemble in principle some of the early Buddhist monolithic stela at Bamiyan and the more sophisticated stelae and reliefs in India. In the same way as the Buddha, bodhisattvas, or saints were said to intercede and were themselves the interface between the human world and the divine so among the Maya the same idea held sway. Some archaeologists were moved when writing of Mayan cosmic iconography that this "tree was the conduit of communication between the supernatural world and the human world" and that the "souls of the dead fell into Xibalba along its path, the daily journeys of the sun, moon, planets, and stars followed the trunk"[27]. They further noted that the Vision Serpent, so clearly inspired directly from the torana-makara in India symbolised communion between the human priests or rulers as the rightful intercessors between the ruling families and their ancestors in the world of deities and gods. The ruler was considered the World Tree made flesh!! It would appear that these elements of imagery are those depicted on Pacal's funerary slab.

These aspects of philosophic speculation are so similar to later Buddhist iconography from the early first millennium A.D. that the Mayan model must have been influenced from the earlier and contemporary Indian. The identification of the ruler in Mayan rites and iconography with the World Tree has its parallel with the identification of the Buddha with the World Tree or Axis Mundae so frequently depicted in the iconography of India. The Mayan rulers in Central America, or the Buddha in India, therefore were considered the centre of the cosmic world. Upon them devolved the belief that they symbolically focused the cosmic order and as the World Axis it was around them that the ecliptic, zodiac or sky band was centred as the central spindle was for the astrolabe.

The first division of the year in India was determined from the winter solstice, Capricorn, whose symbol was the makara and this marked the beginning of the Sun's northward course culminating six months later in the apogee of mid-summer. The

4.60 Mayan dignitary with a Garuda/ Principal Bird above and makaras/ caimans appearing to extend from the sides of the head in the exact manner found in Indonesia and India. Yucatan, DSouthern Mexico, Late Classic.

4.61 Buddhist bodhisattva with a ceremonial bar terminating in makara heads. This is clearly the model for the Mayan iconographical element shown in *4.60*. Chandi Medut, Java, Indonesia, 8th., century, AD.

4.62 Highly expressive depiction of two makaras with godlings riding on their backs similarly found among the Mayans. Pattadakal, Central South India, 7-8th., century, AD.

4.63 Early carving of the Buddha seated on addorsed lions similar to depictions of rulers seated on addorsed jaguars at Palenque. Makaras/caimans extend from the shoulders facing outwards identically to similar depictions in Indonesia and among the Maya. The makaras were in fact the visible ends of a ceremonial bar found identically among the Maya. Nasik, West Central India, 2-5th., century, A.D.

4.64 Expressive depiction of two makaras/caimans facing a deity with godlings riding on their backs - a motif found also among the Maya at Palenque. The makara tails were usual that of a fish but in South India the tail became foliated and then, as here, the tail of a peacock. Pattadakal, South Central India, 7-8th., century, AD.

4.66 Remarkable headdress as a makara-torana where jaguar heads are substituted facing outwards at each side of the baseline above the shoulders. This must have been derived in principle from India. Huastec, Veracruz, East Coast Mexico, 9-10th., century, AD.

4.65 Makaras with riding godlings disgorging the sky arch or torana. The tails reflect the development from the original fish-tail into that of a peacock favoured particularly in South India. Kailasanatha Temple, Kanchipuram, South India, 7-8th., century, AD.

4.67 Makara heads extending outwards from central point possibly inspired from the traditional makara ceremonial bars. The traditional disgorging Simba head surmounting all is probably the protoype for the disgorging monster mask carved over doorways among the Maya. Kallesvara Temple, Huvinahadgalli, South India, 12th., century, AD.

4.68 Outward facing makaras with peacock tails based on the long traditional Buddhist makaras. These appear to be the prototypes for the disgorging caimans in Mexico and Central America. Kailasanatha Temple, Kanchipuram, South East India, 7-8th., century, AD.

4.69 Finely carved high relief panel, with outline profile above, clearly inspired by the ceremonial bar . The makara heads at each end are clearly traditional in form similar over many centuries and adopted from the Buddhists by the Hindus. These in turn are virtually identical to those of the Maya and particularly those displayed on the Rosalila structure at Copan *4.71-3.* Bhimesvara Temple, Nilagunda, South Central India, 12th., century, AD.

4.70 Makara heads inspired from the traditional ceremonial bar of the Buddhists adopted by the Hindus. This group forms one of many in a register around the temple and typical in Late Chalukyan work. Jain Temple, Lakkundi, 12th., century, AD.

4.71 Two makara ceremonial rods are clearly apparent on the facade of the Rosalila Structure when other details are suppressed. Copan, Honduras, 8th., century, A.D.

4.72 Conjectural elevated arched reconstruction above the surviving Rosalila Structure's ceremonial rods. The two eagles as Principal Birds flank the temple entrance at ground level. Copan, Honduras, 8th., century, A.D.

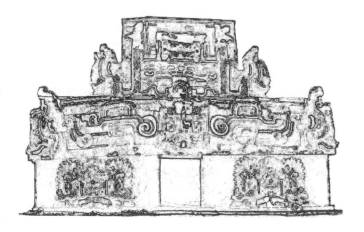

4.73 Perspective view from a photo-graph illustrating the near completed Rosalila Structure as it would have been seen by the Mayans before it was over-built by later temple construc-tions. Copan, Honduras, 8th., century, A.D.

beginning of the year, and therefore Capricorn, was called the "mouth" of the year[28] and this, no doubt, was a reference to the ancient depictions of the makaras disgorging the sky arch or torana. The "mouth" was perceived as disgorging the year to come and this was reflected in the zodiacal symbolism of the sky band or sky vault - an act earlier noted as Pabhavali. The ceremonial bars with the sky band panels so noted in Mayan iconography, held by rulers in examples from many of the ceremonial sites, probably symbolised the sky band as the ecliptic. The Vision Serpent heads, usually shown disgorging a deity, were no doubt the "mouth" referred to in the ancient texts of India and identified with the New Year, and their version of the makara similarly extended to incorporate the two heads of the serpent deities or demons of the ecliptic in India, Rahu and Ketu. Many other elements of Mayan iconography have their parallels in that of India both contemporary with, and earlier than that of the Maya and these are considered in "Mayan Genesis".

In extending the interest in the makara or its Mayan equivalent, the Vision Serpent, there are other aspects which relate to Palenque and Pacal's Slab. The makaras in India are often depicted with "cherubs" or "ganas" - dwarf cavorting figures - which are shown riding or standing on the back of the makaras [*4.58; 4.59; 4.64; 4.65*]. In the Palenque example shown in the triple-headed form known in India [*4.83*] depicts a makara or caiman in the Cauac form with a frontal gaping maw flanked each side with the respective side view facing outward. Seated on each of these side profiles is a deity or godling which clearly mimics those prototypes in India [*4.64*]. Of special interest, and unusual in the surviving makaras in India is the frontal view preserved at Paharpur which is more closely similar to the Mayan reliefs found on the stuccoed mansard surface at Palenque than other examples in India [*4.84*]. This suggests that the Mayan influence may have later been itself intrusive as a counterflow into the Ganges Delta after originally having been exported from India to Central America. The Palenque examples date from the late 7th to the 8th., century A.D. while this one illustrated from Paharpur dates from the later 8th., century, A.D..

It was noted by several Victorian and later researchers that there were many cultural aspects of the Naga tribes in Assam to the North of the Ganges and Brahmaputra Deltas which they considered to be closely similar to the Central American peoples leading to suggestions that they were connected. These connections may indicate that they were perhaps peoples who in part were, from the early Buddhist period, the traders and mariners who sailed for South East Asia, Indonesia and onward to Central America, and who returned from there bringing cultural influences and perhaps pilgrims back to India over many centuries. Clearly many of these mariners and traders left trading stations, or colonies, on many islands and intermarried with the local women. Certainly the close similarities in myths and deity names, distributed throughout the Pacific Ocean, cannot be coincidence. These connections from the Ganges Delta through Indonesia, Melanesia and Polynesia suggests that mariners for many generations had transferred aspects of their myths and culture from South Asia all the way to the Marquesas Islands, the furthest land east in the Pacific Ocean ultimately pointing towards Central America.

The profiles of the Palenque triad of makaras or cauacs [*4.83*] with the seated godlings or deities exhibit another iconographical element which is a trefoil placed on the snout. This element appears to derive from a similar trefoil or trilobe placed behind the gills on an early makara from Mathura[29]. The Palenque trefoil is in a style identical to that found among the Southern Chinese and the Buddhist imagery in particular which is commonly shown with "flames" extending from it. This element of iconography is identical to the same imagery so famously found on the belly of the great cauac or caiman, monolith at Copan [*4.86*]. The early trilobe at Mathura is virtually identical to a fine stone relief of a caiman head profile found at Kaminajuyu[30].

In some cases the makaras are facing inward and they appear to be disgorging an arched form which represents the sky arch. All of these examples depict the foliated tails which replaced the earlier, simpler fish tail [*5.60*] but appear also in the Buddhist reliefs at Ajanta by the mid-first millennium A.D. and were incorporated into the first stone temple prototypes at Pattadakal [*4.64*] often with Ganas or dwarfs riding on the makaras back. Those in South East coastal India in the Pallava dynasty developed the lower half incorporating the peacock's tail [*4.64; 4.65*]. The many aspects of Buddhist iconography influenced that of the Hindu at Kanchipuram, 70 km (43 miles) from Madras on the East Coast of South India, and these indicate individuality disciplined within the existing traditions displayed by the silpins, or artists and craftsmen. The Pallava dynasty, appearing to have been the dominant dynasty over many centuries in South East India from about the 2nd., century B.C., appears to have been greatly influenced by the temple developments under the Chalukyas at Aihole and Pattadakal in South Central India - influences that flowed both ways. Cave and temple building in Kanchipuram, and the other temple towns of the Pallavas, reflect much from the development under these Chalukyas and they spread this influence abroad into South East Asia. The Pallavas and later Cholas were particularly noted for extending their empire into the Western Indonesian islands of Sumatra and Java. One of the most interesting, and mysterious of any of the peculiarities is the unexplained symbol of the inverted "V" found in the Tripurantakesvara temple in Kanchipuram [*4.85*] dating to about the 7-8th., century A.D. This appears to be identical to the year sign found also among the Mexicans and may be an item of iconography suggesting links between the Pallavas and Central America.

There are many examples from Mayan iconography clearly deriving from the makaras of India. However, among the Mexicans located on the North Gulf Coast the Huastec depict in at least one of their surviving sculptures a headdress which is clearly intended to reflect the sky vault or arch [*4.66*]. At the lower ends of the headdress there are jaguar heads facing outwards overall reflecting the arched sky band in the same manner as the toranas of India. The shoulders and upper chest of the figure displays what are believed to be tattoos and many of the designs of these from Huastec imagery have close parallels to those of the Marquesan Islanders in Eastern Polynesia[31].

Vision Serpent:
Unfortunately for Central American iconography and mythology the imagery of the

so-called "Vision Serpent" has not continued down to the present day with associated myths and ceremonies as other elements of Mayan religious life have. Available iconography depicted in bas-reliefs, codex illustrations and ceramic decoration must provide the material for the deductions, which for the most part, and as far as they go, are probably reasonably accurate. The Vision Serpents are mostly associated with the rites and rituals enhanced by hallucinatory substances[32].

In the rituals associated with the Vision Serpent sacrificial blood from the supplicant was burnt in a ritual vessel and from the smoke the Vision Serpent was considered to be vitalised. From the serpent's mouth was perceived to emerge the deities or ancestors who had been summoned to appear before the priest or earthly ruler or other important propitiants or sacrificers. So much blood was drawn that the Maya understood that a state could be entered where hallucinatory drugs were not required to produce visions[33]. The rite associated with drawing blood was retained until after the Spanish Conquest and it is noted at first hand and described by a Spanish priest, Fra. Delgado, demonstrated by a Manche Chol man[34]. The achievement of the hallucinatory state through extreme loss of blood is a fact known also to present day medical research but among the Maya this was one of a number of means of attaining the desired visionary state.

In the well-known Hauberg Stela[35] the ruler Bac-T'ul[36] is shown in what is considered a bloodletting ritual and the result of this ceremony is depicted as the World Tree emerging from his right shoulder down which the upper half of human bodies are falling into the Underworld. The Vision Serpent emerges also from the same place and extends upwards to form a "canopy" over his head, possibly intended to imitate a parasol. Interesting also is the sky band belt since this is closely similar to those found in India over many centuries in the first millennium A.D.[37]. The half-bodies falling down to the Underworld are highly reminiscent of many myths of half-humans in Indonesia and India. More particularly it may be a memory of the early Brahman penalty which was the threat of severing at the waist of any who betrayed a single word of the sacred Vedas to any other than those of their own caste[38]. However, the sky band belt is evident among both the Maya and ancient religions of India and was known among the latter as a symbolic separation of the Upper World and the Lower World reflecting the body of the ruler or priest as Cosmic Man . The imagery on the Hauberg Stela suggests a belief that the half-bodies representing the higher Self may be the only part surviving with the Soul or as a representation of it depicted here on its way to the Lower World to await ultimate rebirth. The Vision Serpent in this depiction in forming an arch terminating in a parasol form appears to suggest that it may owe something to myths of the great Buddhist serpent Muchalinda[39], the resident serpent who dwelt in the roots of the Bo tree, who raised himself over the Buddha to protect Him during his long meditation to achieve enlightenment.

The serpent among the Maya was also associated with clouds and lightning[40], no doubt because of the serpentine shape of lightning, and the serpentine shape of a river was not lost on the Ancient Americans, reflecting similar beliefs in India. The Vision Serpent was the extension in a tubular form of the line of communication

4.74 Carved Buddha in cave shrine showing the makara ceremonial bar extending from the top of the throne back. Buddhist Caves, Aurangabad, Central West India, 6th., century, A.D.

4.75 High relief stone carving showing a makara ceremonial bar supported on the throne back behind the throne. Ajanta, 2-5th., century, A.D.

4.76 Rubbing of a relief carving of a Mayan ruler or deity holding a ceremonial bar with makara/ caiman ends disgorging manikin figures. Disgorging makaras are known in early Buddhist iconography. Lintel 4, Bonampak, Chiapas, Southern Mexico, 8th., century, AD.

4.78 Fine high relief stone carving showing the makara ceremonial bar extending behind the standing deity. Note stylised makaras with riding godlings in each of the higher corners. Goddess Parvati, Bengal, Bangladesh, 12 century, A.D.

4.77 Detail of high relief carved stela showing a makara ceremonial bar supported on pillars or back panel. Flying deities, found also in the Americas, are shown in the upper corners. See *4.78*.

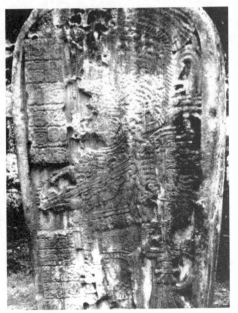

4.80 The successor to Buddha, Kasyapa, depicted with the sacred staff and trilobe finial. Lung-men Caves, Western China, c4th., century, AD.

4.81 Mayan rulers with sacred staffs and "leafed" finials similar to those found among the Buddhists of Lung-men. Lintel 9, Yaxchilan, Chiapas, Southern Mexico, 8th., century, AD.

4.79 Mayan ruler with "lozenge" ceremonial bar apparently derived from similar designs in India and Indonesia. Tikal, Guatemala, Late Classic.

4.82 Traditional ceremonial bar placed typically behind deity resting on the back of the throne. The lozenge design appears to be the proto-

formed by the curling, serpentine shape of the vapour or smoke from the copal or blood offerings. This is reminiscent of the similar rites in India where the perfume and smoke associated with tobacco, incense and flower garlands was considered to attract the attention of the gods and ancestors. Blood rites were well-known among the Tantric sects of Hinduism and Buddhism and also among the Aboriginal Tribes in North India. In South India piercing and lacerating the flesh are still inflicted in some of the less purged of the peripheral Hindu and Aboriginal rites.

The Mayan imagery and rites associated with their Vision Serpent suggests that there was a substantial influence from the pre-Aryan Naga peoples who so influenced the Buddhists that their imagery ultimately permeated every aspect of their religious iconography. The idea of the "mouth" of the year being identified with the makara may be pre-Aryan or derived from ancient Iran but the form of the Mayan Vision Serpent's head appears to have been totally influenced by the Buddhist depictions of the makara itself. In virtually every portrayal of the Mayan, and Mexican, Vision Serpent or caiman - the cauac, the upturned upper jaw is identical to that of the makara [*4.60*; *4.61*; *4.64*; *4.86*; *5.22*], often together with the equivalent emerging head of an ancestor or deity shown in a wider variety of examples in "Mayan Genesis".

The profile of the makara remains almost identical in its long and popular inclusion in the stone carvings and reliefs through many dynastic styles throughout India. The Buddhist style is always recognisable and most often associated with a sky arch or torana or as the ecliptic forming a ceremonial bar. In Hindu building that association is augmented in some cases, such as that so superbly shown on the makara-torana of the Muhktesvara temple at Bhubanesvar in Orissa [4.49; 4.50]. In the South of India this association of torana and makara is retained but the makara is often used as a "supporter" for platform dados or other decoration [4.69]. In Indonesia, so influenced from the Pala Dynasty in North East India and the Pallavas and Cholas in South East India, the ceremonial bar placed at the back of the seated Buddha of ruler in emulation of the universal display of the enthrone Buddha is of special interest. The slightly modified style of the Makaras shown either side of the seated figure are virtually identical to those found among the Maya. The figures of cosmic deities shown with their ceremonial bars in Chandi Mendut [4.61] are carved identically to those found in the Mayan figurine from the Yucatan [4.60] among others. They are so similar that they appear that they could have been carved by the same person or school. Such close similarities among so many other aspects of cultural imagery and iconography cannot be a coincidence.

In the first group of representations of the makaras depicted as supporters they need to face inward to disgorge the sky arch or torana as a whole. In other images of the sky arch the tails of the makaras extend upward to form the arch and therefore the heads and bodies at both of the springing points at the base of the torana turn outward. The makaras forming the terminals at each end of the ceremonial bar turn outward and are always found this way in India, Indonesia and among the Maya. However, in some of the later carvings of dados in the South Indian temples the makaras reflect a somewhat changed, although still recognisable, form. It would be easy, and logical to suggest that these were the natural evolution of the element of iconography and the style developed by a particular dynasty or region. Allowing for the devolution of the makara being assimilated from early Buddhist imagery into Hinduism it would be expected that the makara would become more and more an element of decoration outside of its use as a specific element of cosmic lore.

The clear export of the later form of the makara ceremonial bar from Indonesia to the Maya in about the 7-8th., century A.D. clearly indicates that India through Java and Sumatra was influencing the Maya and beyond in Central America. It has already been suggested that elements of iconography such as the frontal cauac, or caiman depicting the "sky monster" at Paharpur [4.84] may derive from the Maya since it so closely emulates the examples at Palenque rather than those locally known in the usual tradition from North India. It may be therefore that the "year sign" at Kanchipuram may not have been the only other influence derived from the Maya. Carved dadoes in South India exhibit profiles of makaras seemingly to be influenced by those shown on ceremonial bars, particularly those on Indonesia and among the Maya. In many cases the corners or ends of the dado are treated as if they are in fact ceremonial bars [4.69] in buildings from the late Pallava and Chola dynasties from, or near Lakkundi [4.67; 4.70] and this seems to be reflected in the almost identical makaras used in the same way on the so-called Rosalila Structure at Copan dated to the 5th., century A.D. [4.71-4.73].

The defined outline of the makara's profile in some of the depictions from the Kailasanatha Temple in Kanchipuram show both inward and outward facing makaras dating to about the late 7th., century A.D. The internal facing makaras [4.65] form the usual sky arch but the outer facing example [4.68] is less usual since they do not form a recognisable element of imagery and suggests they are moving towards decoration. Both examples at the same temple, however, reflect the profile exhibited by that of the earlier Rosalila Temple at Copan.

The gradual evolution of the makara under the South Indian dynasties could have been entirely a development within the regional kingdoms of India without influence from abroad - either from Indonesia or Central America. However, the heads of the makaras on the Rosalila Structure at Copan in Honduras are so similar to those in the later resurgence of Chalukyan temple building at Lakkundi, which proliferate on the lower registers of the dados, that coincidence seems impossible. It may be therefore that the Lakkundi temples were influenced from Kanchipuram on the South East Coast of India where more similar contemporary styles existed. Originally it appears that the early craftsmen from India, or their Mayan pupils, inspired the iconography of India to be transferred and assimilated into the Mayan style. It is probable that some returned to India, but more likely their mixed race descendants in later centuries, and they would also have transferred or injected some ideas into Indonesian temple building or into the long traditions of India developed at Mayan ceremonial sites. It must not be forgotten that the traditions of India are notoriously conservative and Professor Louis Fabri noted that there are examples of temple being built sometimes centuries out of their time in an archaic style such as the great temple of the Sun at Konarak dated to the 13th., century A.D.[41] and this may also be the case in terms of the makara styles.

The retention of temple styles in India, and therefore accurate dating of them, is one of the most problematic areas of the study of ancient architecture in India. The successive dynasties and regions developed their own styles but are not always greatly different from those immediately before or after. Because of the vast areas covered by the Sub-continent, the break-up of the Mauryan empire, the spread of their introduced styles from Iran meant each regional kingdom developed its own style based upon those introduced along with the crafts and skills developed in the preceding empire. As the major empires that followed usually reduced the subjected capital of the ruling dynasty to rubble a new capital elsewhere was the norm and from this the dating of a major dynasty with its own influences is more certainly dated. These later Buddhist or Hindu empires were never as extensive as the Mauryan under Asoka and their influence was limited and took generations, if ever, before styles and techniques permeated to those outside the area of its immediate control. This meant that in the peripheral kingdoms temple and palace building techniques and styles tended to remain faithful to the architecture that it knew and copied known local traditions as and when necessary. The same is true to this day and temple building complete with sculpted reliefs, stone sculpture and ornamentation is virtually identical to the local style known dating from many centuries, sometimes a millennia or so, before. Only when exceptional sites for wealthy rulers or patrons were being constructed silpins or

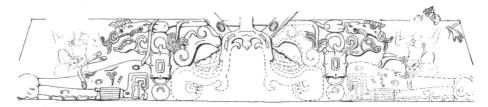

4.83 Remarkable stucco facing to mansard at Palenque. The gaping frontal caiman's jaws are closely similar to those depicted in one found at the Buhhist vihara at Paharpur in Bengal *4.85*. Palenque, Chiapas, Southern Mexico, 8th., century, AD.

4.84 Krishna supporting the sky. The Sky is clearly that of a crocodile/caiman as a makara, but frontal, rare in India but closely similar to that of the caiman at Palenque *4.83*. Paharpur, Bangladesh, 8th., century, AD.

4.85 Inverted "V" representing the year sign in Mexico but unusual in India. Tripurantakesvara Temple, Kanchipuram, South East India, 7-8th., century AD.

4.86 Cauac or caiman shown disgorging a deity head at the left and a demon head at the right. The rear end head, right, displays a year sign in the headdress similar to that at Kanchipuran in India *4.85*. Copan, Honduras, 8th., century, AD.

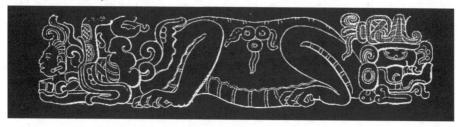

artisans move across boundaries introducing more up-to-date styles but still incorporating much that was recognisable from earlier cultures.

In Nepal, isolated and retaining their independence from the kingdoms of North India, J.C. Harle noted that the "centuries old isolation, allied to a very strong sense of cultural identity, have meant that in many areas time has virtually stood still for the past four hundred years or so, so that art flourishes in the living context in which it was created"[42]. He notes that many of the buildings are of brick and wood sheathed in metal and required replacement over the centuries but they had faithfully copied the original building and its style reflecting the exactitude with which they had been originally constructed. Finally he states that "the country remains unique in its fifteen-hundred-years-old heritage, nourished at virtually a single source - India in conditions of near-total political independence". The same could be said to be true for certain periods among the Maya, Central America generally and Mexico.

In Nepal, on the northern boundary of India, they of course received occasional impetus from the high culture dynasties of India but assimilated only that which was acceptable to them and to their own taste and style. It is clear that there were at least several regions at any one time in India reproducing archaic styles in symbols, particularly the very popular ones such as the makaras, and that these remained a source for any who may wish to reintroduce a particular image type or style into later temple building. It is clear therefore that although there may not have immediately appeared to have been a direct continuity between one form of the makara and another it is likely that in an adjacent region one form was preserved while in another some other variation was being adopted or developed. This is certainly true of the masonry and symbolic depictions remaining in Java and Sumatra showing the regional styles of the Pala in the North East of India, and the Pallava and Chola in the South East.

The Ceremonial Bar:

The Rosalila Structure at Copan appears to be deliberately constructed to display the ceremonial bar as a major element of iconography on the building. Undoubtedly it was a proclamation of the right to rule by the Mayan ruler of the first dynasty of early Classic Copan. The ceremonial bar is found repeatedly in the iconography of the Maya and some of the most attractive designs in Mayan art are those portraying this sacred symbol [*4.76*].

In the bas-reliefs of early India the ceremonial rod or bar occurs so frequently that it is almost ubiquitous in the surviving works. It occurs among all three major religions, the Buddhist Hindu and Jain, but it would appear that it developed first among the Buddhists and adopted in their style from the very earliest centuries of their establishment in North India. In the caves at Ajanta and elsewhere the Buddha is almost invariably depicted seated on his throne with a ceremonial bar apparently supported behind usually set across the top of the throne back. Even if the throne back or the rod or bar itself is not shown the two makara heads extending in opposite directions from the ends of it are clearly depicted [*4.74*; *4.75*]. Buddhist iconography included this important element in their temple construction at least to the 8th., century A.D. since it appears behind two cosmic deities in Chandi Mendut in Java [*4.61*] in the exact form it appears among the Mayans [*4.60*]. In later Hindu stelae and sculpture the ceremonial rod is clearly of importance prominently displayed in its form as a rod or bar [*4.77*; *4.78*]. In the many sculpted works of India the ceremonial rod is almost invariably confined to the same location in a somewhat rigidly defined canon. Behind standing figures the ceremonial rod is often displayed supported by two pillars or supports indicating that it was meant to be an independent object and not part of the furniture decoration [*4.77*].

Recent archaeologists and historians have equated the Mayan ceremonial bar with the sky serpent where the heads "symbolised the path of communication between the supernatural world and the human world"[43]. In several depictions the ceremonial bar is rigid with a makara's or caiman's head at each end sometimes with a deity head emerging[44] while in others it is serpentine in the form of an arch as at Palenque on

Pacal's Slab. In some cases the bar has manikins emerging from it [*4.76*] and in others it become a staff [*4.79*] which is clearly based on the lozenge shapes in a ceremonial rod from India [*4.82*]. It has been posited that the ceremonial bar has been developed from Olmec symbols of kingship[45] but whether this is so or not does not invalidate the transfer, augmentation and assimilation of elements of culture with associated symbols and techniques from Asia. This is the process of evolution that has regenerated and revitalised all other cultural movements in the world and is clearly indicated in the history of the Maya.

Of special interest is the introduction in some of the Middle Classic Mayan sites of the staff god or identification of the ruler with such a figure [*4.81*] here a detail from Lintel 9 at Yaxchilan dating to the 8th., century A.D. The staff is of interest since it closely emulates that of the Buddhist forms found in Central Asia [*4.80*] depicted in this illustration held by the missionary saint Kachyapa, successor to Buddha, from the caves of Lung-men. These caves display another element which is clearly reflected in a group of celebratory stelae celebrating the accession of young Mayan rulers so notable at Piedras Negras [*5.05*]. The Central Asian cultures were known to have influenced the North Indian dynasties over many centuries with some clans retaining tribal memories claiming descent from Scythian ancestors when the British began to record the tribal histories over a century ago. The evidence for cultural connections transferred from Central Asia through the Tibetan mountains to the Ganges and Brahmaputra Deltas and ultimately to the Bay of Bengal was noted by these early British researchers and historians in India. Not least among these were the District Officers who were sent to govern whole tribal districts in the remote regions of North East India and Assam. This is an area of research largely forgotten today but deserves attention since there are undoubted Buddhist cultural influences that entered via this route from Khotan and Western and Central Tibet assimilated into the art and architecture of Burma to a great degree and from there were transferred to Indonesia and Central and South America.

In India the ceremonial bar undoubtedly relates to the ecliptic as it did among the Maya, but in the latter examples it appeared to indicate more completely the idea of rulership whereas in India it tended to be more confined to religious authority. This divergence can only be expected in the adaption and assimilation of symbols from one culture to another, particularly so very distant from each other. One of the more interesting aspects of the adoption of this symbol of power by the Maya was their release of the item itself in its portrayal in iconography being expressed more freely than limited in the rigid confines of canon in India.

CHAPTER 5
CAVE DEITIES through to ECLIPSE
SERPENT and SKY BAND SYMBOLS

Buddhist Caves - Deified, Closetted Deities - Accession Stelae:
Initiated in the 5th., century A.D. the occupation and elaboration of the caves at Lung-men in Honan province in Central China reached their apogee under the Tang dynasty in the 8th., century. The earliest period reflects the Indian missionary style while the later period displays the assimilation to the flowing, more convoluted Chinese style. Available evidence suggests that Buddhist monks entered China by invitation from the Chinese emperors and gradually spread their influence through their missionary zeal to Western Tibet and into Central Asia. One of the most important, and lesser known developments in Buddhist culture was the great cultural centre known as Khotan. All these regions were influenced from India and those at Khotan and Western Tibet were established and flourishing Buddhist centres by at least as early as 2nd., century A.D. but it is more likely that incursions into this region were initiated from as early as the Asoka missions of the 3rd., century B.C.

These missionaries were sometimes wanderers not staying longer than necessary at any centre after establishing a base, training local converts, and then moving onwards to new fields of endeavour. Inevitably the Buddhist traditions became permeated with local styles and details and this is particular evident in Tibet where Buddhism never fully converted the people. As a result Buddhism was never purged of the wrathful forms of deities that are so much a feature of the indigenous Bon Po religion. These influences were conveyed by missionaries, traders and perhaps migrations from the highlands of the Himalayan regions from Tibet through into Burma. These integrated with the indigenous traditions and styles of Burma along with the prototypical North Indian forms giving its resultant architecture and arts its own particular exotic style.

The great difference in the Burmese style compared to its parent country, India, with its land bridge on the north west border region with East India, should be an object lesson to those who insist that the greater the divergence of cultural expression the less likely there is a connection. The earliest detectable incursions into Burma were from Buddhist and then Brahmanic India and the early temple constructions reflected the religious and cultural expressions of their respective dogmas. Interestingly it appears that Burma was the last to be influenced from these high cultural points in Northern India where Indonesia seems to reflect their attentions at least as early as the first centuries of the first millennium A.D. Burma, however, preserves certain iconographical elements from the later expansion of Buddhism from Central, Asia and Central and Western Tibet.

Of particular interest among these elements of iconography are the depictions of the Buddha in the cave shrines which are sometimes the only surviving feature to indicate any settlement in these frequently remote and barren regions. Not only do these cave shrines exhibit the larger-than-life image of the Buddha but architraves clearly reflecting common origins with the jataka panels surrounding the inner portals of the cave shrines of Ajanta and other cave sites in North India. A special feature of these caves shrines in the mountain highlands of Tibet, China and Central Asia is that they were frequently depicted with curtains or drapes rolled and tied up under the upper portal opening [*5.02*].

The date of the Lung-men cave carving is 5-6th.,century, contemporary with Ajanta, and it is interesting to note that some folk images in Burma [*5.07*] from the second half of the second millennium A.D. are clearly inspired by the same idea of a rock cave far to the north in the great Himalayan - Tibetan Plateau. The characteristic plan is of a Buddhist temple precinct with the main central tower and four smaller shrines, one at each of the cardinal points, with the extended upper central pagoda supporting an open shrine accessed by one sacred portal through which can be seen the Buddha or saint. This example is in fact a crude image of a central stepped pyramid with a shrine on its upper level. In reality the shrine itself usually had a curtain fixed to the upper architrave which could be rolled up when worshippers were attending. Of special interest in this example is the great ceremonial bar or rod thrust through the upper level of the pagoda with a makara head extending from each end which resembles those among the Maya so closely - and those of Indonesia. The great ladder shown extending from the base up to the shrine itself clearly derives from memories of the ancient cave shrines in the Himalayas and beyond where retractable ladders afforded the caves and their attendant monks the necessary protection from marauding bandits and hostile opponents.

When viewed from the front the inspiration for the Mayan stelae at Piedras Negras [*5.03*] becomes obvious and is reflected also in some of the "ladder" carvings found at Bilbao on the Guatemalan coast [*5.01*]. The Bilbao carving depicts a rayed "headdress" worn by an elevated deity or ancestor in the form of a halo found in Iran and occasionally in India but extremely unusual for Central America. This figure is being approached by a ruler or priest and there is in fact displayed a ladder shown in side view fixed to the face of the vertical surface in front of him up to the ledge occupied by the deity or ancestor. Compared to the niche stelae at Piedras Negras it appears that this is intended to be a sectional view through a niche or a monolithic stelae of substantial depth. In fact it is almost certainly reproduced from the memory of cave shrines in Central and South Asia that were approached by retractable ladders as indicated in the Lung-men and Burmese examples.

At the rear of the niche, recess or cave in the Bilbao illustration there appears to be the indication of bones and it is particularly interesting that relics were of great importance to the ancient Buddhists and also to the Hindus. This bone structure may be a reference to the philosophic speculations, probably descended through the Vedic Aryans to the Buddhist and Hindus, that the spinal cord was the path along which enlightenment was attained and this element of India philosophy appears to be illustrated by the carved monolith shown in "Mayan Genesis" (p76/2;3;4). This group of carvings at Bilbao on the coast of Guatemala and at Piedras Negras near the Mexican border are consistent with imported iconography assimilated and adapted to the social and religious requirements and development of the Maya at that time.

5.03 Carved stela depicting a deitifie
ancestor seated in a niche. The architraves are carved sky panels arranged i
the manner of Buddhist caves even
reflecting the rolled curtain screen
above the niche. The niche is clearly
intended to represent a cave and the
ladder up to it is copied from those of
the Buddhist caves. Stela 11, Piedras
Negras, Guatemala, 8th., century, AD.

5.01 Relief carving of hero/preist
climbimg a ladder to a cave deity. Bilbao,
Santa Lucia Cotzumalguapa, Guatemala, 4-
7th., century, AD

5.02 Carved Buddha seated in cave with relief
carving of a curtain screen over the opening.
Side architrave niches are similar to those of
Ajanta and probably the inspiration for those of
the Mayan sky band *5.05*. Lung-men, Western
China, 5th., century, AD.

5.04 Inner Buddha shrine showing the jataka
panels carved on the architraves appearing to
have been the prototypes for the Mayan sky
band doorways and niches. See full colour
image *3.48*. Ajanta Cave 2, West Central
India, 5-6th., century, AD.

5.05 Mayan stela with deified ances
tor seated in the Buddhist manner. Sky
band reflects the carved architrave
Jataka panels of the Buddhists with
Pricipal Bird (eagle) over the portal in
the Hindu manner. Stela 25, Piedras
Negras, Guatemala, 8th., century, AD.

The social climate at Piedras Negras and contemporary sites near or along the Usumacinta River appears to have been receptive to these foreign influences and the dating of their apogee in the 8th., century A.D. corresponds to major conflict and migration in North and Central India. This was as a result of instability among the Hindu kingdoms and the later Muslim conquest which continued until the 12th., century but never conquered the whole of the Sub-continent. Although there are many aspects of iconography appearing much earlier among the Maya reflecting that of India, particularly of the Buddhists, it is in the Late Classic period that this imagery become almost ubiquitous at Copan, and along the Usamacinta River to Palenque itself. This suggests that those who were refugees from the instability in India and wished to escape what seemed to be the total overrun of the whole of India may have used the long established sea trade to save themselves or their religious beliefs by settling far away in Indonesia and Central America. Among them may have been Mayan pilgrims visiting India and returning home to Central America.

In terms of the theme of this book Stelae 11 from Piedras Negras [*5.03*] reflects exactly the image a pilgrim from Central America, or anywhere else for that matter, would return with in his own mind after visiting the rock caves Tibet and of the Ajanta and other sites in India. It is a three dimensional subject carved in a two-dimensional manner with all the design and technical problems entailed in such a work. It does, however, convey the subject remarkably well and coherently to any viewer who had not seen the original. The subject of another at Piedras Negras stela, Stela 25, is clearly an ancestor or deity viewed through the sacred portal which includes the sky band architrave and an eagle, the Principal Bird, over the lintel or head of the portal. The divine figure appears to be seated in a large niche or cave since

5.06 Detail of the Buddha in The Tavatimsa Heaven shown in *5.07*.

5.07 This figurine clearly imitates the Buddhist saints and hermits from the Himalayas where their cave sanctuaries became adored shrines and places of pilgrimage - *5.02*. The ladder from the ground to the shrine/cave became a revered symbol and is identical to the iconography found in Central America on the coast of Guatemala - *5.01*; *5.05*. Moulmein, Burma, 19th., century, A.D. or earlier. *Courtesy of the Victoria and Albert Musesum, London.*

5.08 Full height carved stone portal depicting in an early example the Garuda (eagle deity) surmounting the doorway holding the tails of two serpents, each one extending down opposite sides of the opening. These serpents end with three nagas (serpent) bodies one above the other on each side. Aihole, South Central India, 5 century, A.D.

5.09 Fine example of Garuda (half-human, half eagle) shown holding the ends of the two serpents representing the two halfs of the ecliptic in Hindu myths. Aihole, South Central India, 5-6th., century, AD

5.10 Carved stone portal showing a Garuda or Principal Bird over the opening holding the tails of two serpents. The serpent scales can be clearly seen. Aihole, South Central India, 5-6th., century, AD

5.11 Carved portal architraves showing the Garuda centred over the doors and holding the tails of serpents one extending down each side of the opening. The Naga endings of the serpents are also evident near the ground. Aihole, South Central India, 5-6th., century, AD.

5.12 Portal to sacred shrine from mandapa or porch. One of the two serpents extends down opposite sides of the opening each one represening the two halves of the ecliptic. The portal is considered the entrance to the inner sanctum as the interface with heaven. The lower ends of the serpents are shown as adoring Nagas (serpents). Aihole, South Central India, 6th., century, AD.

5.13 Finely carved elaborate representation of the Garuda sky bird holding the two ecliptic serpents, Rahu and Ketu by the tails. Durga Temple, Aihole, South Central India, 5-6th., century AD.

5.14 Another view of the elaborately carved Garuda above the portal opening holding the ends of the ecliptic serpents, Rahu and Ketu. Durga Temple, Aihole, South Central India, 6th., century, AD.

5.15 A further example of the Garuda holding the ecliptic serpents by the tail. Mahakuta temple complex, Badami, South Central India, 5th., century, AD.

there is a considerable step up to the base of this niche. Outside the architraves there is Mayan glyphic writing and at the base there are designs which may indicate a platform, dais, or perhaps a symbolic floor pattern. The "base" on which a ruler or dignitary is seated, possibly on a palanquin, shown on Stela 10 from Piedras Negras in illustration *5.19* shows a series of sky band glyphs which are remarkably close to those depicted in India already noted. The style and the similarity at this date suggest closer ties with India indicated in much of the iconography among the Maya at this time.

Piedras Negras Stela 11 therefore appears to be based on Central and South Asian carved cave facades and it does seem to reflect a composite of the pilgrimage shrines in India. The architrave and overall appearance of the stela reflects the shrine portals in the Buddhist cave temples shown in *3.48* (Cave 2, Ajanta) where the jataka, or event or myths from the life of Buddha are replaced in the Mayan stela by sky band panels. This would be the most obvious thing to do if the actual panels designs could not be remembered or were not of particular interest to a non-believer. In India it is quite usual for members of one of the three major religions, Buddhist, Hindu and Jain, to pay respects at the shrines of the others and to modify and incorporate elements of one set of iconography into their own. The Piedras Negras stela appears very much in the form that a pilgrim would view the inner cave shrines from Ajanta, even as he would today, since no access is allowed inside the shrine itself apart from priests or officials. This is demonstrated in illustration *5.04* where the figure of the Buddha fills the view through the portal and the architraves flanking this ceremonial door are carved with panels which here are depictions from the life of the Buddha but in Stela e 11 and 25 at Piedras Negras are replaced with sky band panels. This inner shrine at Ajanta is more clearly depicted in colour in *3.48*.

Of particular note on the Piedras Negras stela is the depiction of the eagle, or Principal Bird, Vucub Caquix over the door. So much of the Mayan iconography

5.16 Tlaloc with serpentine sky-arch or torana held above his head representing the sky. His running/ kneeling posture is identical to that of Hanuman and other deities in India. Stela 19, Kaminaljuyu, Guatemala, Late Preclassic.

5.17 Serpent sky arch or torana with caimans/makaras disgorging ancestor/ deity heads from each end surmounted by Garuda as Principal Bird. Carved wooden lintel, Temple IV, Tikal, Guatemala, 8th., century, AD.

5.18 One or two serpents displayed around a portal in the palace complex probably inspired by the ecliptic serpents found in India. Palenque, Chiapas, Southern Mexico, 8th., century, AD.

reflects imagery borrowed from Ajanta, but the eagle surmounting the sacred portal is not to be found there. It is primarily a Hindu element reflecting the sky bird, Garuda, already of note as the opponent of the Nagas or serpent worshippers. The Garuda is, however, found frequently surmounting the sacred portal in another place of pilgrimage having also numerous elements appearing to also be transferred into Mayan iconography. This is Aihole in South Central India, the capital of the early Chalukyan dynasty, and said to be the birthplace of Hindu stone carved temple building.

The Garuda, Sky Bird, or deified eagle is found carved above the sacred shrine portals throughout Aihole, but it is always depicted in a mature style suggesting that a period of evolution and development was undertaken elsewhere. This motif was not exclusive to Aihole (also Awali) but is found surviving here in more temples in one place than perhaps anywhere else. The earliest known stone temple still standing in South India is at Chikka-gudi, near the Mahakuta temple complex, dated to the 4-5th., century, A.D. and reflects Gupta dynasty building techniques and style in North and Central India. The Chalukyan temples at Aihole are the earliest apart from this and are mostly 5-6th., century A.D. and they are remarkable for the number of iconographical elements and details found almost identically among the Maya.

In Aihole the Garuda surmounting the sacred shrine portal is invariably depicted clutching the tails of two serpents, or nagas, indicating his supremacy over these earth-bound creatures. Several illustrations of this combined motif of eagle subjugating two serpents are included since it is critical to the theme of this book. In "Mayan Genesis" an extended review of some of the texts and myths relating to the eclipse demon, a cosmic serpent personifying the ecliptic, relates that it was said to have been split into two by the discus of the supreme Hindu sky god,

5.19 The lower part of this stela preserves 8 glyphs having their virtual identical counterparts in the iconographic panels of India. Stela 10, Piedras Negras, Guatemala, 8th., century, AD.

5.20 Seated ruler or deity on what appears to be a palanquin or scaffolding displaying glyphs relating to the sky band. Stela 32, Naranjo, Guatemala, 8th., century, AD.

5.21 Simba (lion) disgorging deity in traditional disgorging symbolism of India. Nolamba, Hamavati, South East India, 10th., century, AD.

5.22 An caiman or serpent head disgorging Quetzalcoatl linking this deity to India and cross-Pacific mariners. Codex Borgia, Mexico, Pre- or Post Conquest Period.

5.23 A caiman disgorging a deity or ancestor, possibly Quetzalcoatl. Santa Rita, Belize, cLate Post Classic.

Vishnu. This is consistent as a basic principle of the "twin", or "light" and "dark" half cycles that are the basis of the philosophic constructs of Ancient Vedic India. Each half of the ecliptic serpent deity became either Rahu, the light half cycle governed by the Moon's North Node, or Ketu, the personification of the dark half governing the Moon's South Node.

The ecliptic was the path along which the planets were believed, and now known, to travel in a circular orbit around the earth and was therefore depicted as a sky band much as depicted in the cave ceiling of Ajanta. The sacred portals of the shrine, similar to those at Bhubanesvar in Orissa, were therefore also considered in the Hindu temples to be the ecliptic through which the sky world was approached from the outer, mundane world of the Earth. The only difference is that the Orissan temples utilised the abstracted depictions of the Buddhist sky bands around their portals while at Aihole the more immediate symbology of the Eagle as Garuda and two ecliptic serpents, Rahu and Ketu, were favoured but apparently derived from elsewhere.

The serpents are very realistically presented and in most cases even the scales are depicted [5.09; 5.13; 5.14]. The tails of both serpents are clearly grasped by the Garuda and the other ends display heads depicting the serpent as a born-again Nagas worshipping the deity Vishnu having been forcibly persuaded to reject their own gods [5.11]. As representative of the great god Vishnu, and as his vehicle, being often depicted carrying this deity on his back, the Garuda holds the serpent tails reflecting his delegated authority from this supreme Hindu sky god. He is frequently depicted as half-human and half-eagle and it is in this form that he is represented over the shrine portals [5.09; 5.12-5.14]. In other representations of the Garuda he is depicted as an eagle-headed human, found more particularly in Indonesia, and this may be the prototype of the Mexican Ehecatl[1], or fully as an eagle favoured in the Far East and Southern China[2]. The Piedras Negras Stela 25 [5.05] appears to derive the Garuda either from Aihole, or Indonesia, but there can be little doubt that its origins are in India.

The myths associated with Rahu the eclipse demon are found throughout India but is probably the most dispersed myth known in the Oceanic world but also along the Pacific Rim. The belief that the eclipse was a great serpent attempting to swallow the Sun is known all along the oceanic marine highways in the Pacific Ocean following the sea currents from Indonesia to North and Central America. It can be of little surprise, therefore, that the serpent should be associated with the sacred portal among the Maya, with or without the eagle as Principal Bird, since the original myth of the eclipse serpent Rahu exists without the Garuda. At Palenque an incomplete stucco relief of a serpent is shown extending around a doorway [5.18] and this appears to derive from memories of the Chalukyan serpent portals at Aihole.

The Palenque serpent portal dates to about the 7-8th., century A.D. but an earlier depiction carved on a monolith from Izapa, always appearing to be the entreport and apparent prototypical inspiration for the Maya from the Pacific Ocean trade, reveals a serpent form appearing to indicate a deity associated with the sky serpent or sky arch [5.16]. Interesting also is the unusual timber panels, depicting a deity or ruler standing, it is thought, on a palanquin[3], but with a sky arch formed by a double-headed serpent almost certainly illustrating a connection with the eclipse demon myths from India. This panel was found in a tomb in Tikal and dated to about 747 A.D. being contemporary with the Palenque portal [5.17].

One of the most remarkable iconographical references surviving in both India and among the Maya is a variation on the Garuda bird holding the tails of both halves of the ecliptic demon serpent as Rahu and Ketu. This is a Sun god holding the ends of two foliated serpentine forms of the what is intended to be lotus plants probably representing and derived from the two halves of the mythical ecliptic serpent. Flanking both ends are two sky supporters that are identical to the Mayan Pauahtuns so widely found in Central America. One of the finest representations is that depicted in a carved relief on the Parasuramesvara temple in Bhubanesvar in Orissa dated to about 6th., century A.D. [5.26]. The fine craftsmanship and iconography appears to derive from Buddhist prototypes since another remarkably fine bas-relief is found in the very heartland of their ancient monastic centres at Sarnath a little to the north east of Varansi. This carved relief is part of a complete series covering the lower half of the great circular stupa known as the Samekh or Damekh dating to the 6th., century, A.D. [5.24] - although the foundation of the stupa itself dates back to Asoka in the 3rd., century B.C. Adjacent to this particular section are the many panels appearing to have been the prototypes for the mosaics found at Mitla in Southern Mexico.

The Damekh stupa bas-relief depicts a deity, probably the Buddha, sitting, or squatting on a lotus but looking as if the representation of Him is borrowed from the dwarf-like sky-supporters so common in earlier carvings in Mathura and Bodh Gaya [5.25]. In both of these representations, from Orissa and Sarnath, the seated sun god or Buddha holds the ends of the foliated serpentine lotus forms as the Garuda does with the serpents tails at Aihole [5.31; 5.32] and elsewhere such as at Tigawa in North Central India [5.30]. In some of these depictions in India, such as that in the Durga temple at Aihole [5.31], the finely carved Garuda appears to have inspired those of the Principal Bird depicted over the Mayan portals epitomised by that shown on Stela 25 at Piedras Negras.

In the latter case, where the serpent is replaced in Buddhist iconography by the sinuous forms of the lotus held by the Sun god in place of the serpent, it finds an almost exact equivalent in a vase from Guatemala [*5.27; 5.28; 5.29*]. This red-ware vessel comes from San Agustin Acasaguastlan and dates to the Early Classic from about 400-600 A.D. and was once thought to be a fake although there is little else similar upon which a fake could be based. The Sun god in this example holds the tail of two Vision Serpents with their heads at each end disgorging a deity head. Of particular interest is that these serpents appear to be influenced by foliated designs and this rare example seems to merge both the serpent and foliated forms that must have originated in India. The detail showing the Sun god from this vase is shown holding the ends of the tails from the serpents and the hands are turned upward in the form of a mudra, or handpose so well-known in Buddhist and Hindu iconography. The whole duplicates exactly the two serpents representing the two half cycles of the ecliptic in India and personified as the serpent demons Rahu and Ketu, subjected by the Sky god

5.24 Relief carved surface displaying central section reminiscent of Mixtec work at Mitla. The lowest register reflects a variation of the Sun god holding foliated serpentine forms. Damekh Stupa, Sarnath, North Central India, 5-6th., century, AD.

5.26 Sun god holding the ends of serpentine lotus forms with sky bearers, similar to the Mayan Pauahtuns, at each end. This relief is closely similar to a Mayan vase decoration *5.27*. Parasumesvara Temple, Bhubanesvar, Orissa, North East India, 6-7th., century, AD.

5.25 Detail of central figure (Buddha?), holding serpentine lotus forms. Damekh Stupa, Sarnath, North Central India, 5-6th.., century, AD.

5.27 Rollout of carved redware vase depicting the Sun god holding two Vision Serpents by the tails. At each end a serpent head disgorges a deity or ancestor. San Agustin Acasaguastlan, Guatemala, Early Classic, 400-600 AD.

5.28 + 5.29 *5.28* Redware vase showing the carved relief surface displayedin the above rollout *5.27*. *5.29* illustrates the detail of the Sun god holding the Vison serpent tails identically to those shown in India.

5.30 Sun god holding the tails of the ecliptic serpents similar to Mayan iconography in *5.27*. Mahakosala style, Rajim, North East Central India, 700-725 AD.

5.31 Typical early style Garuda (Sun eagle) holding the tails of the ecliptic serpents - the probably model for the Mayan version in Guatemala. Aihole, South Central India, 5th., century, AD

5.32 Garuda holding serpent tails in the intermediate period. The scales or the serpent tails are clearly visible. ???? Temple, Aihole, South Central India, 5-6th., century, AD

as ruler of the ecliptic or Garuda, the eagle, as his representative.

Ecliptic Iconography and Sky Band Serpent:

Numeration in the Mayan system is based on the vigesimal (times 60 or division by 60ths) system and in listing was reckoned from bottom to top[4]. This meant that in a list of numbers, where a dot equalled one and a bar equalled five, the bottom place in a list meant in simple combination the lowest number was a bar with a dot and equalled six and so on for increasing bars and dots.

Many Mayan glyphs relating to calendrical constructs or references are found in the few surviving codices and among these are glyph groups appearing to relate specifically to the ecliptic. The ecliptic in India has been shown to relate to the serpent Rahu who was the Moon's North Node, and Ketu who was the Moon's South Node. The eclipse cycles were of great importance for the Hindu and Buddhist astronomers and they calculated that it took a little over 18 years (and a few months into the nineteenth year) for these nodes to complete one cycle of the ecliptic or zodiac. The symbolic directions developed in astrology based on the astronomical cycles used a "day-for-a-year" to issue predictions for the future and this is noted more fully in "Mayan Genesis".

Clearly the Moon is related to its own nodes and in virtually all higher cultures the Moon is associated with water and this is evident to all those who live near tidal regions of the world. There were several lunar calendars in ancient India used before the general acceptance of the solar calendar introduced from Greece. The lunar calendars composed either of 12 or 13 months lunar months in the year and these were never satisfactory since there was no exact correspondence between them and the yearly cycle of the Sun. In astronomically-based astrology the Moon has long been thought of as the polar opposite to the planet Saturn and the twenty-year cycle of this planet with Jupiter was considered of great importance in the West, Ancient Middle East, India and in Central America. The correspondence between the Moon and Saturn seems to derive from the fact that Saturn orbits the Sun, as seen from the Earth, once in twenty-eight years while the symbolic directions of the Moon at one day for a year is twenty-seven years plus (into the twenty-eighth year). The importance of the

5.33 Some of the finest art from India has survived from Amaravati - a major Buddhist pilgrim centre. The solar disk at the far right with foliated rays shows a centre is identical to that found widely among the Maya representing the Sun. This centre is depicted with a central point and four inside the perimeter representing the cardinal points. Amaravati, Godavari Delta, Central East Coast india, 3rd., century, AD.

5.34 - 5.38 Five vignettes from the Codex Dresden showing deities associated with sky bands, except *5.35*, reflecting a skeletal deity seated on a central lotus with side views at each end identical in principle to those in India. Pre- or Post Conquest Mexico.

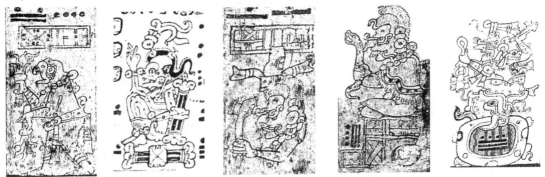

5.39 Cosmic serpent depicted appears to be associated with a total eclipse indicated by the bi-lobed glyph linked by a Sun circle glyph, bottom right. Codex Tro-Cortesianus, Pre- or Post Conquest Mexico.

5.40 Cosmic serpent with a deity appearing to be inspired by the axe deity of India Parasu Rama. Codex Tro-Cortesianus, Pre- or Post Conquest Mexico.

5.41 A cosmic depiction showing mythic turtles in myth that are closely similar to those in Indian beliefs. The bi-lobed glyph in the bottom left show the light and dark half of the ecliptic typical of India. Codex Tro-Cortesianus, Pre- or Post Conquest Mexico.

5.42 Serpent disgorging deity/ancestor. The deity holds a sun symbol identical to that found in India 5.33. Codex Tro-Cortesianus, Pre- or Post Conquest Mexico.

5.43 Pauahtuns as sky-bearers which are identical to the ganas or sky-supporters of early India. The upper register shows a caiman disgorging a deity. Codex Tro-Cortesianus, Pre- or Post Conquest Mexico.

Saturn-Jupiter conjunction appears to be in that one orbit of Jupiter around the Sun occurs, seen from the Earth, every twelve years and therefore was perceived to link it directly to the twelve months of the solar year.

The usual geocentric observations of planets in conjunction is not always determined when the two bodies first appear from the Earth to come together since they may do so three times. This is due to the fact that the Earth, the platform from which the motions are determined, is moving in the same direction as the two planets being observed and both the planets, quite obviously, are doing the same but in varying orbit distances from the Sun. Because the nearest of the two planets being

5.44 - 5.46 Ouroboros or encircling serpent around number 18 seems to indicate the Moon's Node 18 year cycle. Note long nosed Chac deities which appear to be derived from stylised depictions of elephants in India and Indonesia. Codex Tro-Cortesianus, Pre- or Post Conquest Mexico.

5.47 Chac rain deity with long elephantine trunk and year sign headdress found also in Kanchipuram in South India *4.85*. The sky band panels reflect sky loops and Sun symbol identical to those in India. The posture of the Chac is clearly derived from that of the flying deities ubiquitous throughout India *5.50*. Codex Tro-Cortesianus, Pre- or Post Conquest Mexico.

5.48 Ritual scene with footprint on the cape of one of the participants. The footprint is also the symbol of the Buddhists and later Hindus. The number 19 above the altar seems to indicate a link between the eclipse or the Jupiter/Saturn conjunction. The altar is identical to West Asian types found over millennia. Codex Dresden, Pre- or Post Conquest Mexico.

observed, is moving faster, but the Earth is moving faster still being in an orbit nearer the Sun, the two planets further out will come together in conjunction and the faster, and nearer will continue onwards for a short time before appearing to stop and then commence a retrograde motion. After a period of up to about four months the inner planet will continue to move backwards, forming another conjunction with the other planets and continue on its retrograde motion before appearing to stop and then move forward again to approach the planet for a third time. This will be the last co-joining of the two planets before another complete orbit of the Sun and this will not be for another twenty years in the case of Jupiter and Saturn conjunctions. The time difference between the first, second and final conjunctions may take many months and variable within a couple of months. This is characteristic of all the conjunctions of the outer planets to a lesser degree and that of Jupiter and Saturn occurred usually late in the nineteenth year after their last conjunction, co-joined again in the twentieth and toward the twenty-first year formed the final conjunction occurs before continuing on separately in their own orbits. This time cycle appeared to be the origin of the importance of the number twenty but it appeared not to be missed by ancient observers that the beginning of the Jupiter and Saturn cycle was sometimes in the nineteenth year corresponding to the cycle of the Moon's nodes. This gave a double link between Saturn and the Moon and emphasised the numbers eighteen and nineteen. In the Mayan numeration system at the base of their sacred calendar the two principal numbers are thirteen and twenty suggesting that this is a combination of the thirteen months of the lunar calendar and the twenty-year cycle of Jupiter and Saturn reduced to simple numbers.

In Mayan codices, particularly in the Codex Dresden and Codex Tro-Cortesianus, many iconographical references appear to relate directly to the eclipse serpent in exactly the same way as found in India. One of these is the repeated depiction of a serpent linked to the simple numbers eighteen or nineteen. Of particular note are the "long-nosed" gods associated with them, or Chacs - rain gods. The Chacs have been shown to reflect the profile of elephant deities, the Gadjas of Indonesia, or Ganesa of India, and this is expanded to some degree in "Mayan Genesis". In a vignette from Codex Dresden one depiction is of a "long-nosed god" emerging from the open jaws of a Vision Serpent [5.38], the equivalent of the Makara in India. The serpentine form of the Vision Serpent is depicted as an ourobos or a snake completing the circle often shown holding its own tail in the imagery of India through to the Mediterranean. Inside the circle formed is the number nineteen - four dots = 4; three bars = 3x5 = 15. This would suggest that this is linked to the nineteenth year cycle of the Moon's nodes and possibly directly to the eclipse myths of Rahu the eclipse demon of India.

Three other linked vignettes, *5.44; 5.45;* and *5.46,* the same figure of the rain god, Chac, is seen holding a torch before a serpent encircling the number 18. Since these are linked in series along with one other this suggests that they are referring to the cycle of the Moon' nodes. In the symbolic meanings of India, many of which derive from Greece or the Middle East, the raised torch means "life" while the opposite meant the extinguishing of "life". This interpretation would seem to be appropriate considering the fear in which eclipse cycles were held since it was believed both in Asia and the Americas that the demon serpent was attempting to swallow the Moon and, or the Sun and this act would extinguish all life. Each of the Chacs is characteristically depicted by the Maya with a long drooping nose and this is augmented in the even more exaggerated example in the lower register in *5.44.* The Chac depicted supported by a serpent in the lower register of *5.45* also displays an exaggeratedly long nose. This appears to derive from the earliest examples known of this type of illustration of an elephant, a personification of Ganesa the god of luck and of travellers, shown in the Mahakuta complex dating to the 6th., century A.D. in South Central India [*5.105*].

Another vignette from the Codex Tro-Cortesianus depicts a deity or ancestor, emerging from the Vision Serpent's mouth, and he holds a Sun symbol clearly relating again to the ecliptic, the notional orbit of the Sun and planets around the zodiac, and the eclipse demon Rahu [*5.42*]. Of interest also above this depiction is the eclipse symbol in two dark halves, or lobes, joined by another Sun symbol. This corresponds perfectly to the half-cycles in the philosophic constructs of India where all orbits or cycles including the Sun's yearly orbit, and the ecliptic, were considered to be half cycles, one ascending or lightening and the other descending or darkening. In this Mayan glyph it would appear that this related to a total eclipse where the light is completely extinguished.

In some vignettes the great Vision Serpent does not appear to be referred to since they more clearly relate to the eclipse demon rather to any visionary rites. In several faces of the screenfold the serpent is shown centrally placed "writhing" its serpentine form across these "pages" behind rows of glyphs. On one of these pages the complete serpent, depicted as a rattlesnake and therefore a warning of danger, is shown with a glyph adjacent to its tail [*5.39*]. This glyph appears to be a caption to indicate that this is indeed the eclipse demon since it shows the Sun glyph holding the two halves of the ecliptic together. Clearly this indicates an eclipse since both "lobes" or halves are blackened probably referring to a total eclipse.

An interesting page from the Codex Tro-Cortesianus depicts a reptilian bird disgorging the blackened halves of the ecliptic linked with the Sun glyph and surmounted by a three-panel sky band. The serpent here is clearly intended to represent the Mayan version of Rahu attempting to swallow the orbs of light, the Sun and Moon, and therefore possibly resulting in the end of the world. The shape of the serpent head is clearly derived from that of the makara of India and the bone on which it rests usually represents the end of life and the possibility of rebirth in both the myths of India and among the Maya.

One of the most interesting of the screenfold page faces depicts a deity in the "flying" posture so widely known in India with the identical depictions found in Mexico and among the Maya [*5.47*]. This deity is clearly intended to be a Chac or rain god and of particular interest is the prominent year sign he wears in his headdress and this is the symbol found in a temple in Kanchipuram in South East India [*4.85*]. The Chac is shown spotted, linking to the Sun as Night Jaguar, tending to indicate a period of darkness or lack of sunshine. The half-cycle glyphs shown above the sky band appear to indicate clouds since they do not block out the light completely and there are lines of "rain" descending from them. This probably indicates a period of floods and there are legends and myths indicating that there were periods of great rains and at other times periods of extended darkness. The sky band panels are also of interest since the middle glyph depicts overlaid loops appearing to be derived from similar sky loops in India, significantly among the Buddhists [*3.15; 3.17*]. The serpent shown with the Chac appears to be a water serpent and the number thirteen, relating to the Moon's yearly cycle survives in the bottom right hand corner.

Another illustration from Codex Dresden shows an old god seated on a stepped platform intended to depict a cranked sky band [*5.48*]. The number nineteen is indicated on the first step and this may indicate a reference to the conjunction cycles of Jupiter and Saturn - the latter as god in Western myth also being considered the "old god". This same god is depicted conducting a ceremony before an altar [5.38] identical to those known in the Hittite, Western Asia and Middle East and in later South Arabian and Ethiopian cultures. This old god faces across this altar another "old god" who wears a cape with a footprint displayed upon it. Both gods have curved fangs at the edges of their mouths - a motif found also in ancient India. The footprint was long used to indicate the presence of the Buddha since images of Him were forbidden in the early centuries after his death in the middle of the first millennium B.C. This second "old god" would appear to represent the Buddha or a missionary representing Him, but it is also true that the symbolic footprint was adopted by both the Jains and Hindus. The ceremony appears to relate to a rite requiring the sacrifice of a chicken, a common element in many tribal cultures in the world and known in Indonesia through to the tribal Aborigines in India and the Nagas of Assam. In India the high cultures of Buddhism, Jains and Hindus became permeated with elements of tribal culture in the peripheral regions of their influence and this ceremony may well be one from those regions or incorporated on the way or in the Americas before appearing in the Mayan codices.

In a final vignette from the Codex Tro-Cortesianus a glyph showing the light and dark halves of the eclipse or solar cycle, in the philosophical constructs of India, is shown held together with the Sun glyph [5.41]. Of particular interest are the two long-nosed deities one of which is shown, it would seem, from the back, while the other is shown descending in an upside-down pose. The back view is extremely unusual in Mayan iconography but a particular feature among the religious imagery of India. The back views are particular noted of the early Buddhist imagery and is shown repeatedly from the earliest depictions at Sanchi and other Mauryan, Sunga and Andra sites and particularly fine in examples from lower part of the roundel from Amaravati [5.94] and in the higher register at Sanchi [5.95].

The second upside deity is found widely among identical "diving" deities among the later Maya and clearly derives from identical examples from India through South East Asia to Indonesia. The diving deities among the Mexicans and Maya are associated with Quetzalcoatl [5.67-5.71]. In India the upside-down deities are very common and some very fine examples related to acrobat performers seem to have been

5.49 Ganas or sky-supporters in India identical to the Pauahtuns of the Maya. Chalukya Dynasty, Badami, Central South India, 6th., century, AD.

5.50 Fragments of extensive carved stonework typical of Buddhist viharas. Upper register displays typical flying deities and both lower ones depict sky-supporters. Both these godlings are found identically among the Maya. Ratnagiri, Orissa, North East India, 5-8th., centuries, AD.

5.51 Stone altar with ganas or sky-supporters carved around the base surfaces. These are identical to those found among the Maya *5.52* and *5.43*. Nalanda (near Bodh Gaya), Bihar, Noth Central India, 1-5th., century, AD.

5.52 Of all the Mayan sites Copan and Palenque exhibit iconography more completely and less diluted from India than any others. This finely carved bench depicts sky-supporters or Pauahtuns virtually identical to those of India *5.51*. Copan, Honduras, 8th., century, AD.

an inspiration, if not origin, of these descending deities or godlings [*5.72-5.76*]. The fine bas-relief from Pattadakal displays the acrobats in the highest register while the main figure exhibits the broad-hipped style so common in India but also notable among the Maya [*5.76*].

Ganas; Sky Supporters; Pauahtuns:

No aspect of the iconography of India is found so completely represented with so little change than the Ganas, or sky supporters called Pauahtuns in Central America. The mythology associated with these godlings has been considered to a large degree in "Mayan Genesis". The imagery of these dwarf "beings" is so widespread in the regions of India that they are found represented at all the sites which are considered here to be the major influences on Palenque and Copan among the Maya.

In the Codex Tro-Cortesianus a depiction of "Pauahtuns" or sky bearers is displayed across two faces of the screenfold. Three of these are depicted in illustration *5.43* and they show the characteristic seated and running/kneeling pose so well known in the iconography of India particularly associated with the monkey scribal god Hanuman [*5.54*]. These "pauahtuns" in the Codex, depicted holding up the sky are found most closely similar of all in those of ganas as supporters of an altar at Nalanda (Bodh Gaya) dated to the early centuries of the first millennium A.D. [*5.51*]. These dwarf sky supporters are found in many locations on the important sites in India and those shown from Badami [*5.49*], near Aihole - a Chalukyan site, and those from

5.53 Running/kneeling pose of Mayan monkey deity identical to the mankey god of India, Hanuman. Copan, Honduras, 8th., century, AD

5.54 Hanuman, the Hindu monkey god of India shown trampling a skull, a motif typical also in Mayan iconography. North Central India.

5.55 Hanuman in characteristic running/kneeling pose. The lower half is virtually identical with that of the monkey god at Copan *5.53*. Pallave Dynsty, Sri Ekambaranathur Temple Temple, Kanchipuram, South East India, 7th., century, AD.

5.56 It is typical in Indian temples for guradian figures to be carved on either side of the main shrine doorway. This principal is applied even to cave shrines. The diety is often Hanuman in India and this is also the case at Copan *5.61 + 5.62*. Aihole, South Central India, 5-6th., century, AD.

5.57 Door guardians, or dvarapalas, are often Nagas in Buddhist iconography shown here flanking a cave shrine with a statue of the Buddha seated in the shrine itself. Aurangabad Caves, 6th., century, A.D.

Ratnagiri [*5.50*], north of Bhubanesvar in Orissa, show the similarity so closely that they must indicate a common origin with those of the Maya, particularly those indicated on the ceremonial bench at Copan [*5.52*]. The upper register of the relief carvings from Ratnagiri show flying deities which closely copied in Central America [*5.50*] but more fully explored in "Mayan Genesis".

Above the register depicting the sky-bearers or "pauahtuns" in the Codex Tro-Cortesianus [*5.43*] a deity is seen emerging from the maw of what seems to be a serpent and this again appears to be based upon imagery borrowed from that associated with the makara in India. These serpent forms disgorging or otherwise, appear throughout the Codex Tro-Cortesianus and are clearly associated with the "ecliptic" by the glyph formed by two halves or lobes linked by the solar disk glyph. This solar disk

5.58 + 5.59 Two guardian caimans identically displayed in a manner to makaras long traditional in India *5.60*. Copan, Honduras, 8th., century, AD.

5.60 Makara roundel in traditional form with vertical tail as depicted over centuries in India identically found at Copan. Bharhut, North Central India, 2nd., century, AD.

5.61 + 5.62 Dual guardian monkey deities with a torch identical to Hanuman's club, the monkey deity of India, and disposed either side of a plaza stair also in the identical manner. Copan, Honduras, 8th., century, AD.

5.64 Typical guardian deities flanking cave shrine leaning on clubs. Note also portrait niches at high level. Pallava Dynasty, Trichinopoly Temple, South India, 6th., century, AD

5.63 Fine craved portal with "gelbai" motif and a group of paired guardian deities. Parasumesvara Temple, Bhubanesvar, Orissa, 6-7th., century, AD.

5.65 Nagas (half-human serpents) with their interlocked tails forming a sacred knot found widely in India, and in Mexico and among the Mayans. Brahma Temple, Vidisha, West Central India, 2-6th., century, AD.

5.66 Serpentine Nagas interlocking to form a continuous architrave of sacred knots terminating at the base in a guardian hooded Naga either side of the door opening. Brahma Temple, Gyaraspur, Central West India, 8th., century, AD

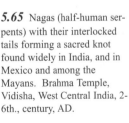

5.67 Diving deity particularly favoured in the Yucatan. Yucatan, South East Mexico, Late Classic.

5.68 Diving deities are found in the codexes up until the Spanish conquest. Codex Dresden, Pre- or Post Conquest Mexico.

5.69 Finely carved monolith depicting a diving deity usually associated with Quetzalcoatl identical to that found in Bali, Indonesia *5.21*. Huastec, Veracruz, East Coast Mexico, 8-10th., century, AD.

5.70 Diving deity considered to be Quetzalcoatl with sky band and feet attached to bi-lobed eclipse symbols identical in principle to the Indonesian example *5.71*. Codex Dresden, Pre- or Post Conquest Mexico.

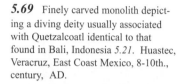

5.71 One of a pair of diving deities from a temple on the Indonesian island of Bali identical to those found among the Huastec in particular, the Maya and Mexicans. North Temple Gate, Pura Dalem, Jagaraga, Bali, Indonesia, 12-13th., century, AD

appears as a circle with four "dots" equally spaced inside the rim and a central one and this would suggest that they represent the cardinal points of the ecliptic with the centre indicating the Axis Mundae is identical to that found among the earliest Buddhist representation [*5.33*]. The same ground plan symbolism was applied to the sacred temple precincts and this is illustrated by the later Burmese folk sculpture shown in *5.06*; *5.07* where the main shrine was centrally placed and the four subsidiary shrines placed at the cardinal points. In this Burmese example the cardinal points are represented by the corners of the temple precinct but in other, earlier examples the layout was in fact circular.

The first (left side) pauahtun or sky supporter depicted in the Codex Tro-Cortesianus displays the characteristic running/kneeling pose found so typically of Hanuman, the monkey scribal god of India, as noted above. This posture is found also at Copan in a fine example of Mayan carving displaying the monkey head of the scrib-

5.74 Acrobat which may have inspired Mayan diving deity. Chalukyan, Pattadakal, South Central India, 6th., century, AD.

5.73 Acrobat or yogi performing an asana or pose. This may have been an inspiration for the Mayan diving deity. Aihole, South Central India, 5-6th., century, AD.

5.72 Pillar detail showing an acrobat performing a handstand which may have been an inspiration for the Mayan diving deity. Aihole, South Central India, 5-6th., century, AD.

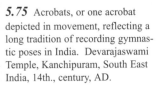

5.75 Acrobats, or one acrobat depicted in movement, reflecting a long tradition of recording gymnastic poses in India. Devarajaswami Temple, Kanchipuram, South East India, 14th., century, AD.

5.76 A fine relief panel carved at the height of the Chalukyan Dynasty's power. The highest register shows acrobats, but more likely sadhu (holy men) performing asanas, or ritual poses. These were probably one of the inspirations that the Mayan converted into the diving deity of the Late Classic period. Pattadakal, South Central India, 6th., century, AD.

al gods [5.53; 5.61; 5.62], not only of the Maya but also identical to the original in India, Hanuman [5.54]. The running/kneeling posture is not exclusive to Hanuman and is found among several other deities in India [5.55]. Among the Maya this running/kneeling deity, usually associated with one of the two scribal brothers, Hun Batz or Hun Chuen, is found as a door guardian exactly as they are in India. Similar door guardians in Central America are extremely rare and this example at Copan emphasises the identical nature, style, and intent clearly derived unchanged from India. This could only have occurred where there was direct and immediate transfer by those who witnessed, as pilgrims or artisans, the exact nature and intent as it was found in India so frequently, before it faded in personal memory. In other words it had to transfer within a generation and this could easily be achieved since Thor Heyerdahl half a century ago sailed his raft Kon Tiki one third of the distance from South America to Asia in 101 days and therefore it was not out of the question to complete the journey in one year.

Among the high cultures of India these door guardians were usually called "dvarapalas" and occupy a prominent position flanking either side of virtually every sacred portal in India [*5.63; 5.64*]. Serpents, earlier noted carved around the door representing the ecliptic, were often intended to represent also dvarapalas and extremely elaborate and symbolic designs of the serpent forms interlocking as sacred knots (see "Mayan Genesis") are common [*5.65; 5.66*]. Some of the earliest forms are the most direct and effective [*5.64*] since many became so ornamented as to loose their intent to create fear in those of ill intent.

The Mayan examples of these door guardians are so unusual that it cannot be a coincidence that Copan has not one set of these dvarapalas, in the exact style of India, but two. The most prominent pair are the two monkey faced "pauahtuns" holding a club-shaped torch flanking the stair to the main temple structure facing the West Court [*5.61; 5.62*]. Directly above them on the face of this building are a pair of reptilian forms with a trefoil disk behind their ears in the identical style of the makaras in India [*5.58; 5.59*]. As noted in "Mayan Genesis"[5] the trefoil closely relates in the identical position in makaras from the early Mathura school in North India and the Mayan forms are clearly derived from them (see "Mayan Genesis" P12/1,2;p82].

"Turned Foot" Deities:

The early sculptures of India dating from the third century B.C. during the Mauryan dynasty indicate all-pervasive architectural and sculptural influences from the contemporary Achaemenid dynasty of Iran. The fine polished realism carved into the hardest stone represent some of the finest known achievements in the art of India. They were essentially realistic in their portrayal of human subjects and anthropomorphic deities and this direction was augmented by the Greeks who remained, or followed after, Alexander the Great's invasion of North West India in 326 B.C. The influences of the Greeks who remained in the states of Parthia and Bactria to the North West of the Indus Plain and the later influences from these regions permeated the realism of Gandharan art in the region of what is now North Pakistan. The art and sculpture of this period was wholly orientated towards creating anthropomorphic portrayals of the heroes, gods and deities based on the human reflection of the highest and finest examples of human form and elements of ritual objects to indicate the status of the personage portrayed. The sculptures of Gandhara reflected the highest achievements of the Greeks transferred to this South Asian state and any adjustment in technique of element, symbol or form was not a result of incompetence but a logical expression of a thought out process to accommodate technique and artistic form in the material and palette available.

In accommodating the perspective problems of portraying a three dimensional form, such as a human figure in a two-dimensional carving or surface such as bas-relief has been one of the most difficult problems to resolve in sculptural technique and perspective. Carving into a flat surface to convey the reality of the full roundness and depth of the human figure is a test of very great skill but depending on the overall allowable depth the master masons demonstrated that they were successful

5.78 Detail from relief carving shown in *5.80*. Two panels show a deity with a turned foot - the upper left and lower right. The upper right depicts a normal side view. Stela D, Copan , Honduras, Late Classic Period, 8th., century AD.

5.79 Detail from under niche showing two panels of figures with the turned foot motif. Parasumesvara Temple, Bhubanesvar, Orissa, North East India, 6-7th., century, AD.

5.77 Finely carved niche surround with a band of 6 panels under the niche itself. The panels are composed of figure groups appearing to have been the inspiration for those of the Maya *5.80*. Parasumesvara Temple, Bhubanesvar, Orissa, North East India, 6-7th., century, AD.

5.81 Detail from under niche showing panels of figures which may have inspired the Mayan glyph designs at Copan. Parasumesvara Temple, Bhubanesvar, Orissa, North East India, 6-7th., century, AD.

5.80 Copan is noted for its remarkable stelae and finely designed and carved glyphs. Among the finest of these groups of glyphs is that carved on the back of Stela D. These glyphs are formed of figure groups and appear inspired by examples found on the Parasumesvara Temple in India. Stela D. Copan, Honduras, 8th., century, AD

evidenced in most of the surviving carvings. One of the most problematic parts of the body when the human form is seated on the ground are the legs and particularly the feet. Where the depth of carving in a bas-relief was appreciable the foot could be carved reasonably normally with limited foreshortening giving a natural appearance. In very shallow bas-reliefs the carving became extremely problematical since there was no room to sculpt the floor- or ground-seated body where the leg was placed upright in front as was demanded in a number of traditional poses. Since seats or stools were usually reserved for those with status or wealth the larger number religious poses, other than standing postures, were ground-seated poses and this was certainly so for ordinary people generally carved as seen.

The difficulty of the ground-seated pose in bas-reliefs, with the leg in front and the foot naturally projecting outward from the surface presented an almost insuperable problem in frontal poses unlike fully three-dimensional examples. To resolve this problem the sculptors did in fact adjust the poses for the most part by turning the body to depict a slightly side-on view or frequently maintained the flattened three-dimensional tradition but turned the foot to align across the bas-relief in an anatomically impossible position. The long-held custom of placing the statues or representation of deities and gods in niches in a very formal full frontal aspect meant that this was the most immediately recognisable view of that deity or god for the mass of the people and therefore the most acceptable. Turning the foot was the least variable from the original, commonly accepted pose. For a turned foot to be anatomically correct meant that the buttock corresponding to the turned foot would have to be lifted off the floor, or ground, and the pelvis turned to some degree toward the point of the foot.

5.82 The turned foot motif was retained or renewed from Indian contact from the Mayan to the later Aztec in Mexico. Aztec, Central Mexico, 5th., century, AD

5.83 Deity showing seated pose with foot carved normally corresponding to the posture. Jain Temple, Meguti Hill, Aihole, South Central India, 7th., century, AD.

5.84 Male deity displays characteristic turned foot to accommodate lack of depth in relief carving. This is a convention developed many cemturies earliesr and adopted directly by the Mayans and Mexicans. Parasumesvara Temple, Bhubanesvar, Orissa, North east India, 6-7th., century, AD.

5.85 Seated rulers or princes showing the natural disposition of the feet suiting the postures. Chalukyan, Pattadakal, South Central India, 6-7th., century, AD.

5.86 A deity or man with flower or peyote (hikuli) head but in posture which is impossible for the right foot to actually achieve. This has been adopted from India without adjustment. Aztec, Central Mexico, 1200-1521 AD.

5.87 skull-headed deity in seated posture with turned foot. Note also he is seated on sky band probably inspired from India. Codex Dresden, Pre- or Post Conquest Mexico.

5.88 Drawing taken from giant monolith of Chac in seated posture with turned left foot probably inspired from India. Stela D, Quirigua, Guatemala, 8th., century, AD.

5.89 Detail of a deity with the impossible turned left foot for such a seated posture. This is clearly derived from closely similar motifs long known and developed in India. Codex Dresden, Pre- or Post Conquest Mexico.

This in fact occurs in several examples, such as at Pattadakal [*5.85*] in South Central India, copied among the Maya [*5.88*], and it is clear that the sculptor must have been anatomically aware and perhaps had worked from a life model at some time.

The problem of representing the foot of the raised leg must have occupied numerous artisans over the centuries in India at many of the sites since some have foreshortened the foot dramatically in an attempt to achieve a more anatomically correct appearance such as at Aihole [*5.83*]. Others have attempted to adjust the pose to achieve a more realistic result but the most widespread appears to have utilised the traditionally accepted three-dimensional pose flattened into a bas-relief and simply turned the foot to suit.

All of these variations to ground-seated poses have been found among the Maya and the Mexicans and they are further evidence that virtually every prominent element of the iconography was transferred from India to Central America and in some cases with the minimum of adaption. It is again from the many stone carved bas-reliefs on the Parasumesvara temple in Bhubanesvar in Orissa that panels almost identical to the point of mimic of this motif among those at Copan are found. Beneath all of the niches constructed on the external faces of the walls of this temple are six panels which for the most part are depictions of the elephant deity Ganesa, or the lion god Simba [*5.75-79*]. Several of these sub- niche panels are depictions of a pair of ground-seated gods or heroes [*5.77*; *5.81*] in combinations which are highly reminiscent of those at Copan [*5.78*; *5.80*]. Of particular interest are those depicted in *5.79* showing in the two central panels ground- or floor-seated heroes or deities who have their right feet turned inward to accommodate the problems of foreshortening and perspective. Almost identical figures occur in those examples from Copan shown particularly in the middle and second from bottom registers, left panel, and the left panel in the lowest register of illustration *5.80*. These all show the extreme resort of turning the foot inwards to accommodate foreshortening in the identical way to the examples found on the Parasumesvara temple and elsewhere in India [*5.84*]. The examples shown in the photographic illustration *5.78* are limited to the two lowest registers in the drawing itself. The importance of these examples being found in India so similar to those at Copan cannot be underestimated since this is the region where so many other of the aspects of closely similar imagery among the Maya appears to be derived and particularly those related to Pacal's funerary slab.

Early reliefs from Copan's sister site, Quirigua, depict a similar pose which exhibit the foot turned across the body [*5.88*]. Clearly this is probably influenced from Copan but there are much later examples demonstrating that these were not elements that were just imported but mimicked the exact form of the turned foot as exhibited in the same "motif" in India. This indicates that there were contacts with India transferring these influences afresh over 600 or 700 years later. The most important surviving codices are all dated to either the immediate pre-or post-Conquest period in the 15th., to 16th., centuries A.D. These preserve examples of this "turned foot" motif but does not attempt to adjust or correct the sculptor's struggle in attempting to present reality in two-dimensional carving in perspective or foreshortening through drawing but accepts that the figure carved is the correct representation of the deity or god and copies it as it occurs in Indian sculpture. These drawn examples are evident in the Codex Dreden [*5.87*] with the deity seated on a sky band, and a simpler form shown in *5.89* aslo from Codex Dreden.

From the carved Aztec box a figure, said to be a detail of Motechzoma, is shown the exact turned foot as that in India and this is dated late to the 15th., century before the Spanish conquest of Mexico. In a remarkable Aztec three-dimensional figure sculpture of a man holding a peyote (hikuli - see "Mayan Genesis") or flower is shown in a ground/floor seated pose where the foot is turned into the anatomically impossible position exactly as shown in the high relief carvings in India [*5.86*]. This suggests that the two-dimensional view of this deity was accepted as it appeared in either a bas-relief carving or perhaps early codex and then transferred by a Mexican sculptor to the full figure carving without any consideration given to the real anatomical position of the foot.

Among many aspects of transferred formalised religiously influenced figure sculpture one of the most interesting is the depiction of the Hindu supreme sky deity, Vishnu. His many depictions vary according to the aspects and attributions necessary to be projected in any particular representation of Him. As Vishnu Ananlasayana He is shown sleeping on the great World Serpent, Sesha, during the period when the cosmic darkness descended on Creation and a much favoured subject among Hindu sculptors. One of the finest of these carvings is found as a ceiling panel in Temple 9, the Kont-gudi at Aihole in South Central India shown in illustrations *5.91* and *5.92*.

5.90 Reclining cross-legged Mayan figure displayed on the riser of steps clearly inspired from similar Chalukyan examples at Aihole in India *5.91 + 5.92*. Tamarindito, Usumasinta region. Mexico/ Guatemala border, 8th., century, AD.

5.91 Fine ceiling carving of the Hindu Sun God known as Vishnu Ananlasayana in this pose lying on the cosmic Naga (serpent). The cross-legs are virtually identical to those found at the Mayan sites of Tamarindito and Dos Pilas. Chalukyan Dynasty, Kont-gudi, Aihole, South Central India, 5-6th., century, AD.

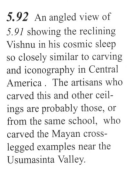

5.92 An angled view of *5.91* showing the reclining Vishnu in his cosmic sleep so closely similar to carving and iconography in Central America . The artisans who carved this and other ceilings are probably those, or from the same school, who carved the Mayan cross-legged examples near the Usumasinta Valley.

5.95 Finely carved torana pillar preserving the original imagery of the World Tree growing out of a mound or platform. Sanchi, North Central India, 2-1st., century, AD

5.93 Siva seated on his throne as regulator of the world cycle. The World Tree above his head symbolised the Axis Mundae and its identification with Siva. Kailasanatha Temple, Kanchipuram, South East India, 7th., century, AD.

5.94 The Buddha seated on His throne with the World Tree emerging from the rear of the throne. This identification is found from the earliest records of Buddhism. Amaravati, South East Coastal India, 3rd., century, AD.

This particular representation of Vishnu is important to the theme of this book since it exists in one of the main centres exhibiting a group of inconographical elements which are also found in Central America. Not only is the memory of the overall physical form transferred to the Americas but in the detail of the carving particularly displayed in the crossed-legs and in the memory of the original appears to be remarkably faithful. Surviving sculpture reliefs among the Maya depict several bound prisoners whose ultimate fate would be a very cruel death and this is particularly well-shown in a carved relief panel from Tamarindito, dated to the 8th., century A.D. [*5.90*]. The general display of the physical form in this Mayan relief appears to be directly copied from that at Aihole with the crossed legs as near identical as could be achieved. The question of why the depiction of a deity should be utilised for that of a captive is of interest since in India imagery related to one religion was, on occasions, used as elements to indicate subjection, indicating the ascendancy of one over the other.

It has been posited that artisans, "silpins", who were known to have been sent to Indonesia to build temples in the Indian style may have also either travelled on from there to Central America or have gone directly. The reliefs in the Mayan example are so similar to those at Aihole it is also probable that it was they who were the artisans who made it to Central America and then simply using traditional forms with which they were already familiar. These they adapted to fit the lintels and upstands as required corresponding to the demands of their new masters regardless of whether the imagery was used to represent deity, ruler or captive. This would explain why there is so little variation from the originals in India displayed in some of the Mayan iconog-

5.96 Addorsed figures supporting a bar of half-lotuses. the Half-lotus motif is found widely in India but also among the Maya. Brahmesvar Mandir, Bhubanesvar, Orissa, North East India, 7th., century, AD.

raphy at Palenque, Copan and some of the other sites such as Piedras Negras and Yaxchilan.

Mansards and Temple Buildings:

The architecture at Palenque is unusual among the Mayan ceremonial sites since the buildings reflect constructional forms not found at other sites. This is claimed by modern-day archaeologists and historians to be a result of the inventive Mayan mind extending the limits of traditional prototypical layouts and constructional methods found at the earlier great sites such as Tikal, and developments such as Cerros, where rapid growth and development, from apparently very little precedent locally, occurred in a very short time frame. The overall site layout at Palenque appears to reflect a more random, less structured planning than at Tikal and other sites and of particular note is the unique construction of the roofs that were mansarded in stone and then stuccoed in a style unique for Central America.

The construction of these buildings and their planning can be found in more detailed descriptions such as Merle Greene Robertson's five volume set "The Sculpture of Palenque" and other references by other well-known researchers[6]. It is sufficient to note here, however, that the mansard roofing utilised at Palenque may have been unique to Central America but is not unusual elsewhere and certainly not in India in the same time frame.

In the first half of the first millennium A.D. depictions occur in rock carvings indicating that mansards were early used in India. Few buildings survive apart from the rock carvings and ruins of temples from that period to preserve any built evidence apart from these illustrations. In attempting to reconstruct the sequences in temple building in Orissa Prof. Charles Louis Fabri's interest was drawn to the intimate involvement of the Buddhist artisans on the designs of early Hindu temple building in Orissa. He noted that "further excavations will, without a shadow of a doubt, support the contention that Hindu temple architecture had burst into perfection so rapidly precisely because the ground has been so well prepared for it by Buddhist monastic and ecclesiastical architecture"[7]. Americanists could do worse than take note of these words for "sudden" or "unexplained" developments in the architecture, planning and iconography in the Americas and particularly at Palenque.

The mansards exhibited in Hindu temple building could easily be taken as the models for Palenque in Central America. Fabri did not consider the export of this roof

5.98 Mansarded temple or palace depicted on a roof vault of a temple. This depiction shows the early form of mansard similar to that found at Palenque. Pattadakal, Aihole, South Central India, 6-7th., century, AD.

5.97 Mansarded Temple of the Inscriptions atop the pyramid at Palenque under which Pacal's tomb was found. The Mayan mansard appears to derive from the early Buddhist types found in early India and particularly in Orissa. Palenque, Chiapas, Southern Mexico, 8th., century, AD.

5.101 Portal to Parasumesvara temple showing the ancient mansarded shrines more typical of early Buddhism at each end of carved door lintel - the probable prototypes of those at Palenque. Bhubanesvar, Orissa, North East India, 6-7th., century, AD.

5.100 Typical mansard of later Hindu architecture - often doubled as shown. Kandagiri, Bhubanesvar, Orissa, North East India, 7-8th., century, AD.

5.99 Typical double mansard of the Hindu period. Eastern Ganga, Orissa, North East India, 13th., century, AD

5.102 Typical double mansarded temple at Palenque - here the Temple of the Inscriptions. Palenque, Chiapas, Southern Mexico, 8th., century, AD.

constructional style but noticed that the earlier Buddhist temple designs were some-what different and he provided in his book a sketch of a typical single shrine temple complete with mansard. It is not necessary to reproduce this sketch here since the almost identical construction is shown flanking each end of a relief from the Parasumesvara temple in Bhubanesvar - the temple city of Orissa and from Pattadakal in South Central India, shown illustration *5.101*. The examples at each end of a ped-iment or lintel panel over the sacred temple door indicates a type of mansard sur-mounting a simple one-chamber shrine which is more typical and the probable proto-type for the Palenque mansards. The relief carved on the Pattadakal temple vault end, *5.90*, shows that early constructional methods include not only one level of mansards but two on most or all the stories of the temples or palaces. Hipped and mansarded buildings in Orissa indicate that multi-registers were used in roof construction [*5.98*] and the eaves were adjusted to extend at a different angle [*5.100*] seemingly to have been the inspiration for a similar eaves line at Palenque.

At Palenque the mansards faces were stuccoed and remarkable reliefs were built up covering the whole of the available surface - a technique usually known as plaster relievo. The designs incorporated on these mansard faces bear remarkable resemblances to some in India reflecting the identical frontal view of the Mayan sky monster or cauac [*4.83*] - the makara of India [*4.84*]. At Palenque stucco was widely used throughout all the temple structures and similarly in some parts of India, and in Orissa in particular stucco became more used in the later centuries as Fabri noted: "It is true that the plain brick wall of the earlier Buddhist monasteries becomes more and more ornate in later, idolatric times, but the tradition of the plain wall changes only slowly by first displaying images in recesses or niches, and then in later days, by increasing the ornamentation by the application of plaster"[8]. This tendency towards plaster decoration is notable in Orissa where the Buddhists were less affected by the Muslim invasions but is also found at the great Buddhist university of Nalanda in Bihar [*3.20*]. It is of interest that the Pala dynasty who ruled North East India, into Bengal (Ganges and Brahaputra Delta) region patronised Nalanda, this site exhibiting many plaster relievo panels, and in the Delta region the great Buddhist centre of Paharpur where the panels were of terracotta and these were similar to the plaster examples. It is here that the makara as sky deity is illustrated [*4.84*] identical to that at Palenque [*4.83*] above noted.

Overall it would seem that the general form of the mansard roof, its stucco relievo finish and even the eaves detailing, was transferred to this main known site in Central America then simplified and adjusted minimally to suit the rulers of Palenque. This transfer must have taken place during the Pala Dynasty in North East India but arriving so late in Late Classic period of the Maya it allowed insufficient time, before the collapse of the Maya, for it to greatly influence their other ceremonial sites. Another aspect of Palenque's originality among Central America cultures was its many examples of realistic portraiture. Figurative art never normally occurs without a long tradition of development and socio-political impetus to preserve the likeness of the patrons or rulers of a particular civilisation. That it suddenly occurs and at one site only suggest that this is an imported art and it can be noted that in India the art of portraiture and figurative art generally was the result of a long, long tradition and greatly influenced by another people with a very long realistic figurative tradition - the Greeks. Together with so many aspects of Orissan Buddhist iconography, imagery and constructional techniques it is clear that Central America, and above all Palenque and Copan, was substantially influenced from the contemporary architecture of India.

Portrait Niches and Cartouches:
In high cultures with traditions in figurative art and particularly portraiture the niche or framed display panels usually go hand in hand. These niches are required either to display the portrait or bust or the full-figure sculpture and occurred for the most part in traditions that have developed the need to display images of their rulers, heroes or deities. Such niche traditions occur among the Egyptians, Greeks, Romans and others of antiquity and later among the Classically influenced, three major religions of early India. The low relief stucco "niches" or cartouches occur at Palenque in considerable number and their form is highly reminiscent of the "portrait" niches or "gavaksas" ("bull's eyes") in India. In Palenque the niche form is built up in plaster on the stucco face [*5.106*; *5.107*] providing a frame in which the portrait head or bust is then also built up [*3.50*]. In a few surviving instances a cartouche form is built up in plaster on the stucco wall surface [*5.103*] and these also incorporate the image of a deity, ruler, or elite person [*3.51*]. In the finished design the walls and each element is colour-coded[9] from one of three colours plus orange - red, blue and yellow. However the colouring must be approached with caution since it has been shown that layers of colour under the last applied were in fact sometimes another of the three possible colours in the code and therefore were changed either from taste or more likely for symbolic or ceremonial reasons. This colour coding was applied to all the architectural surfaces and associated features such as murals and it likely therefore that it was also intended to apply to Pacal's funerary slab. No attempt it seems to construct a finite set of colours that the Mayan priests would have used in colouring of the slab for Public interest have been released from the researchers who have access to the slab. The colour coding identified from the rest of the architecture and decoration has been applied to the funerary slab design shown in *3.49* and the colours indicated in this illustration are therefore reasonably faithful in terms of the known colour coding but are still conjectural until proven otherwise.

In India the "gavaksa" or "bull's eye" was almost universally used from early Buddhist work through into the last Hindu dynasties in South India as decoration and display on all levels of their building. These niches are often equally spaced across a lintel or pediment or grouped in special displays and in Orissa [*5.108*] are frequently outlined with "pearling" [*5.109*] and is a feature also of some Mayan and Mexican work. For the most part they occur with their portraits at head or lintel height [*5.104*] or on the many levels of a sikhara, or tower, but also occur at the lower levels on the registers of the temple platforms near ground level [*5.105*] or on massive stone balustrades [*5.110*]. Even the "foliated" designs at Palenque, extending around or from the niche perimeter is repeated in principle diverging little from the variations found in this display niche in India. In some cases the earlier examples of niches reflect the arched torana with a makara facing outward at the springing point of the arch [*5.109*] while illustrating the stylistic change towards the foliated design which is reflected in the later niche outline.

In "cartouche" design at Palenque shown in illustration *3.51* the colour coding determined by recent research is again applied as near as possible to reality but of interest is the sky band surround and the two variations in serpent head, or makara designs at both ends all of which appear to derive in principle from originals in India but assimilated in a truly Mayan manner. This same colour coding used in all the colouring of the architecture is applied to a particularly fine portrait head of a young

5.103 Alfred Maudslay sketch of mansard stucco mural at Palenque with sky band border and portrait cartouche. See *3.51* for coloured version of handed face. Palenque, Chiapas, Southern Mexico, 8th., century, AD.

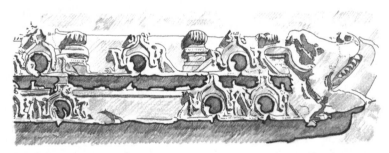

5.104 Carved lintel ending in a makara with portrait niches called gavaksas. These were probably the inspiration for the Mayan medallions, roundels, or cartouches found at Palenque. Palenque, Chiapas, Southern Mexico, 8th., century, AD.

5.105 Carved platform register displaying elephant and lion profile types less often seen in India but frequently adopted in Indonesia indicating the influence that the Chalukyan style had upon the Cholas and Pallavas in turn influencing Indonesia - Java in particular. Mahakuta Temple Complex, Badami, South Central India, 6th., century, AD.

5.106 + 5.1
Two portrait roundels or medallions pr ably influence by the portrai niches of Indi Palace Structu Palenque, Chiapas, Sout Mexico, 8th., century, AD.

5.108 Finely carved but eroded niche gavaksa or portrait niche. These were probably the prototypes for the Mayan portrait roundels. Jain Temple, Meguti Hill, Aihole, South Central India, 7th., century, AD.

5.109 Gavaksas or portrait niches ubiquitous on the architecture of India in the first millennium AD and later. Temple 2, Nalanda, Bihar, North Central India, 5-6th., century, AD.

5.110 Finely carved portrait roundels surmounting sky-supporter or pauahtun panels. Stylised makaras flanking the roundel have become foliated. Cave Temple, Badami, South Central India, 6th., century, AD.

5.112 Two portrait heads contained within a niche less usual in India More than one head in a niche is found also in the architecture of Palenque. Vaikunta Perumal Temple, Kanchipuram, South East India, 7-8th., century, AD.

5.111 Detail of the construction of a portrait head with rough stone armature covered with stucco or plaster is similar to Palenque. Vaikunta Perumal Temple, Kanchipuram, South East India, 7-8th., century, AD

ruler, relief number 34, on the north face of the upper platform substructure on which the Palace has been constructed [*3.54*]. The overall surface colouring of the stucco appears almost invariably to be red as was the skin colouring of the ruler typically and it is interesting to note that in India, in cases where plaster was not used to surface the stone carvings, red stone was much favoured where possible as exemplified in illustrations *3.52* and *3.53*. These portrait niches are unusual since the heads appear to sit on an upstand dividing the niche projecting from outside, a design technique found also nearby at Badami [*5.100*].

In a few cases the Mayan cartouches incorporate more than one portrait and it is interesting to note that more than one occurs in a gavaksa or niche in the architecture of the Pallavas in South East India at Kanchipuram [*5.112*]. At Kanchipuram also plastered stonework with much and very fine surface detail painting was the great hallmark of the dynasty from about the 7th., century through until the end of the Chola dynasty some 6 centuries later. In some examples in need of repair the construction of the portraits can be seen as rough stone armatures placed in an approximate form and plastered over to provide the shape for the finished result [5.111] - the exact same constructional detail found in the Palenque examples. The plaster portrait niches at Palenque remain without any full-faced portrait surviving but enough fragments exist for general portraits to be sketched in to give some semblance of their appearance intact [3.51; 3.50]. The long rows of these existing niches at Palenque are adequately depicted in open-fold coloured sketches in Merle Greene Robertson's work indicating that they must have endowed the palace buildings with Classic majesty.

Serpent Footed Gods:

The manikin sceptre said to represent God K in Palenque and of particular prominence in its iconography[10], found widely at other Mayan sites, and is frequently depicted as a serpent-footed deity [5.114]. This element of imagery has long been a mystery to archaeologists and historians but in fact this god almost certainly has been derived in terms of imagery, but not necessarily meaning, from the Naga or serpent supporters flanking in relief panels depicting the Buddha [5.115].

The Palenque serpent-footed deities were painted blue, the colour of divinity as also were dwarfs and the serpent-footed babies, so frequently depicted in the Palenque ceremonial panels, identifying the rulers at birth with these deities[11]. The serpent was also a symbol associated with divinity and the divine right of the rulers and found clearly displayed in these terms at Palenque[12]. The serpent baby identified with the birth of the ruler was usually painted blue but this belies the fact that earlier it was painted red so colour coding was not necessarily fixed for all time[13]. In India the serpent deities, called Nagas were subsumed to Buddhism at least by the third century B.C. and permeate Buddhist iconography from that date.

Magician's or Ceremonial Apron:

Although the remarkable "diamond bead skirt", as it is referred to by the archaeologists at Palenque, so very prominent in the "pier" panels at Palenque [4.35-38; 5.116], little attempt has been made to explain its intent or origin[14]. These "skirts" are found worn by priests or officiants at ceremonial occasions often related to the serpent-footed baby identified with God K. The fact that this element of the priest's regalia is much less usual at other Mayan sites while forming such a major proportion of the iconography at Palenque suggest again that this has been developed and borrowed from elsewhere. In the design on Pacal's funerary slab Pacal himself is depicted wearing this same "skirt" [4.53] suggesting that it is connected to an ancestral element which is necessary to assume to be able to reach the land of the ancestors.

It has been shown that although there are many aspects of the Mayan iconography, and that at Palenque in particular, found almost identically in major cultural regions of India and in similar contexts it is in Orissa that the most important and most

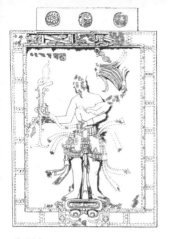

5.114 Vision Serpent disgorging a deity but with its tail forming the right leg/foot of the manikin deity (left) also known as God K. This imagery probably developed from serpent-footed Nagas in India *5.115*. Ceramic rollout, Tikal(?), Guatemala, Late Classic Period.

5.113 Palenque panels showing a serpent-footed baby identified with the ruler. The panel is seen through a sky-band portal. Chiapas, Southern Mexico.

5.115 Finely carved panels showing the Buddha flanked by two adoring Nagas both serpent-footed. Nagarjunakonda, South East India, 3rd., century, AD.

5.116 Palenque panels showing a serpent-footed baby identified with the ruler. The panels is seen through a sky-band portal. Chiapas, Southern Mexico, 8th., century, AD

5.117 Ruler displayed in ceremonial kilt or "magician's apron" identical to that derived from the Bon Po in early Tibetan Buddhism *5.118*. Stela 8, Piedras Negras, Guatemala, 8th., century, AD.

specific influences are found. Links with Paharpur in the marshlands of the Ganges Delta appears to have a special influence since the frontal makara found at Palenque [*4.83*] is virtually identical to the only known similar example found in India [*4.84*]. It is therefore not surprising that Paharpur was the major intermediary of influences from Central Asia via the great Buddhist centres in Western Central Tibet and the Ganges Delta region through to Burma and to the South East. In Tibet the Buddhist missionaries fought hard and long against the indigenous animist religion known as Bon Po and never completely succeeded in the Central and Eastern regions directly to the north of Bengal and Burma.

The celebrated sites of Khotan and the centres in Western Tibet were well established by the third century A.D. By the 7th., century A.D. the central regional llamaist

5.118 Tibetan Buddhist priests in regalia derived from the earlier Bon Po religion of Tibet. Late 19th.- early 20th., century, AD.

Buddhist religion had been established but had been permeated to a considerable degree with the rituals and symbols of the Bon Po religion. Among the elaborate regalia used by the Bon Po is what might be called the "magician's apron" [*5.118*] which is identical to the ceremonial "skirt" shown in so many images at Palenque [*4.37; 5.116*]. The ceremonial "skirt" is also shown worn by rulers outside Palenque at Piedras Negras [*5.117*]. It is clear that the Buddhist influences actually transferred this item of regalia from the Tibetan highlands across the Pacific along with the many aspects of Buddhist iconography. It is probable that this item was transferred through Paharpar, by sea south to Orissa, Amaravati and Kanchipuram in Central and South India, then eastward on through Indonesia directly across the Pacific Ocean to Central America. For the "magician's apron" or ceremonial "skirt" or kilt to have survived so completely unchanged from the Tibetan prototype meant that it had to be achieved within one generation or sooner so that the memory or example transferred did not decay.

CONCLUSION

In this brief examination of the origins of the iconography preserved on Pacal's funerary slab it must surely have been shown beyond doubt that virtually every element depicted has been influenced from India and more particularly relate to Orissa in maritime North East India. The fundamental symbol of the World Tree, identified with the sacred Mayan tree the ceiba, where even the name is virtually the same as the Sema (cotton tree) in India is a central element in Buddhist iconography in particular. This emphasises that these elements absorbed into the Mayan culture have been assimilated and reflected in terms of the local Central American traditions which date back to at least the 4th., millennium B.C. and are not simplistic copies.

The many various myths related to the World Tree growing out of a deities' or ancestor's skull as depicted on the Pacal's slab are found all along the island cultures flanking the maritime highways defined by the equatorial currents flowing directly from Asia to Central America and return with the prevailing winds across the Pacific Ocean. This emphasises the maritime connections between the Americas and Asia and the enormity in effect of the transfer of the elements of culture, myths and iconography by mariners, missionaries and traders.

The regions of specific contact that the Central Americans had with India are indicated in the broader design and particularly in the details of the iconography on the funerary slab. The ceremonial bar with its Vision Serpent terminals, so clearly deriving from the original local examples of the traditions in Orissa and Indonesia, where these latter are undoubtedly the prototype for that on Pacal's funerary slab. The sky band border depicted on the funerary slab is quite evidently derived from the sacred portals of India. It has been shown that the border is a merging of that seen from the pilgrims' view through the sacred portal framing the red-painted Buddha images inside the shrine and the sky band panels of Orissa at the "temple city" of Bhubanesvar.

Several associated or peripheral items of iconography have been considered from Palenque but all find their parallels and prototypes in India. Elements including the rock cave imagery from Central Asia and Western Tibet are found recognisably at Izapa and the ceremonial staff clearly derives from the same region and is likely to have been the inspiration for closely similar staffs among the Maya. The same is true for the ceremonial bar reflecting the Indian form with a lozenge design and this is true also for all other iconographical aspects considered here.

There can be no doubt that there had been a long tradition of transfer of culture from Asia to Central America by the middle of the first millennium A.D. This contact could only reasonably have been by sea and this is likely to have commenced as far back as the second or first millennium B.C. This is far from unrealistic since the evidence for sea migration from Asia and or trading is recognised to have occurred in the fifth millennium B.C. and is later exemplified by the Lapita culture which spread from South East Asia into northern Melanesia and West Polynesia from 1500 B.C.

Conclusion

Although so much of the Mayan iconography, particularly in the later centuries of the Classic period, reflects cultural imports from India in particular it is also clear that these aspects had great influence upon the ruling clans among the Maya themselves. However, it must not be ignored that there are aspects of Mayan art and iconography appearing to have been transferred from Central America to India in a counter-flow and this may be evident in Bengal, particularly at Paharpur and among the Nagas of Assam.

The disparity of temple styles in Burma (Myanmar) and its parent in India, countries with a common border, should warn that, along with language, the convention that temples styles and constructional techniques should diverge with the distance and time from the land of origin is a dictate that is far from certain. It might be expected that the taste of a particular people might diverge to a certain extent from another but that the overall aspects of iconography and technique would remain recognisably similar within a few generations. It is more obvious that the long cultural history of a country like China would assimilate foreign cultural influences more completely and reflect their own traditional styles and techniques more completely. This is certainly true of Buddhism where the similarities with India, the land of its origin, diverge remarkably. It is therefore important to note that the iconography clearly identical to that with their origins and context in India among the Maya reflects only the most limited adjustments in taste and style in Central America with its own long cultural history. This suggests that the iconography must have been transferred not through a filtration process over many generations moving across the various cultures from India through Indonesia and the Pacific to India but within one generation with the minimum of deviation or variation. The imagery thus barely assimilated would require revitalising by successive contacts to ensure that it remained recognisable in the original Indian form over generations.

This study is far from exhaustive and the subject of the connections between the iconography of India and Central America deserves a much more complete study. It can only be deplored that so many Americanists eschew any contact between the high cultures of Central America and Asia and refuse for the most part to even consider the evidence let alone initiate any research into the possibilities of cultural transfer. The present climate suggests that there will be no real interest displayed from those professionally interested in the Mayan ceremonial sites in the near future. It is necessary for those prepared to present serious studies on the subject of cross-Pacific contacts to stand alone or seek long and hard for support even just to be heard.

In reality there is abundant evidence for contacts between the Maya and Mexicans and Asia, and with Indonesia and India in particular, and it is hoped that this small volume will illustrate the necessity of further serious research in this field. Although Pacal's skeleton survived in his tomb at Palenque, DNA tests appear not to have been done to determine hereditary. If there is no complete direct line, that is if all the males are not all from India, then the male line will not indicate relationship through the Y-chromosome and no direct relationship with India can be proved or disproved. If there is no direct inheritance in the female line, that is if all the females are not from India including Pacal's parents, then the mitachondrial DNA (mDNA) will be of no assistance. But the iconography preserved on Pacal's funerary slab clearly indicates that, if there is no biological descent from India, then the sepulchral imagery of the slab itself clearly indicates a cultural descent. This is a cultural relationship which was able to be transferred and revitalised by later transfers over at least several hundred years from India to the Maya and Central America from the Pre-Classic to Late Classic period.

SUPERSCRIPT NOTES

INTRODUCTION

1   Irwin; C. - 97-105
2   Coe; M.D. [M.] - 52
3   Coe; M.D. [M.] - 66
4   Coe; M.D. [M.] - 111
5   Coe; M.D. [M.] - 118

CHAPTER 1

1   Landa; D. de - 46
2   Kearsley; G.R. [M.G.] - 360; 367; 379
3   Kearsley; G.R. [M.G.] - 940/1; 945/6
4   Kearsley; G.R. [M.G.] - 6/7; 513/4; 558; 1010-12
5   Kearsley; G.R. [M.G.] - 443-7
6   Coe; M.D. [M.] - 180
7   Coe; M.D. [M.] - 52
8   Kearsley; G.R. [M. G.] - 204/5; 734
9   Coe; M.D. [M.] - 112
10 Coe; M.D. [M.] - p115
11 Coe; M.D. [M.] - 112
12 Kearsley; G.R. [M.G.] - 594; Schele; L. + Miller; M.E.] - 112
13 Kearsley; G.R. [M.G. - 595/6
14 Freidel; D. + Schele; L. - 217
15 Freidel; D. + Schele; L. - 218
16 Weaver; M.P. - 326
17 Townsend; R.F. - 43
18 Kelley; D.H. - 96
19 Miller; M. + Taube; K. - 129
20 Schele; L. + Miller; M.E. [B.K.] - 79
21 Schele; L. + Miller; M.E. [B.K.] - 81
22 Kelley; D.H. - 96
23 Kearsley; G.R. [M.G.] - 961/2
24 Coe; M.D. [M.] - 191
25 Coe; M.D. [M.] - 194
26 Coe; M.D. [M.] - 196
27 Coe; M.D. [M.] - 199
28 Weaver; M.P. - 113
29 Kearsley; G.R. [M.G.] - 287; 360; 367/8; 379
30 Kearsley; G.R. [M.G.] - 279
31 Coe; M.D. [M.] - 87
32 Schele; L. + Miller; M.E. [B.K.] - 71

33 Freidel; D. + Schele; L - 51
34 Fash; W.L. - 19
35 Fash; W.L. - 64
36 Fash; W.L. - 54
37 Freidel; D. + Schele; L. - 309
38 Freidel; D. + Schele; L. - 315; M.G. - 172-6
39 Weaver; M.P. - 287
40 Aveni; A.F. - 4
41 Coe; M.D. [M.] - 87
42 Kearsley; G.R. [M.G.] - 144-54
43 Coe; M.D. [M.] - 98
44 Coe; M.D. [M.] - 184
45 Landa; D. de - 61
46 Kearsley; G.R. [M.G.] - 613; 618; 629; 631
47 Coe; M.D. [M] - 200
48 Kearsley; G.R. [M.G.] - 614
49 Coe; M.D. [M.] -187
50 Aveni; A.F. - 17
51 Sharer; R.J. - 219
52 Liebert; G. - 174
53 Liebert; G. - 177
54 Liebert; G. - 87
55 Kearsley; G.R. [M.G.] - 171-4
56 Liebert; G. - 294/5
57 Leibert; G. - 105
58 Liebert; G. - 302
59 Liebert; G. - 339
60 Kearsley; G.R. [M.G.] - 414; 416
61 Kearsley; G.R. [M.G.] - 752-67
62 Harle; J.C. - 490
63 Russell; R.V. + Hira Lal; - v1-108
64 Elwin; V. [M.M.I.] - 4
65 Kearsley; G.R. [M.G.] - 850-4
66 Russell; R.V. + Hira Lal; - v1-170
67 Russell; R.V. + Hira Lal; - v1-171
68 Kearsley; G.R. [M.G.] - 211-33

CHAPTER 2

1   Thurston; E. [C.T.S.I.] - v1-24
2   M.G. - 631-6
3   Danielou; A. - 77
4   Danielou; A. - 178
5   Kearsley; G.R. [M.G.] - 701-6
6   Sastri; H.K. - 151

7   Kearsley; G.R. [M.G.] - 462/3; 466-8
8   Danielou; A. - 160
9   Danielou; A. - 161
10 Danielou; A. - 162
11 Thompson; J.E.S. - 44/5
12 Kearsley; G.R. [M.G.] - 629; 631
13 Danielou; A. - 91
14 Kearsley; G.R. [M.G.] - 987
15 Kearsley; G.R. [M.G.] - 988
16 Kearsley; G.R. [M.G.] - 118; 720/1
17 Danielou; A. - 91/2
18 Danielou; A. - 91
19 Danielou; A. - 95
20 Danielou; A. - 158
21 Danielou; A. - 316
22 Danielou; A. - 143; 308; 315
23 Mills; J.P. [A.O.] - 289
24 Mills; J.P [A.O.] - 53
25 Handy; E.S.C. - 232
26 Handy; E.S.C. - 233
27 Schele; L. + Freidel; D. - 177
28 Miller; M.E. + Taube; K. - 17
29 Kearsley; G.R. [M.G.] - 80/1
30 Miller; M.E. + Taube; K. - 182
31 Kearsley; G.R. [M.G.] - 443-7
32 Elwin; V .[M.M.I.] - 62-4
33 Miller; M.E. + Taube; K. - 57
34 Miller; M.E. + Taube; K. - 57/8
35 Miller; M.E. + Taube; K. - 99/100
36 Miller; M.E. + Taube; K. - 137/8
37 Vogel; J.Ph. - 62
38 Vogel; J.Ph. - 63
39 Vogel; J.Ph. - 25
40 Vogel; J.Ph. - 25
41 Kearsley; G.R. [M.G.] - 56; 57; 111; 646
42 Vogel; J.Ph. - 29
43 Vogel; J.Ph. - 29
44 Vogel; J.Ph. - 30
45 Kearsley; G.R. [M.G.] - 487/8
46 Danielou; A. - 119
47 Danielou; A. - 118
48 Danielou; A. - 119
49 Danielou; A. - 143
50 Danielou; A. - 308
51 Danielou; A. - 163
52 Danielou; A. - 57
53 Danielou; A. - 80/1
54 Danielou; A. - 81

55 Danielou; A. - 91
56 Danielou; A. - 106
57 Danielou; A. - 66
58 Danielou; A. - 106
59 Danielou; A. - 107
60 Danielou; A. - 130/1
61 Vogel; J.Ph. - 32
62 Vogel; J.Ph. - 34
63 Vogel; J.Ph. - 32
64 Vogel; J.Ph. - 33
65 Kearsley; G.R. [M.G.] - 987/8
66 Kearsley; G.R. [M.G.] - 522/3
67 Lishk; S.S. - 227
68 Kearsley; G.R. [M.G.] - 195; 909
69 Bradley-Birt; F.B. - 9-11; Vogel; J.Ph. -
       245/6; Roy; S.C. [M.] - 135
70 Schele; L. + Miller; M.E. [B.K.] - 114/5
71 Howitt; A.W. - 584/5
72 Spencer; B. + Gillan; F.J. [T.N.T.C.A.] -
       471
73 Mountford; C.P. [A.L.] - 479/80; 488/9;
       493; 495
74 Danielou; A. - 229-31
75 Ereira; A. - 63/4; 66/7; 88; 115-
       8;131/2;176/7
76 Spencer; B. + Gillan; F.J. [T.N.T.C.A.] -
       621
77 Kearsley; G.R. [M.G.] - 701; 703-6; 816
78 Howitt; A.W. - 578
79 Howitt; A.W. - 578
80 Malinowski; B. - 433/4
81 Popol Vuh - 118/9
82 Popol Vuh - 120-3
83 Seligmann; C.G. - 381/2
84 Thurston; E. [C.T.S.I.] - v4-226/7
85 Thurston; E. [C.T.S.I.] - v7-197
86 Sastri; H.K. - 7
87 Sastri; H.K. - 151
88 Hutton; J.H. [S.N.] - 357/8
89 Speiser; F. [T.Y.N.W.P.] - 264/5
90 Kearsley; G.R. [M.G.] - 742-4
91 Riesenfeld; A. - 94
92 Riesenfeld; A. - 100/1
93 Riesenfeld; A. - 323
94 Riesenfeld; A. - 299
95 Riesenfeld; A. - 402
96 Kearsley; G.R. [M.G.] - 655/6
97 Howitt; A.E. - 376

98   Roy; S.C. [H.B.O.] - 270/1
99   Crooke; W. - v2-137
100 Schele; L.+Freidel; D. - 342
101 Vogel; J.Ph. - 49
102 Miller; M.E. + Taube; K. - 63
103 Kearsley; G.R. [M.G.] - 262/3
104 Weaver; M.P. - 366
105 Miller; M.E. + Taube; K. - 64
106 Kearsley; G.R. [M.G.] - 67/8
107 Miller; M.E. + Taube; K. - 64
108 Miller; M.E. + Taube; K. - 148-50
109 Roys; R.L. - 42/3
110 Elwin; V. [M.M.I.] - 354; 367-9
111 Kearsley; G.R. [M.G.] - 209-11
112 Miller; M.E. + Taube; K. - 181
113 Miller; M.E. + Taube; K. - 184
114 Leon-Portilla; M. - 49

CHAPTER 3

1   Coe; M.D. [M.] - 52
2   Roberston; M.G. - v1-11
3   Schele; F. + Freidel; D. - 184
4   Russell; R.V. + Hira Lal - v1-58
5   Russell; R.V. + Hira Lal - v1-376
6   Kearsley; G.R. [M.G.] - 918-21; 804-7
7   Roy; S.C. [M.] - 446/7
8   Thurston; E. [C.T.S.I.] - v4-294/5
9   Thurston; E. [C.T.S.I.] - v4-306
10   Kearsley; G.R. [M.G.] - 547/8
11   Thurston; E. [C.T.S.I.] - v2-243
12   Thurston; E. [C.T.S.I.] - v2-354; v6-389
13   Thurston; E. [C.T.S.I.] - v2-357; v6-207
14   Thurston; E. [C.T.S.I.] - v5-67
15   Thurston; E. [C.T.S.I.] - v5-106
16   Thurston; E. [C.T.S.I.] - v5-127
17   Thurston; E. [C.T.S.I.] - v5-295
18   Thurston; E. [C.T.S.I.] - v6-364-6
19   Thurston; E. (C.T.S.I.] - v5-295
20   Thurston; E. [C.T.S.I.] - v7-198
21   Thurston; E. [C.T.S.I.] - v6-371
22   Coe; M.D. [M.] - 68/9
23   Kearsley; G.R. [M.G.] - 20
24   Kearsley; G.R. [M.G.] - 82; 84
25   Rawson; J. - 14/5
26   Akerblom; K. - 134-6
27   Akerblom; K. - 45

28   Kearsley; G.R. [M.G.] - 341
29   Popol Vuh - 174
30   Popol Vuh - 174
31   Popol Vuh - 174
32   Kearsley; G.R. [M.G.] - 1006-17
33   Kearsley; G.R. [M.G.] - 907-9
34   Elwin; V. [A.] - 2; 19; 28
35   Elwin; V. [A.] - 89
36   Kearsley; G.R. [M.G.] - 78
37   McGee; R.J. - 65
38   Schele; L. + Freidel; D. - 107
39   Schele; L. + Freidel; D. - 66; M.G. -
     764/5
40   Reichard; G.A. - 18; 464-6
41   Kearsley; G.R. [M.G.] - 471-4
42   Kearsley; G.R. [M.G.] - 1023-5
43   Kearsley; G.R. [M.G.] - 348
44   Kearsley; G.R. [M.G.] - 631-637
45   Kearsley; G.R. [M.G.] - 804-807; 918-
     21

CHAPTER 4

1   Kempers; A.J.B. - 11; 12
2   Kearsley; G.R. [M.G.] - 969
3   Fabri; C.L. - 50
4   Fabri; C.L. - 55
5   Fabri; C.L. - 55
6   Stierlin; H. - 65
7   Fabri; C.L. - 67
8   Fabri; C.L. - 48
9   Fabri; C.L. - 72
10   Fabri; C.L. - 78
11   Fabri; C.L. - 68
12   Kearsley; G.R. [M.G.] - 79
13   Steirlin; H. - 68
14   Kearsley; G.R. [M.G.] - 82-97
15   Spinden; H.J. - Part2, PlateLI, p125
16   Kearsley; G.R. [M.G.] - 632-7
17   Danielou; A. - 316
18   Danielou; A. - 315; 316
19   Liebert; G. - 106
20   Danielou; A. - 312
21   Danielou; A. - 158
22   Liebert; G. - 165/6
23   Liebert; G. - 165/6; 331
24   Liebert; G. - 166

25 Russell; R.V. + Hira Lal, - v1-13
26 Liebert; G. - 166
27 Schele; L. + Friedel; D. - 91
28 Kaye; G.R. - 30
29 Kearsley; G.R. [M.G.] - 82
30 Kearsley; G.R. [M.G.] - 82
31 Kearsley; G.R. [M.G.] - 947; 951
32 Schele; L. + Miller; M.E. [B.K.] - 46/7
33 Schele; L. + Miller; M.E. [B.K.] - 177
34 Schele; L. + Miller; M.E. [B.K.] - 180
35 Schele; L. + Miller; M.E. [B.K.] - 191
36 Kearsley; G.R. [M.G.] - 898
37 Kearsley; G.R. [M.G.] - 898; 900
38 Kearsley; G.R. [M.G.] - 471-4
39 Cotterell; A. - 80/1
40 Miller; M.E. + Taube; K. - 181
41 Fabri; C.L. - 166
42 Harle; J.C. - 467
43 Schele; L. + Freidel; D. - 342
44 Miller; M.E. + Taube; K. - 150
45 Weaver; M.P. - 128/9

CHAPTER 5

1   Kearsley; G.R. [M.G.] - 74
2   Kearsley; G.R. [M.G.] - 71
3   Coe; M.D. - 102
4   Coe; M.D. [M] - 184/5
5   Kearsley; G.R. [M.G.] - 82
6   Coe; M.D. [M.] - 108-15
7   Fabri; C.L. - 106
8   Fabri; C.L. - 127
9   Robertson; M.G. - xi; 17/8
10 Robertson; M.G. - v1-9
11 Roberston; M.G. - v1-18
12 Robertson; M.G. - v1-35
13 Robertson; M.G. - v1-37
14 Robertson; M.G. - v1-40

BIBLIOGRAPHY

AKERBLOM: K. - "Astronomy and Navigation in Polynesia and Micronesia", Ethnological Museum, Monograph Series, Publication No. 14, Stockholm, 1968.

AVENI; A.F. - "Archaeoastronomy in Pre-Colombian America", University of Texas Press, 1975.

BRADLEY-BIRT; F.B. - "Chota-Nagpore", Smith Elder + Co., 1903; 1910.

COE; M.D. [M.] - "The Maya", Thames and Hudson, 5th., Edition, 1993.

COTTERELL; A. - "World Mythology", Oxford University Press, 1979/91.

CROOKE; W. - "Folk-lore of Northern India", 2 Vols., Archibald Constable + Co., 1896.

DANIELOU: A. - "The Myths and Gods of India", Princeton University Press, 1985/91.

ELWIN; V. (A.) - "The Agaria", Humphrey Milford/ Oxford University Press, 1942.

ELWIN; V. [M.M.I.] - "Myths of Middle India", Vanya/Oxford University Press, 1949/91.

FABRI: C.L. - "History of Art in Orissa", Orient Longman Ltd., 1974.

FASH; W.L. - "Scribes, Warriors and Kings", Thames and Hudson, 1991.

FREIDEL; D. + SCHELE; L. - "A Forest of Kings", William Morrow + Co., (N.Y.) 1990.

HANDY: E.S.C. - "The Native Culture in the Marquesas", Bernice P. Bishop Museum Bulletin 9, 1923.

HARLE; J.C. - "The Art and Architecture of the Indian Subcontinent, Yale University Press, 1994.

HOWITT; A.E. - "The Native Tribes of South-East Australia", MacMillan + Co., 1904.

HUTTON: J.H. (S.N.) - "The Sema Nagas", MacMillan + Co., 1921.

IRWIN; C. - "Fair Gods and Stone Faces", W.H. Allen, 1964.

KAYE: G. - "Hindu Astronomy", Memoirs of the Archaeological Survey of India No. 18, 1924.

KEARSLEY; G.R. (M.G.) - "Mayan Genesis - South Asian Myths, Migrations and Iconography in Mesoamerica", Yelsraek Publishing, 2001.

KELLEY; D.H. - "Deciphering the Maya Script", University of Texas Press, 1976.

KEMPERS; A.J.B. - "Ancient Indonesian Art", Harvard University Press, 1959.

LANDA, D. de - "Yucatan Before and After the Conquest", The Maya Society, Baltimore, 1937.

LEON-PORTILLA: M. - "Pre-Colombian Literature of Mexico", University of Oklahoma Press, 1969/86.

LIEBERT; G. - "Iconographic Dictionary of the Indian Religions", E.J. Brill, Leiden, 1976.

LISHK; S.S. + SAJJAIN SINGH - "Jaina Astronomy", Vidya Sagara Pub., Delhi, 1987.

MCGEE; R.J. - "Life, Ritual, and Religion", Wadsworth Pub. Co., 1990.

MILLER; M.E. + Taube; K. - "The Gods and Symbols of Ancient Mexico and the Maya", Thames and Hudson, 1993.

MILLS; J.P. [A.O.] - "The Ao Nagas", MacMillan + Co., 1926.

POPOL VUH (Morley; S.G. + Goetz; D.) - "Popol Vuh - The Sacred Book of the Ancient Quiche Maya", University of Oklahoma Press, 1969.

RAWSON; J. - "Ancient China", Trustees of the British Museum (B.M.P.) 1980.

REICHARD; G.A. - "Navaho Religion", Bollingen Series xviii/Princeton University Press, 1990.

ROBERTSON: M.G. - "The Sculpture of Palenque", 5 Vols., Princeton University Press, 1983.

ROY; S.C. (H.B.O.) - "The Hill Bhuiyas of Orissa", Man in India Office, Ranchi/India, 1935.

RUSSELL; R.V. + HIRA LAL - "Tribes and Castes of the Central Provinces", MacMillan + Co., 4 Vols., 1916.

SASTRI; H.K. - "South Indian Images of Gods and Goddesses", Government Press, Madras, 1916.

SCHELE; L. + MILLER; M.E. - "The Blood of Kings", Sotherbys Pub., 1986.

SHARER: R.J. - "The Ancient Maya", Stanford University Press, 1994.

SPEISER; F. - "Two Years with the Natives in the Western Pacific", Mills and Boon, 1913.

SPINDEN; H.J. - "Maya Art and Civilization", Falcon's Wing Press, 1957.

STIERLIN: H. - "The Art of the Maya", MacMillan, 1981.

THURSTON; E. [C.T.S.I.] - "Castes and Tribes of Southern India", 7 Vols., Government Press, Madras, 1909.

TOWNSEND; R.F. - "The Ancient Americas", Prestel, 1992.

VOGEL; J.Ph. - "Indian Serpent Lore", Arthur Probsthain, 1926.

WEAVER; M.P. - "The Aztecs, Maya, and their Predecessors", 3rd., Edition, Academic Press, 1993.

INDEX

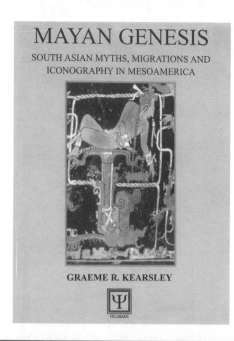

MAYAN GENESIS

SOUTH ASIAN MYTHS, MIGRATIONS AND
ICONOGRAPHY IN MESOAMERICA

GRAEME R. KEARSLEY

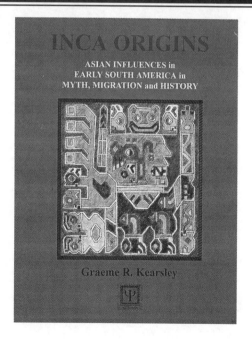